KINGDOM OF
TEN THOUSAND THINGS

ALSO BY GARY GEDDES

POETRY
No Easy Exit
Light of Burning Towers
Girl by the Water
The Perfect Cold Warrior
Active Trading: Selected Poems, 1970–1995
Flying Blind
Skaldance

FICTION
The Unsettling of the West

NONFICTION
Letters from Managua: Meditations on Politics and Art
Sailing Home: A Journey through Time, Place and Memory

DRAMA
Les maudits anglais

TRANSLATION
I Didn't Notice the Mountain Growing Dark,
poems of Li Bai and Du Fu

CRITICISM
Conrad's Later Novels

ANTHOLOGIES
20th-Century Poetry & Poetics
15 Canadian Poets Times 3
The Art of Short Fiction

Gary Geddes

Kingdom of Ten Thousand Things

An Impossible Journey from Kabul to Chiapas

STERLING

New York / London
www.sterlingpublishing.com

Kingdom of Ten Thousand Things:
An Impossible Journey from Kabul to Chiapas

STERLING and the distinctive Sterling logo are registered trademarks of
Sterling Publishing Co., Inc.

Library of Congress Cataloging-in-Publication Data Available

2 4 6 8 10 9 7 5 3 1

Previously published by HarperCollins Publishers Ltd.
Published in 2007 by Sterling Publishing Co., Inc.
387 Park Avenue South, New York, N.Y. 10016
© 2005 by Gary Geddes.

Distributed in the United Kingdom by GMC Distribution Services
Castle Place, 166 High Street, Lewes, East Sussex, England BN7 1XU
Distributed in Australia by Capricorn Link (Australia) Pty. Ltd.
P.O. Box 704, Windsor, NSW 2756, Australia

Manufactured in the United States of America.
All Rights Reserved

Sterling ISBN-13: 978-1-4027-4363-4 (hardcover)
ISBN-10: 1-4027-4363-7

Sterling ISBN-13: 978-1-4027-5344-2 (paperback)
ISBN-10: 1-4027-5344-6

For information about customs editions, special sales, premium
and corporate purchases, please contact Sterling Special Sales
Department at 800-805-5489 or specialsales@sterlingpublishing.com.

CONTENTS

PRELUDE

"KABUL? You've got to be kidding." Kim, my local grocer, was brandishing the single banana from my pile of groceries as if it were a revolver about to be aimed at my head.

"Yes, I'm leaving for Afghanistan. Next week." Then, as a dubious consolation, I added, "Via Pakistan."

Kim stepped back, still holding the banana, her other hand resting on the glass cabinet that housed an assortment of doodads for sale, a pink ceramic unicorn with sugary wings, glass candleholders, miniature cloth flower arrangements, and a merry-go-round with three horses that cranked out a syncopated version of the theme from *Love Story*. Light from the fluorescent tubes on the ceiling fell on Kim's long auburn hair, a little gray at the roots, giving her an air of luminosity.

Owner of the French Beach Mini-Mart, less than a mile from my house, Kim was no prude or stay-at-home. As a young woman, she had quit London to see the world, holing up for a spell Down Under. She trained as a dancer, ran a pub, and worked at a variety of jobs before emigrating to Canada. Out here on Vancouver Island, on the edge of the Pacific, where rain is a constant in winter, and fog in summer, and where cougars and black bears frequently cross her gravel parking lot, Kim has eked out a living from a smattering of dis-organized hermit-residents like myself and from the seasonal influx of curious tourists heading to Port Renfrew to test their mettle on the West Coast Trail, a suicidal assault course over jagged rocks, slippery moss, rotting logs, and swollen streams on a forlorn but spectacular shoreline known as the Graveyard of the Pacific.

"Afghanistan!" Kim rolled her eyes and gave me a withering look. "Why?" She shook her head as she weighed the perishables, then passed the other items in front of the bar-code reader. Although small—an elf with Rapunzel hair—she is not a person to argue with, having chased a black bear out of the store with a rolling pin, its moist snout quivering at the aroma of early-morning pizza and sausage rolls.

Feeling a little perishable myself, I evaded Kim's question and its underlying concerns, though she was expressing exactly what family and friends had been telling me for months.

"Why not?" I replied breezily, stepping through the beam of the newly installed security system and setting off the buzzer. As I turned to wave, I noticed for the first time a poster on the wall—a doubly whimsical version of the *Mona Lisa*, her cheek bulging from the chunk of apple she has bitten and is now holding in her lap. The image of Mona Lisa bore an uncanny likeness to Kim.

As I drove home with my groceries, I wondered why I had not given Kim the true story of my attraction to such a volatile part of the world, where Westerners are not exactly welcome and where dust on the horizon heralds yet another invasion. How to explain my thirty-year fascination with a fifth-century Buddhist monk and his epic peregrinations?

Huishen—his original name in Sanskrit is not known—was a monk from Kabul who fled to China to escape persecution from the Hephthalites, or White Huns, nomads from Central

Asia who regularly raided the Afghan area, trashing monasteries and slaughtering the inhabitants. There is no record of his arrival in China. However, he is reported in the *Liang Shu*, the records of the Liang Dynasty, to have sailed from China to the Americas in AD 458, a distance of twenty thousand *li* (seven to ten thousand miles), returning in 499 to tell his story to the emperor and the court historian.

My religious education had taught me that forty days and forty nights in the wilderness was an honorable length of time for self-analysis or the testing of one's mettle; forty-plus years was in another league altogether. If such a journey took place, then our assumption that Europeans were the first outsiders to reach the Americas—that is, after the ancient migrations—was badly in need of revision. This possibility appealed to me greatly as a young man; it still does. The arrogance and ethnocentricity of civilization in the West—evident not only in our writing of history, but also in our attitudes toward the rest of the world—could, it seemed, use a good shaking up.

I was alerted to the story of Huishen in the early 1970s through the writings of historian Harold Griffin, the author of *Radical Roots*, who gave it a local spin: "Whether Hoei Shin actually visited what is now British Columbia is a long-disputed point, but his account of the natives and their customs, particularly their use of the bark of a giant tree for textiles and their extraction of oil from a fish which could only be the eulachon, or candlefish, suggests that he may have." Having grown up on the West Coast, where connections to Asia are very much a part of our consciousness, I was intrigued by this hypothesis. Little is known of Huishen's journey. Was it motivated by missionary zeal or by a wise assessment of

Chinese politics in which the future of Buddhism was, at best, precarious? Most likely, both. Yet here was a man of courage and faith, setting out into the great unknown to cross a perilous ocean in a small vessel, to risk everything for a dream. As a young boy, I had imagined becoming a missionary and doing the same thing, in the opposite direction. That project, and the faith that fueled it, eventually gave way to the equally rigorous dream of art, a different sort of religion and one that promised as little in terms of money or recognition or success. As a writer, I could identify with the renunciation that surrounded Huishen's remarkable journey into the unknown. Over the years, I became the keeper of the tale. It was incorporated into my social repertoire, a story I told so often that one of my friends used parts of it in a book of poems.

As I discovered, I was not alone in my fascination with the idea of Buddhists sailing from Asia to the Americas long before Columbus and how that possibility radically challenged our perspective on the past. Sporadic accounts had been written on the subject, including several books and a spate of newspaper articles and popular essays. One of those essays appeared in a book called *Chinook Days*, published in 1926 by the Vancouver poet, lawyer, and bon vivant Tom MacInnes.

I located a signed first edition of *Chinook Days* in a locked and cobweb-shrouded glass case at the back of McLeod's bookstore on Denman Street in Vancouver. The slim, leather-bound volume, a collector's item, was expensive but definitely worth the price. MacInnes added his own coloring to the story of Huishen's voyage, giving the monk's ship a name and a specific link with the West Coast. He suggests that Nootka, on the northwest shore of Vancouver Island and now more or less abandoned, was a trading center long before several European nations began to contend for dominance there at the end of the eighteenth century. According to MacInnes, "the devout and courageous visionary, Hoey Sien . . . in his gospel junk the *Tai Shan* came to Nootka . . . to speak the knowledge of the Lord Buddha and the Mahayana, the Wide Raft of Salvation, among the aborigines. Leaving three monks at Nootka, after having wintered there, he sailed south, seeking a harbor and finding none until he came to Acapulco in Mexico, which land . . . he described under the name of Fusang when he made an official report to the [e]mperor on returning to China."

Fuller accounts of the Huishen story appear in Edward Vining's *An Inglorious Columbus* (1885) and Henriette Mertz's *Pale Ink* (1954), interesting and substantial books by two true believers. Vining's book is a scholarly account of arguments for and against the Huishen voyage, while Mertz's study attempts to link Huishen's account of his travels with geographical references found in the four-thousand-year-old Chinese text *Classic of Mountains and Seas*, a work that is viewed by most Chinese scholars as myth. Mertz, who is more enthusiast than scholar, claims that Huishen was none other than Quetzalcoatl, the plumed serpent of ancient legend in the Americas. Neither skeptic nor convert, journalist Scott Lawrance published a short, whimsical piece in *Raincoast Chronicles* in the 1970s with the catchy title "Buddhist Columbia," citing rumors of bronze Chinese coins, a small statue of the Buddha, and an ancient Japanese sword discovered on the coast or inland, and all of unknown or doubtful provenance. Without realizing it, I was becoming initiated into what British sinologist Joseph Needham described as the "lunatic fringe," that group of amateurs and pseudo-archaeologists given to unscientific practices and shameless speculation.

Still, it was comforting to know that other writers had been captivated by the same story, never mind the liberties they took with the material. Three monks dropped off at Nootka? Having read a translation of the original Chinese text, I knew the Nootka reference was apocryphal; so, too, was the reference to an ancient junk called the *Tai Shan*. Perhaps MacInnes was anticipating the junk *Tai Ping (Great Peace)*, which would set sail from Shanghai in 1939 under the command of John Anderson, with his wife and a crew of four, to prove the seaworthiness of this ancient workhorse. In October 1939, a month after the outbreak of the war in Europe, the *Tai Ping* was forced to seek shelter from fierce storms in Quatsino Sound on Vancouver Island. Two weeks later, it was blown north and wrecked on Princess Royal Island, captain and crew saved by a passing fisherman. The wreck was towed to Ocean Falls, where it rotted away. Along with the *Tai Ping*, there were constant reminders on the West Coast of our connections with Asia, not least of which were the glass fishing floats from Japan that showed up with great regularity on the beaches, bright bubbles of possibility.

Huishen and his story had stayed with me for three decades, like some sort of double or shadow self, an alternative history, a road not taken. Despite its leisurely gestation, I felt a certain urgency to be delivered of this project. The past had broken out in my heart. I was beginning to understand what was meant by the phrase "the ventriloquism of history," that muffled voice from earlier times, insistent, demanding to be heard, set down. I recalled an image in a book: ventriloquist Edgar Bergen, in a bright Hawaiian shirt and shoes without socks, bending over to remove his monocled and top-hatted dummy, Charlie McCarthy, a pile of clothes in an old suitcase about to be brought to life.

Which one was I, Edgar or the dummy? Was I writing history or was history writing me?

When I left for Afghanistan in early August 2001 to follow the path of Huishen, I could not have imagined how world events would overtake me or how my quest for an obscure Buddhist monk would be framed and informed by war and rebellion, with the Taliban at one end and Zapatistas at the other. Neither could I have anticipated, in the eighteen-month interregnum, surprise after surprise that would be my constant lot as a traveler. My journey took me on a cavalcade of jets, buses, taxis, pickup trucks, trains, donkeys, camels, and ferries, a container ship, and several small river launches, through twelve countries and through war zones, desert, jungle, mountain passes, muskeg (bog), ancient ruins, floods, and a chicken sacrifice.

And all this against the wise counsel of shopkeepers and ancient philosophers who insist: the farther you go, the less you know.

*What surrounds us, here and now, is not guaranteed.
It could just as well not exist—and so man constructs
poetry out of the remnants found in ruins.*

Czeslaw Milosz, *The Witness of Poetry*

*If a traveller does not meet with one who is his better,
or his equal, let him firmly keep to his solitary journey;
there is no companionship with a fool.*

The Dhammapada,
trans. F. Max Muller

CROSSROADS

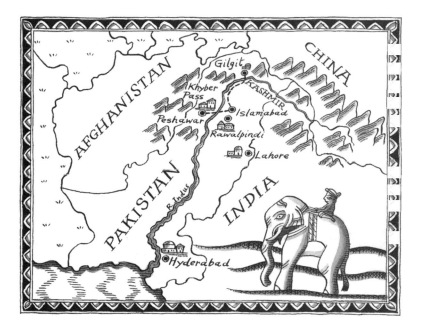

ONE

SHORTLY AFTER the plane from London touched down in Islamabad, Pakistan, at 5:00 a.m. on August 9, 2001, I spotted in the
terminal an employee of the Pearl Guest House B&B with a
sign for a MR. GALI GUESS, which was close enough to my name
to inspire confidence. A prescient misspelling, I thought, given
the questions and uncertainties surrounding my journey. I bade
farewell to Akhtab Khan, the charming Pakistani businessman
who had sat next to me on British Airways flight 129 and
who had offered to help expedite my visa to Afghanistan if I
encountered difficulties.

Earlier, as the plane passed south of Vilnius then Moscow, I
noticed we had left behind the North Atlantic cloud cover and
the random helter-skelter of pack ice. Akhtab had been telling
me about his thirty-one years in business. He lived in England
but traveled widely and spent at least four separate weeks each
year in Pakistan, some of them accompanied by his family. I was
grateful for the conversation but more than a little distracted,
wondering what awaited me on the ground. On the port side,
I saw the lights of Samarkand as we lost altitude and began our
descent toward the western extremities of the Hindu Kush, a
rugged mountain range that is a southwesterly extension of the
Pamirs and Himalayas and that, across the border, dominates
the landscape of Afghanistan. Each name carried its own exotic
associations and produced a rush of excited thoughts: the

crossroads of history, where the Persian conqueror Darius I had built a highway in the fifth century BC to facilitate trade in silks and lapis lazuli, and whose lush grazing and agricultural lands came to be known as the Gardens of Asia, or the Granary of the East. Armies of Greeks, Huns, Arabs, Ghaznavids, Ghorids, Mongols, Timurids, Uzbeks, Safavids, Moguls, and Persians had swept back and forth across these same mountains and territories, leaving in their wake devastation, new religions, languages, art, architecture—all the remnants of culture—and, of course, an altered gene pool.

Like the constantly shifting political and ethnic map of Central Asia, this trip, I knew, would be about change, dislocation. Change had been subtly evident as early as the flight from Vancouver to London, on which I drank Schweppes Indian Tonic Water and listened to a Danish steward speak six languages and talk intelligently about Arundhati Roy's novel, *The God of Small Things*. Security was tighter at Heathrow Airport than in Vancouver, the X-ray monitors picking up my folding fish knife with a five-inch blade. When I explained its domestic use, I was allowed to keep it in my hand luggage. Complexions were darker, and a faint smell of curry from unpacked catering hung in the air. Even the first-class seats looked different, facing forward and aft in a reclining position, like dueling dental chairs. With no Dari, Pashto, or Urdu, and with very little Chinese, I would be at the mercy of my various hosts, including the gods of things both large and small.

Unlike the ancient cities with their topsy-turvy patterns, Islamabad, a recently built capital, was laid out in a grid pattern, each district or zone numbered—not that this made things easy to find. After toast and tea at the Pearl Guest House in

Sector 7/A, I flagged down a taxi driver who spoke no English but assured me he knew exactly where I wanted to go, nodding his head to all my questions. As we plunged pell-mell through Islamabad traffic without seat belts, with a CD-ROM disk that contained verses of the Quran swinging back and forth from the rearview mirror, the driver ignored my futile jabs at the map. He not only spoke no English, he was also illiterate. He stopped half a dozen times to ask directions in Urdu of passersby and other drivers. It would take several days before I learned to hire only the local yellow cabs, not the black ones belonging to drivers from nearby Rawalpindi, who were less than familiar with the streets of the capital.

By trial and error, we approached the Blue Zone, which is not, as it sounds, a haven of illicit delights, but a comparatively trendy area of hotels and shops in downtown Islamabad catering to a crowd of well-heeled civil servants and diplomats. Two blocks south of the Blue Zone, we turned into a small lane, where a huge crowd of hopefuls was lined up outside the visa office of the Danish embassy. A hundred yards farther along was the compound of the Islamic Emirate of Afghanistan, with an armed guard and two assistants out front who directed me down a narrow, overgrown path between two converging plaster walls. Through a door on the right, I approached what looked like a cowshed, a small whitewashed structure with a corrugated roof that extended to protect petitioners from heat and rain, the latter now beating a gentle rhythm on the metal. A dozen men and two small boys, all wearing white Muslim caps and *shalwar kameez*, sat on benches waiting for the visa window to open. Their matching knee-length cotton shirts and pajama-like baggy trousers made much more sense than my tight-fitting getup, though I'd already stripped down considerably because of the heat. The only other foreigner was a Belgian hoping to get from Pakistan into Afghanistan on a tourist visa. We nodded, exchanged a few words, but quickly fell silent, conscious of the possibility that there might well be a limit on the number of Westerners admitted this week.

A thin young man in a black turban emerged, asked me in English what I wanted, then disappeared back into the shed. Eventually, a better-fed specimen in a white turban came out to ask the same questions. Neither introduced himself.

I'm a writer and teacher, I said, and then, as an afterthought, I mentioned I was also a journalist, feeling my nose grow several inches. A young Spaniard I'd been in touch with by e-mail had warned me that tourist visas were not being granted—his own request had been refused—but that journalists still seemed to be getting into Afghanistan despite the bad press they continued to generate for the Taliban, their fundamentalist hosts.

"Show me your passport and journalist's card," White Turban said, managing to look both bored and impatient.

"I don't work for a single newspaper, so I don't have a union card. I'm a freelance writer and journalist."

I knew this sounded fishy and unconvincing, so I pulled out a string of membership cards I'd taped together from various organizations—the Writers' Union of Canada, the League of Canadian Poets, the Playwrights Union of Canada—and offered them as proof, however dubious, of my professional status. I also produced from my canvas bookbag letters from the editors of two major Canadian dailies, indicating they would be happy to consider any stories I might wish to submit.

"What do you want to do in Afghanistan?"

The dynamic of power was quickly established. I was the supplicant here, wanting something, anxious to find words that would enable me to get it. My interrogator's task was to assess my credibility, weigh my potential for trouble. I muttered something about medical and relief facilities in Kabul, Herat, and Mazar-i-Sharif. "Canadians are very interested in knowing the situation in your country," I added, feeling my nose grow another inch. Before I could explain that I had several friends who worked for aid agencies in Afghanistan, White Turban directed me to a chair and disappeared back into his office.

As soon as the cooling rain stopped, the blast furnace took over. Black Turban sat on a chair and leaned back against the wall, eyes closed. He looked decidedly friendlier than his boss, a curious reversal of the good cop/bad cop routine. I hadn't said a word about the monk Huishen, the object of my Afghan quest, and certainly had no intention of wearing a scarlet letter *B*, for *Buddhist*, on my forehead. To add to my concerns about religious intolerance, already heightened by the Taliban's recent destruction of the Bamiyan Buddhas, the world's largest and most famous sculptures of the Buddha, I'd just read a report in the morning paper at the Pearl Guest House suggesting that the few Sikhs remaining in Afghanistan might soon be required, like the Jews in another era, to wear identification patches.

After fifteen minutes, White Turban returned with an application form and a sheet of paper on which I was to write out the reasons for my visit. I had extra photographs, but I'd forgotten to make photocopies of my passport and supporting documents, which entailed a quick walk through mud and wet grass to the Blue Zone. When I returned, the young Belgian, who had written his "rationale" on a sheet of lined paper he tore from a ring binder, was asked to rewrite it on the white sheets provided. I was instructed to redo my carefully printed letter as well—I didn't need to explain why I should be admitted to the country, only what I wished to do there. I was being politely put in my place. I did not mind the attempt at intimidation, only the growing conviction that they'd assessed me as a total fraud, despite my identification papers and carefully cultivated beard, still a couple of inches too short to meet Taliban standards.

White Turban skimmed the revision, then slipped it into the folder of photocopies I'd given him. Before he turned on his heel, he looked me in the eye, and with the faintest hint of a smile, told me to come back in two weeks, which I took to mean "You've got to be kidding."

I now had time to explore bits of the Punjab and of the North-West Frontier Province, the two volatile northern Pakistani provinces bordered by Afghanistan and the disputed Kashmir region in India. But first I needed to make some contacts in the aid agencies. On my way back from a fruitless visit to the Canadian embassy, I noticed the bloated corpse of a tabby cat on what passes for a sidewalk in Islamabad. Its four ramrod legs pointed up to a sign for the United Nations Information Centre. Since the scorching midday sun was quickly sucking up every drop of moisture in the streets and in my body, I took the sign and the dead cat as omens and ducked into the air-conditioned offices, where I was ushered upstairs to meet Iftikhar H. Shah, head of information. I was glad to escape the smells, the noise, and that other sleek animal—a weasel, most likely—I'd seen slithering through the bush where a man and two children were foraging in a garbage-laden drainage ditch.

Iftikhar H. Shah—a presence, an emanation—sat on his throne before a cluttered desk and a huge computer monitor, his personal eye on the universe. This deputy divinity wore a brightly colored tropical shirt and sported the most amazing corona of reddish-orange hennaed hair that linked him at once in my mind with the fiercely comic deities of Indian mythology. I must have been standing with my mouth open, as he rapped on the desk with his knuckles. I explained that I needed the names and addresses of contacts in several aid agencies. He was neither pleased with my unannounced intrusion into the thought-control center nor amused by my offhand remark that I was a poet and retired academic traveling in disguise as a journalist. He rolled his eyes, peered at me over the top of his reading glasses, and then rang a colleague downstairs on the phone.

"Give this gentleman a catalog that he can study in the Reading Room."

That was it—short shrift, audience over. I thanked this high priest of information, abandoned the questions I'd intended to ask him, and took a last glance at the piles of unanswered petitions on his desk. As I removed myself from his exalted presence, I could only imagine what demonic, or wildly erotic, shapes might be cavorting across the screen of his computer monitor. Perhaps it was nothing more than a jigsaw puzzle, the successful completion of which would restore order to the universe or at least pacify the warring factions in Asia.

Fortunately, the lesser deities whose names and telephone numbers I copied from the catalog proved more approachable.

Letizia Rossano, field operations officer for the United Nations Development Program (UNDP), (Afghanistan), explained that her organization was trying to strike a balance between general humanitarian assistance and specific developmental programs. With seven agencies on the ground, this was no easy task. She worked closely with the World Food Bank, overseeing implementation and matching grants. "You had to juggle food for work, food for seed, food for asset creation; and you could not," she added as I took notes, "expect children to study on empty stomachs."

There were five thousand Afghans employed in the Mine Action Program, chipping away at (or, more likely, delicately probing) the twenty million land mines in Afghanistan. I asked her about donors, whether nations were giving as much as usual. And if not, why?

"Perception," she said, leaning back in her chair in the semi-gloom of the small glass-walled conference room with its oval conference table. "We call it the 'OBL' syndrome."

I stopped writing briefly and looked up from my notebook, eyebrows raised. I could see a man and a woman conversing outside the glass doors. The woman placed the fingers of one hand lightly on the man's forearm. They could be setting up a rendezvous, deciding what to have for supper, or closing a deal that would affect tens of thousands of lives. Letizia's voice was barely audible over the hum of the air conditioner.

"OBL: Osama bin Laden. Afghanistan's stocks have gone down since the Taliban gave shelter to bin Laden. It's a major problem. People say that in the post-Soviet period, the West has forgotten Afghanistan. That's not true—it's one of the UN's major priorities—but aid distribution seems less important to some countries these days than information-gathering." I assumed she was alluding to the United States.

Samantha Reynolds, who worked for the United Nations Human Settlements Program (UNCHS Habitat)—was convinced the funding problem was racist in origin. She told me she'd had personal experience with anti-Islamic sentiment in the West, because her husband was a Muslim. She had experienced racism in airports where customs officials gave her the raised eyebrow and a once-over when she mentioned her husband's name. And she believed aid to Muslim countries had a lower priority in the minds of Westerners. I told her I'd heard from several sources that less than 2 percent of the moneys given for foreign aid through the UN actually gets to those on the ground who need it. I did not mention I'd also been told that many UN employees are overpaid, underqualified, and get a new car every year.

"That's ridiculous," she insisted. "The cost of administration, including salaries, et cetera, averages between 5 and 13 percent. Another 13 percent goes to the implementing partners—truckers, contractors, people delivering the aid. You do the math. Beyond that, there is the cost of food, tents, buildings, et cetera." I also wanted to ask Samantha about the reliability of UN staffers and about the stories I'd heard of private contracting, small fortunes being made on the side by UN employees, which involved exploiting child labor in the weaving trade. However, it seemed impertinent and somewhat disloyal to focus on rumors at a time when there was such stiff competition for donor moneys and when public perception was all-important.

My third taxi ride across Islamabad brought me to Denise Brown, a Canadian employee of the World Food Program.

"Canada provides a pittance," she said, with a gesture of dismissal. "The $78 million in aid we administer is mostly American." One of Denise's responsibilities was to produce a diversified food basket for people, including lentils, oil, and blended foods. She talked about the problem of breastfeeding when there is too low a caloric intake. While acknowledging a high-stress factor in her job, she seemed more concerned about the different "degrees of desperation" among Afghans and about the fierce competition for resources. I learned a lot from Denise. She told me that the average size of an Afghan family, including adults, is 6.5; she recommended two books by political historian Barnett Rubin, *The Search for Peace in Afghanistan* and *The Fragmentation of Afghanistan*. Denise was passionate about her work. She not only had at her fingertips all the nitty-gritty, including the exact cost of buying and shipping a metric ton of wheat flour to Afghanistan—US$318—but also could wax rhapsodic about a family of nomadic Kuchi—an Afghan equivalent of the Bedouins—and their string of several hundred camels she'd seen descending a narrow trail from the mountains.

"Try to locate David Finkel's articles in the *Washington Post*," she said as I stood up to leave. "He followed an Afghan family and wrote about them in a very personal way." After telling me about the internally displaced persons (IDP) problem, with forty-five thousand people fleeing conflict and drought in the Herat region, she wrote on the back of a business card the name of a British journalist who had visited *madrassas* in Pakistan—fundamentalist Muslim schools for boys, mostly orphans—and written about their influence in recruiting and shaping the minds of young Taliban. I lost the card during the taxi ride back to the Pearl Guest House.

I'd been reading and talking to enough people to realize it was not just the "OBL problem" or anti-Muslim sentiment that was slowing down aid to Afghanistan. The burka was competing for the world's attention. This sacklike covering that the Taliban obliged Afghan women to wear, with its peephole netting resembling a cage, was the perfect symbol for Western feminists, who saw it as a stark reminder of the universal oppression and confinement of women. With international media focused on Afghan girls denied education and on women forced to remain at home, the mood of foreigners had shifted from sympathy to rage. However, drought and civil war had brought Afghanistan to its knees, destroying crops and infrastructure alike. The woman inside the burka, who might well be trained in one of the professions but not allowed to work and who had children to feed and educate, had been displaced by a symbol. I thought of the discussion I'd had a few days before my departure with my Afghan friend Gulalai Habib, who had recently emigrated with her family to Vancouver.

"Women in Afghanistan have been covering their heads in one form or another for twelve hundred years," Gulalai insisted as I sat with her and her husband sharing some food in their living room. "The burka is not the major issue. Food is the major issue and jobs to earn money for food."

Having arrived early for my first meeting with this Afghan couple, I had parked a few blocks away, beneath the concrete supports of the Greater Vancouver's light rapid transit line. While I looked over some notes and questions, an attractive dark-skinned man in a blue T-shirt glanced at me as he passed. I remembered having read that bare arms were impolite in Muslim society, so I quickly changed into a shirt with full sleeves. When I arrived at their door, the same man in the T-shirt welcomed me and introduced himself by his surname, as Habib. He had a master's degree in engineering, he told me, but had been unable to find employment in his field in Canada. He now worked renting bicycles near Stanley Park. His wife, Gulalai, wore neither a burka nor any sort of head covering, though she was a devout Muslim. She, too, had a master's degree. They had been forced to flee Kabul to Peshawar in Pakistan when rival mujahideen factions started fighting for control of the city after the Soviets decamped. They had lost everything, only to find that they were not welcome in Pakistan. Work at the UN had helped them survive, but the future offered little hope for their children. They jumped at the offer of Canadian visas. These witty, elegant people were grateful for the refuge Canada provided, but their hope of employment in their professions had been disappointed. They were amused to learn of my pursuit of an Afghan Buddhist monk but not half so amused as when I confessed that I'd changed into a long-sleeved shirt in the car in case they were strict Muslims.

I gathered my papers and said good-bye to Denise Brown. I was humbled by the scope and immensity of the task faced by aid workers and conscious too of the apparent insignificance and self-indulgence of my own peregrinations. I would not have lasted a week at Denise's job without shouting about deadlines.

Afghanistan and the area it shares with the North-West Frontier Province of Pakistan have constantly paid the price of being at the crossroads of history. When the Hephthalites invaded Bactria, as it was then called, and, pushing south of the Hindu Kush, started their long slaughter of Buddhists and sacking of holy places in the first half of the fifth century, Huishen and his associates would have wasted no time embarking on their long journey east toward China, where the religious climate was reportedly more favorable. They would have gone in disguise, traveling by night or joining a caravan, and taking nothing that might identify or incriminate them. Peshawar, once known as Purushapura, the City of Flowers, would have been a first stop along the way, where traders paused to recuperate and exchange a wide array of goods, and where fresh news of empire was of major import.

Feeling the weight of bureaucracy and officialdom and anxious to experience the older, less sanitized Pakistan, I made my way to Karachi Company, the western terminal in Islamabad, and caught the first bus northwest to Peshawar, which cost less than a dollar for the four-hour trip. When I boarded the small van, it was almost empty, so I assumed there would be plenty of room to sprawl, even in the tightly spaced seats. The illusion was short lived. Women and children piled in beside the driver and in the first full row of seats behind him. A small boy and his blind grandfather occupied seats across the aisle from me; a man with a rooster under his arm plunked himself directly in front. In fact, even the aisle disappeared as spare seats were folded down. Two people squeezed into the single seat next to me, forcing me to keep my legs—at least six inches too long—jammed into the backrest of the seat in front of me, to the dismay and discomfort of both man and rooster.

Yet the atmosphere was congenial. In fact, I'd found Pakistanis to be extremely gracious. Rather than argue about prices, taxi drivers were just as likely to respond to enquiries about price with the disconcertingly polite phrase, "As you wish." In a gesture of goodwill, Khawar Medhi, a "fixer" recommended to me by the UN, came to meet me at the Pearl Guest House at 10:30 p.m. to discuss my visa problem, but we spent an hour talking instead about art and Pakistani politics. I don't know what I'd expected, perhaps some sort of sleazy undercover type from a Graham Greene novel, but Khawar was nothing of the sort. He was bright, urbane, and engaged and called himself a digital nomad—someone caught up in the new technologies of film and mass media. Khawar favored a quiet, nonviolent socialist revolution, which he called the "real" Marxist kind. He'd never been married but claimed to be interested in the idea of a "relationship under contract." Meanwhile, he plied his various trades. He'd just finished working with a French film-maker on a documentary about Afghan women, about their strength and quiet subversion in the home. With the film already "in the can," he was needed in Paris for the editing phase and would be catching a flight in several hours. He gave me his associate's name and phone number in Peshawar, in case I still needed help in securing an Afghan visa.

Traveling by bus in Pakistan, which requires no more than a death wish and a handful of rupees, is never dull. Although listed as a superhighway, the road between Islamabad and Peshawar has to accommodate every sort of vehicle, including donkey carts transporting fifty-gallon drums of gasoline and cyclists with huge bundles of plastic gizmos on their backs and a small refrigerator balanced over the rear wheel. At any given moment, a blind and deaf beggar will launch himself into traffic, guided by faith and instinct, both of which will fail him if an overloaded but brilliantly decorated truck does not slow down or swerve into the next lane—my lane. Protruding pipes and steel rods with no red warning flags attached lie in wait for the unlucky or the merely distracted.

I couldn't move, so the circulation began to fail in my legs. Curtains were drawn on all but the driver's window, though why that was an exception I don't know, as he seemed to be guided by radar rather than eyesight. It was so uncomfortable in the bus and the sun was so hot that no one but me seemed the least bit interested in the view. I was desperate for fresh air and needed a lateral view to distract me, not only from my growing discomfort, but also from the terror of oncoming vehicles. At least there was Rashid, my squashed seatmate, an assistant professor of business administration and dean of his college in Peshawar, who was returning home from a visit to his mother. As he'd traveled extensively and studied in China, we had no shortage of things to talk about.

"Are you Afghan?" Rashid asked.

It hadn't occurred to me before that a professor of business might be so unobservant. Of course, I was as delighted by his question as I was surprised, because I'd been wondering how I could possibly blend into the crowds in Kabul or Mazar-i-Sharif. The beard and the tan must be working. To keep my mind occupied, I told him about the book I was researching. He'd never heard of Huishen, but he knew about the travels of two other famous monks, Fahien and Hsuan Tsang, both of whom made westerly journeys from China to India to bring sacred Buddhist scriptures back to China and wrote about their experiences at length. Rashid had recommended that I visit the ramshackle but archaeologically rich town of Taxila, which we had just passed. Now he was pointing out the window to where the muddy waters of the Kabul River merged with the larger body of the Indus.

"Here is where Punjab meets the North-West Frontier Province."

The Indus River is to Pakistan what the Ganges is to India, a sacred source of life, a force both physical and spiritual. Born in the ice fields of the Karakoram Mountains, it traverses the entire length of the country, emptying into a broad delta on the Arabian Sea. On this alluvial plain once stood the ancient seaport of Banbhore, now some distance inland, which was one of the foremost trading centers two thousand years ago, where spices were dispersed to distant ports in China and Africa and where goods received were transported north on the Indus as far as the Punjab. Given its immense volume and extreme seasonal variations, the Indus has throughout history been both redeemer and destroyer. The Kabul, one of three important rivers in Afghanistan, is, by comparison, a minor enterprise, only two hundred and nineteen miles in length, gushing out of the mountainside at Sarcheshma, crossing into Pakistan through mountains north of the Khyber Pass, and merging with the mighty Indus at Attock, the junction we had just passed. Drought, irrigation, and hydroelectric projects may have reduced the Kabul on occasion to a trickle, but as the muddy, swirling waters indicated, it was still, like the country itself, a force to be reckoned with.

Rashid's thoughts on regional politics proved to be as measured and sensible as those of Khawar Medhi and the Pakistani journalist M. B. Naqvi, whose column I'd read earlier that morning. While Afghan rivers and ethnic groups (mostly Muslim) have readily merged or coexisted with their counterparts in Pakistan, the same can hardly be said for the country of India, which has been at war with its neighbor more or less constantly since Pakistan's tumultuous birth on August 14, 1947. Partition, which divided Bengal and Punjab, resulted in ghastly massacres among Hindus, Muslims, and Sikhs and left unresolved the question of Kashmir. Naqvi urged hard-liners in Pakistan to remember that much Hindu resentment stems from ancient Muslim—and eventually British—domination of India. He encouraged a shift from backward-looking communalism to a celebration of shared values ("language, race, modes of thinking and outlook, even customs, food and dress"). He also pointed out that there are those who benefit from promoting paranoia, namely the military and its corporate suppliers. Unless stopped, he stated boldly, these hard-liners would be the authors of tragedy on a massive scale in the region.

As the pain in my cramped legs became excruciating, several passengers on the bus made it known that they'd prefer my curtain to be drawn. I persisted in taking in the view, which included the occasional hulk of a wrecked car or bus, a water buffalo immersed to the ears in a small slough, and an unending parade of poverty. The bus slowed to pass the scene of an accident, where a crumpled figure lay beside an overturned cart. In the midst of this panorama of insufficiency and need, where children and goats competed for plastics and edibles, a small boy had begun to dance. His shaved head swung in a rolling motion, while his thin body, draped in a dirty, brown *shalwar kameez*, executed a series of intricate steps. His eyes were closed, oblivious to hunger, to passing traffic, and to the unfairness of the world. I could not take my eyes off his hands, fluid, undulating in the warm air like leaves or like seaweed responding to ocean currents, as he heard in his head music you might find any night on Pakistani or Indian television. For a moment, this penniless child was transported, perfectly at ease, singing to himself.

When we reached Peshawar, Rashid shared a cab, then directed it to take me to University Town, an upscale suburb where the offices of most aid agencies are to be found. My luck was good, and I hauled up at the Continental Guest House, which had e-mail—and which turned out to be directly across the street from ACBAR, the NGO for coordinating Afghan relief. My room, though windowless, was comfortable, with air-conditioning and a television. Despite near-death experiences on the road, I felt good and checked the menu for room service. But first, I stripped off my sweaty clothes and stepped into the bathroom for a shower. The face that peered out at me from the mirror looked familiar but strangely altered. I looked fifteen years younger than I had when I left Islamabad five hours earlier. My beard was black and my skin much more tanned than I'd realized. I'd heard stories about the rejuvenating powers of the Orient, but this was extraordinary. If I stayed another week, I'd look as young as my own kids.

But there was a strange line of demarcation around my neck, where the shirt collar had been. Below that line, I was as pale as plaster. I stepped into the shower and turned on the warm water, which did not so much cascade down my body as bounce off my face, repelled by what it encountered. With repeated applications of soap, however, the heavy coating from the diesel fumes gradually broke down. Normality and antiquity returned, hand in hand. My beard was once again indistinguishable from the lather. I shampooed my hair, dried myself off, and waved farewell to that fleeting, theatrical figure in the mirror, liberated from its highway makeup and automotive war paint and slowly disappearing in the steam.

I stepped out of the shower, twirling my towel. Having escaped death on the roads in Pakistan and eternal youth in Peshawar, I was ready for a few pirouettes of my own here in the North-West Frontier Province, a few dervish whirls about the room. I might not be young or beautiful, but, hell, I was alive and moving deeper into history.

Two

"YES, I AM ARMED."

The gaunt, thin-boned Afghan refugee in her early twenties, who looked more like a girl of fourteen, tapped the black canvas shoulder bag on her lap before taking another sip of tea in the lobby of the Continental Guest House. She was one of a wave of four million Afghan refugees to flee their homeland to Iran and Pakistan as a result of ten years of Soviet occupation, drought, earthquakes, and a decade of civil war after the departure of the Soviets.

Marina was waiting with a driver, who doubled as a bodyguard, to take me to several literacy classes for refugees in Peshawar and surrounding areas. The classes were sponsored by the Revolutionary Association of the Women of Afghanistan (RAWA) and ranged from small children to married women, most working as weavers for twelve to fourteen hours each day. Because education was not widely valued among refugee families and because children were potential money earners, RAWA gave each student lunch and 80 rupees (U.S.$1.32) per month for doing a piece of embroidery to placate and assist the student's family. Teachers earned only 1,000 to 1,500 rupees (U.S.$25) per month for teaching the two-hour class each morning. One teacher was an unemployed pharmacist. Another, whose husband was unable to work, had eight children and rented her living room for the morning classes.

One of these women, Marina explained, had a very bright eighteen-year-old daughter who was suffering from depression. As there was no work or chance for further study, the daughter spent her days alone in the house, reading cheap Persian novels, sometimes spreading the family's pairs of shoes in a circle around herself and talking to them. Marina was trying to involve her as a helper in the literacy classes.

As we wound our way through the fumes and cacophony of the ancient city of Peshawar, which has witnessed the rise and fall of so many dynasties, I was struck not only by the fragility of human life, but also by its tenacity. Two small children, most likely Afghan refugees, were sorting through garbage in search of items that could be burned or resold. A man, naked to the waist, struggled past in the opposite direction pulling a huge cartload of coal that must have weighed at least a ton. He balanced and controlled the cart by his grip on the shafts, but most of the weight was distributed throughout his body by ropes attached to a leather strap around his forehead. When a thoughtless truck driver forced him to stop, all that precious momentum was lost, and he had to start again.

"My mother was an early supporter of RAWA," Marina confided as we bounced along the back streets of Peshawar, "but she was arrested and sent to jail. I spent the first four years of my life in prison with her." With neither rancor nor bitterness, she explained that members of RAWA are regularly harassed by the Pakistani police and security forces. RAWA was haven for bleeding hearts but a collective of hardheaded women determined to resist Islamic fundamentalism. Their numerous publications openly criticized Pakistan for its support of Afghan fanatics and demanded the overthrow of the Taliban, whom they dismissed as typical *jihadi* (holy warriors): "All of them have a Kalashnikov in one hand and the Quran in the other to intimidate, detain and kill our people arbitrarily." The publication also described Afghanistan as a launching pad for international terrorism. I could see how RAWA's mere existence might be viewed as an anathema.

"I have to change my address every couple of months. And, of course, we are forced to carry guns because the fundamentalists stir up hatred against us and attack us at rallies, calling us prostitutes. We live in constant danger."

I looked at this young woman, not yet twenty-five, and wondered at the devotion she felt for this work, the perilous path she had chosen. I'd seen the photographs of the bloodied faces of women demonstrators in Peshawar and Islamabad, and I knew that a RAWA cameraman had been kidnapped and was never seen again. As her driver maneuvered the crowded back streets of Peshawar and kept a discreet eye on me in the rearview mirror, Marina explained that RAWA had support among Pakistani intellectuals and even some members of government, who contributed in one way or another but could not openly endorse the organization. Donations and letters of support came from private individuals around the world and from groups as diverse as Italy's Women in Black, students of the York University Law School in Canada, and similar organizations in London and New York; but they had not been able to enlist the support of nongovernment organizations.

"Of course, if we dropped the word *revolutionary* from our name, there would be no shortage of money."

"So why not do it?"

"We began our work as freedom fighters, opposed to the suppression of women, by whatever group. That suppression continues. We're not a political party that can shift from left to right as the wind blows. We attacked the Soviets, just as we attack the mujahideen and the Taliban, not only for their atrocities against women, but also for their destruction of our homeland." As articulate as she was determined, Marina had been shaped by imprisonment, by the martyrdom of Meena, RAWA's leader, and by the dreams of her father, who, I gathered, saw his own revolutionary ambitions being fulfilled by his radical daughter.

I asked Marina what she would be doing if the claims of RAWA were not so pressing. She told me she had studied premedicine and was still taking courses, but that it would take ten or twelve years of full-time devotion to specialize. And even then, as a foreign resident in Pakistan, she would not be able to find a job in the system. Someone whose family had money and influence would snatch up whatever vacancy emerged.

"Besides"—she paused to give the driver an instruction "I could do a lot of useful political work in twelve years."

It was a sobering thought. I had fallen out with fundamentalist Christianity in my youth for its intolerance and its lack of a social gospel. Since that time, liberation theology had mobilized a generation of Catholic priests; and Buddhist monks had set themselves on fire to protest the war in Vietnam. Other than traveling to some of the hot spots and writing about them, what had I done to improve the world, to reduce suffering? And what about the monk Huishen, that fugitive from an earlier period of Afghan violence when he was confronted with the political intrigues and human sacrifices of the Maya and other indigenous peoples of the Americas? Did he counsel peace and harmony? Or had he, too, taken refuge in words?

The first literacy class I visited, taking place in a modest dwelling on one of the unpaved back streets of Peshawar, contained mostly girls and one small boy. These children had so few advantages. Many still suffered the effects of hunger and trauma. Yet it was a joy to see them excited about education, their small hands beating the air for a chance to show the teacher and guests what they'd learned and how they could read. The older girls wore headscarves, some of them brightly patterned, but their faces were not covered. In the second class, held on the roof of a shop in Peshawar, mothers and daughters studied together. The girls learned twice as fast as their mothers and had to help them. I was shown some of their fine embroidery work as well, which is resold to support the activities of RAWA.

Before completing the round of RAWA projects, I was introduced to several of Marina's supporters, including a taxi driver and a gem carver and jeweller from Kabul who was teaching his skills to disabled people. They advised me to talk to Afghans, not to journalists or "authorities," and to share their stories when I returned home. I couldn't stop thinking about the depressed teenager Marina had mentioned earlier, talking to her circle of shoes, each pair carrying stories of better times, different places, exciting or homely events. There's something special about the humble status of shoes, the weight they carry, the abuse they suffer, the tasks they are called on to perform. Besides, you can say things to shoes, in circles or in awkward disorganized heaps at the door, that you can't always say to their owners. Shoes, for all the pretensions we might have about them, are proof that we are all equal in the eyes of Allah.

Jake Stringer, who works for the Holland branch of *Médecins Sans Frontières* (MSF)/Doctors Without Borders, had arranged a trip for me to the Jalozai refugee camp, about an hour's drive west from Peshawar, toward the Afghan border. Medical statistics for Afghanistan were not good. You had a one-in-four chance of dying before you reached age five, and, if you survived unsafe drinking water, starvation, cholera, respiratory infections, and land mines, you'd still be unlikely to live beyond age forty-five. If you were female, the odds were even worse, because women were not allowed to work as doctors, and the one male doctor for every seven thousand persons was unlikely to be allowed to examine you, thanks to strict fundamentalist edicts. Life for the 2.2 million Afghan refugees in several camps in the Peshawar area was slightly better, but you'd need a set of delicate instruments to measure the difference.

We took off at 11:00 a.m. in the intense heat, with a couple of other staffers. Outside the entrance to the camp, a huge culvert spilled its gray-brown contents into a ditch. A dozen children were at play in the outflow, letting themselves be swept over the small waterfall and out along the secondary channel of sewage and human waste, squealing with delight as if they were guests at Club Med. On the road leading into Jalozai, long-term residents had erected mud houses and set up crudely constructed stalls to sell vegetables, meat, flour, and other essentials, such as tools, tents, and bits of hardware, to newly arrived compatriots. It was a measure of how my standards had altered since arriving in

Pakistan that life on the perimeters of Jalozai looked almost normal. I was not prepared for what awaited me inside.

If you blinked in the intense heat, the thousands of ramshackle tents, as far as the eye could see, looked like waves, a vast sea that stretched in every direction, covering more than two square miles and growing more crowded daily. Many of the thousand or more tents were made of cheap plastic that would neither protect against the cold wind from the mountains nor be likely to last the winter. Eight-inch mud barriers, built by the refugees to serve as gutters and windbreaks inside the tents, were in constant need of repair.

Dr. Assad, the camp's chief medical officer, introduced me to the medical and nonmedical staff at the MSF clinic, located in several large tents at the center of the camp. The pathetic scattering of medicines in a makeshift wooden box on the folding table looked more like candy play samples you'd find in a medical kit for dolls. As it was midafternoon, the medical compound was quiet; the refugees, especially the sick ones, were unable to move about in the intense heat and glare. Three men and five women, all overworked and paid a pittance, were preparing to close shop for the day. I accepted the offer of Noo, Dr. Assad's assistant, to show me around the camp. In his late twenties, Noo had been studying medicine in the much-contested northern city of Mazar-i-Sharif when the civil war began in the early 1990s and had fled the atrocities being committed on all sides.

"We never have enough to eat," explained Ibrahim. The bearded patriarch was surrounded by fifteen adults and small children, all relatives, crowded into a patched 8-foot-by-10-foot plastic tent. "And there is no way to make a living here." Despite this disconcerting testimony, he sent his grandson to the canteen to purchase a bottle of orange soda for me, a gesture of hospitality so ingrained in Afghan culture that it does not recognize poverty as an excuse. I knew this orange pop, served up with unclean ice, would be the undoing of me, but I could not refuse it without insulting my hosts. With fifteen pairs of eyes watching me, I tried to appear grateful as I sipped the soda, careful not to drain the glass for fear it might be refilled. Ibrahim and his friends looked for day labor in Peshawar, but the cost of transportation to and from the city was so expensive that the effort was hardly worthwhile. Ahmad, a much younger man, wanted me to understand that many refugees, particularly the newly arrived, had no ration cards at all, and that even among those who had ration cards, adequate food was never guaranteed, because camp officials and army personnel set aside quantities for resale and for their own use. I was told, for the second time in one day, that the good canvas tents supplied by the UN for the refugees could be found in the markets for sale, having been replaced by the local "authorities" with a cheaper plastic variety.

I wondered what these destitute people made of me and the trickle of journalists and curious spectators who show up from time to time, ask the usual questions, then disappear, so often silenced by what they have seen and by the enormity of the refugee problem. The small boy who had fetched my deadly refreshment, one side of his face badly scarred by impetigo, sat quietly between his grandfather and me while we talked, his small eyes darting from one face to another, as if he were at a Ping-Pong match. Words, precious as food or cheap and inconsequential as plastic balls filled with air, bounced back and forth through the dust-filled oven of the tent.

What might be in store for this child in ten years' time, if he survived? Would he return home to the family farm or, tired of hearing useless old men discuss his fate, be recruited into yet another jihad?

Late for the bus, we made a beeline for the clinic. We'd held up the medical team, who were waiting to head back to MSF headquarters in Peshawar for supper. As we arrived at the compound, full of apologies, Dr. Assad ran past, motioning for me to follow. Had he been told of a medical emergency? A helicopter, sending up a huge plume of dust, had just touched down two hundred yards away. However, this celestial chariot was engaged in a public relations exercise, not medical relief; it carried the Japanese foreign minister who planned to say something to the media about his country's support of UN efforts at Jalozai. Surrounded by Pakistani military, he was ushered from the helicopter to a black sedan, sleek and enormous in this wasteland of ragged tents, and whisked off to a large tent for photo ops and a quick news conference. He wore a baseball cap, a blue shirt, slacks, and a photographer's vest with a plethora of pockets. I was not introduced to him or allowed to shake his hand, as two security types who'd been watching stepped between us. Dr. Assad wasted no time on small talk as he outlined the work being done at Jalozai by MSF–Holland.

Before Noo, Dr. Assad, and I reached the waiting bus, the Japanese foreign minister had disappeared into the blue sky, leaving behind another plume of agitated dust to settle on the inhabitants of the Jalozai camp.

» » « «

I'd been so oppressed by refugee problems in the previous few days, I decided to take some time off to look for books about Afghanistan in general and the Taliban in particular. I found them in abundance at Saeed's Bookstore in the Saddar Market in Peshawar. As soon as I picked up a copy of Ahmed Rashid's *Taliban*, the clerk began to bring over dozens of other related titles for my inspection. He even found a new, if somewhat dusty and shopworn, copy of Nancy Dupree's book *An Historical Guide to Afghanistan*, published in the early 1970s, which I wanted to read before meeting her. The service was excellent; so, too, the selection. By the time I finished browsing, I'd spent a hundred dollars for three in-depth books on the Taliban and their rise to power.

As I headed out into the street with my purchases, a young boy about fifteen years old grabbed me by the arm and insisted that I look at his tray of knives. I was not the least bit interested, but he was so determined that I decided to do him the courtesy of examining his wares. This proved to be a mistake. Some of the jackknives had bone handles; others were made of multicolored stone that had the polish, if not the luminescence, of jade. The stainless-steel workmanship was superb. I praised the knives, smiled at the young man in gratitude, and turned to leave.

"Fifteen hundred rupees," he said, thrusting the last-inspected knife in my face. "Cheap."

I told him I did not need another knife, that I already had one in my bag at the hotel, but he was not impressed and insisted these were special knives, that I should buy one for my son. When I confessed to having no son, he suggested giving one to a cousin or uncle. By now, we were halfway down the street, and I was worried about the full tray of knives he'd left on the street in front of Saeed's. He kept pace with me, then deftly cut in front so I was forced to stop.

"One thousand rupees. Special for you. My father makes in Kabul. Good steel from Russian tank." He watched my face closely, my body language. So did a small boy—a brother perhaps, or apprentice—who was tracking a parallel course ten feet to my left.

The kid was an Afghan refugee, like hundreds of others I'd seen scrounging or begging in Peshawar. However, he was doing neither; he had a product to sell, a good-quality product. I should be supporting him and his family, but I was determined not to give in, not to be pressured into buying something I did not want. As I turned the corner, he made what seemed like a final sacrifice.

"Okay, five hundred rupees. Last offer." The price had dropped from thirty to ten dollars. Meanwhile, the little brother had disappeared, doubtless to keep an eye on the tray of unsold knives back at Saeed's. I was angry with this kid but also at my inability to shake him off. I waved my arms vigorously, books and all.

"Look, I'm not interested. Okay?"

Not okay.

"How much, then? Two hundred rupees." He pushed the folded knife into my chest, while I continued shaking my head. I realized how close I was to grabbing and shoving this kid. I tried to brush him off by crossing the street, conscious of other merchants observing this little drama, no doubt a familiar one.

"Please, you buy. How much? How much?" He was blocking my way now, desperate. "One hundred rupees." He practically screamed the price. I couldn't bear it any longer. I thrust a hundred rupees into his hand and turned away, refusing the knife. But he wouldn't let me go. He threw the knife into my bag of expensive books and turned away, humiliation evident in his face, defeat.

After all my sanctimonious deliberations about the plight of refugees, I felt sick. I had come here to do research on Huishen and the Buddhist past, but I was so deeply mired in personal tragedies of the Muslim present that I did not know where to turn. I made up my mind to take a day off. Marina, however, had other plans for me. She insisted on accompanying me to Khewa, an upscale refugee camp an hour's drive from Peshawar. You don't argue with a woman with a vision and a gun.

Khewa, twenty miles east of Peshawar, was well established. The camp had existed long enough to have acquired permanent dwellings and some basic facilities, such as electricity and running water. But my curiosity about the courtyards and small gardens was not to be satisfied, as Marina wasted no time in ushering me into a room of elders and children. A seventy-year-old man with white hair and beard extended his hand. He was the sole survivor of a massacre at a village in the Yakawlang region of Bamiyan Province on January 8, 2000, eleven months prior to the destruction of the Buddhas. Sunni Muslim Taliban, he said, cut throats and skinned people alive—not just the opposing local militia, but also the general Hazara and Sadat populations, all of whom were Shiite Muslims. A twelve-year-old girl in a bright green shawl with a yellow floral pattern, seated between two relatives, was rocking to and fro nervously. When finally allowed to speak, Nastaran could hardly find the words. A comforting hand was placed on her shoulder. Her father, who had fought against the Russians, was tortured by the Taliban, she said, held in prison twenty days, then delivered home dead to the family. Her mother protested, so she too was taken away with Nastaran's little brother, neither of them ever seen again. Nastaran, whose name means "flower," told me she was in the eighth grade and hoped to become a teacher. Like Marina, she wanted the Taliban and mujahideen destroyed.

The dreadful vigil of sharing was not yet over. Satara, a teenager in a pale blue transparent headscarf, insisted on telling me her story but could not do so without weeping. Lips compressed, deep sighs audible, Satara, whose name means "star," nodded as an elder explained about the raids on houses by foreign Taliban soldiers who could speak neither Dari nor Pashto, demanding money, guns, taking away men and boys, sometimes killing them in front of the family. Old men were forced to bury the dead in common graves. How did she feel about this violence, all of which had been committed by men?

"I hate men. I will resist them as long as I can."

These stories confirmed what I'd been told the previous day, at the weavers' guild in Peshawar. According to Hashim, one of the elders, there were rogue elements in the Taliban that could not be controlled. Hashim had lost his five-year-old son in the gunfire at Deh Surkh (Red Village). A friend of Hashim survived the slaughter of his own family and 235 villagers because of a chance encounter with a former student, a recruit in the invading Taliban forces, who interceded with the commanders on his behalf. "I was sitting in my shop," the friend said, "when they burst in the door." The events he described lasted three days, until nothing was left; even the gardens and crops were destroyed, a replay of Genghis Khan's scorched-earth policy in Bamiyan eight centuries earlier.

"I was spared," Hashim explained, "so I must tell this story." He spelled out the names of the butchers for me so there'd be no mistake: Mullah Dadullah, Mullah Satar, and Qari Ahmadullah.

The background to these atrocities is by no means straight-forward or easy to summarize. Although Shia and Sunni Muslim antagonism is ancient and deep-seated, Afghanistan had a tradition of tolerance that allowed Muslim sects, Jews, Hindus, and Sikhs to live together peacefully for centuries. All this began to change in 1893 when Pashtun king Abdul Rehman initiated a pogrom against the Hazaras, destroying mosques, killing thousands, and displacing the population, many of whom were reduced to living as indentured slaves. The Hazara Shia, with military aid from Iran, remained in the forefront of resistance to Sunni Taliban rule and were ferocious in their defence of Mazar-i-Sharif, where they showed no mercy to the enemy. However, by 1998 the Hazara were in disarray as a result of factional in-fighting and severe food shortages. When the military tables turned, old hatreds combined with recent bitter memories led to an unprecedented massacre by the victorious Taliban, who shot men, women, and children indiscriminately on the streets and massacred entire households.

I thought I'd be able to put all of this violence and chaos out of my mind for a day, but the seller of knives had brought it flooding back. To break the tension in the room, I told the guild of weavers a story I'd heard from Dr. Qayoom, who earned thirty dollars a month working full-time at the Jalozai refugee camp. Dr. Qayoom had been a medic on the front lines in the Bamiyan region during the anti-Soviet campaign. I asked if he'd ever felt his Muslim faith threatened by the presence of the colossal Buddhas. Dr. Qayoom laughed. As it happened, he knew the caretaker of the Buddhas, a devout Muslim. Each morning the caretaker would climb the stairs to the top of the largest Buddha, place his prayer mat on the Buddha's head, and direct his prayers toward Mecca. He was grateful for the two giant Buddhas, which brought him closer to Allah. As Marina translated, smiles appeared one by one on the tired faces of the weavers. Because there were young children in the room, I did not repeat the second story Dr. Qayoom had shared with me on the way back from Jalozai to Peshawar at dusk, after telling me about problems of impetigo and dysentery in the camp.

"We Afghans are big fans of Maleka Whiskey," he said with a broad grin as we navigated the shoals of perilous vehicles and suicidal pedestrians on the highway. Dr. Qayoom's paltry salary had not dampened his enthusiasm for life or his sense of humor. I wondered why a good Muslim was talking to me about alcohol, especially whiskey, which must be as rare in Pakistan as in his homeland. I said I'd never heard of a brand of whiskey called Maleka. Was it single malt or blended?

"In Dari, the word *maleka* means 'queen,'" he explained, "and that's how we pronounce her name."

"Whose name?" I turned to my companions after witnessing another near miss on the highway. Dr. Qayoom and his medical associates were in stitches. He pulled himself together, sucked in his cheeks, and said in an exaggeratedly dignified British accent:

"Why, Monica Lewinsky, of course."

THREE

"KACHAGHARAI."

Oazi Imayat-ur-Rahman was addressing his minuscule audience of four as the Toyota van blasted through the moving kaleidoscope of trucks, buses, donkeys, horse-drawn carts, bicycles, three-wheeled motorized rickshaws, pedestrians, and stray goats. He pointed to the mud-brick structures of the refugee camp, outside of which were piled sacks of cement, plastic racks and baskets, ceramic pots, chairs, and bundles of firewood. A man squatted to urinate beside the road as we passed.

"What does it mean?"

"Temporary dwellings," Oazi expounded, with the self-satisfied smile of the pedagogue. Oazi had a degree in history and archaeology and told us he was once in charge of museums in Peshawar and other parts of the country. He was working as a tour guide to finance his retirement.

The 120,000 Afghan refugees of the Nasir Bagh camp, who occupied these crudely built "temporary" dwellings and the thousands of tents and patchwork shelters in the eastern suburbs of Peshawar, knew they might be ejected at any moment by government decree. In fact, a substantial number had already been given the option of returning to their homeland or being relocated to the Jalozai refugee camp by October 1, in six weeks. There was no hope for them in Afghanistan, where drought, fighting, and land mines had rendered much of the countryside uninhabitable, and where any infrastructure that might cushion the return had been destroyed. A family would be given the equivalent of ten dollars in Pakistani rupees and dropped off at the border. Most simply waited until dark and slipped back into Pakistan, to whatever fate awaited them.

Assuming I would not be granted a visa to Afghanistan, I thought I should at least visit the Khyber Pass, where so many armies had clashed and so much blood had been shed. Along this pass, a relatively short route through the Sulaiman Range—the distance from Peshawar to the Afghan border is approximately thirty-four miles—had traveled adventurers, monks, and traders of every sort. There, too, had marched the armies of Darius, Babur, Alexander the Great, Genghis Khan and, eventually, the British. The latter's occupying force of 16,000 soldiers, civilians and their families, after promise of safe passage, were massacred in the Khyber Pass in January 1842 by Akbar Khan's soldiers and Ghilzai tribesmen, who picked them off from the surrounding crags and hillsides, giving credence to Wellington's observation that "it is easy to get into Afghanistan; the difficulty is in getting out." As the van navigated a series of switchbacks, gaining altitude, Qazi pointed out a huge walled compound, the biggest private dwelling in the pass, owned by a man who was in jail in Peshawar on a narcotics charge. The phenomenal geological upheavals that created this rugged terrain seemed to have their human counterpart, as three millennia of invasions, wars, and shifting loyalties had created an unstable society in which criminal and unsavory elements thrived.

Because this region remains outside government control, to enter the pass we were obliged to request permission and hire an armed guard from the Khyber Agency, the authority responsible for policing this section of the Tribal Areas. In the compound, a serious altercation ensued when the guard, armed with a Kalashnikov, agreed to sit in the back of the van, giving the passenger seat to one of the tour trainees. His boss became apoplectic, shouting until the guard resumed his position next to the driver so his presence and automatic weapon could be clearly seen from the road. Kidnappings and robberies were more common than weddings in the North-West Frontier Province. And having read of the dangers we might face, I was glad to have this gentle warrior on board, although it seemed unlikely that in broad daylight we'd meet anyone meaner and nastier than the official we had left glaring in the driveway.

Guns are big business in this part of Pakistan. Every small enterprise or bed and breakfast has an armed guard out front. There are said to be sixty small-arms production units in the Tribal Areas, each with twenty to twenty-five employees; three hundred small gun workshops of four to five technicians; and another four hundred shops selling arms and ammunition. Earlier that morning I had read in the *International News* an article on gun control that described the government's efforts to license automatic weapons. According to the columnist, 88,000 arms had been received in June and 21,461 recovered in the days following the amnesty. When you considered that 1.4 million gun licences were granted between 1981 and 1995, these efforts seemed a drop in the bucket, a public relations exercise.

Gudrun and Ikuko, my companions on the trip to the Khyber Pass, were graduate students in Chinese studies at the University of Heidelberg. They were decked out in head-scarves, *shalwar kameez*, and hiking boots. This was their final excursion in Peshawar, so their expensive cameras were at the ready. We passed the Sphola Stupa, a quaint and unlikely ruin from the Kushan Empire, Central Asian nomads who ruled the region from the second to the fifth century AD. King Kanishka, exceptional for his promotion of art and learning, had set out to humanize Buddhism by focusing on the miracles and personality of the Buddha. A fully intact stupa, with its foundation level, cornices, and seven ascending umbrella stones, or *chatri,* resembled a mushroom-shaped high-rise. According to Nancy Dupree, the stupa was more than a chamber for relics; it also signified the cosmos, the *chatri* representing the various heavenly levels. As they were reported to contain treasure, most had been looted and destroyed.

I was telling my companions about my quest for Huishen and his voyage to the Americas when Oazi, who was eavesdropping, interrupted our conversation to deliver a lecture on the various schools of Buddhism and the peculiarities of the traditional stupa. These shrines, he intoned, are alleged to contain a sacred relic of the Buddha, such as a hair, a bone, or a fingernail. The tone he used for the word *alleged* was not lost on me.

"Of course," he added, with a broad smile and just a touch of sarcasm, "such a broad dispersal would have required a larger-than-life Buddha."

"Oh, like those destroyed by the Taliban?" I was tired of his superior, patronizing air.

Noticing that Gudrun—either sick from the motion or wilting from the heat—was hanging out the window, Oazi tapped her on the shoulder and told her to pay attention to the lecture. While she decided whether to slug him or empty the contents of her queasy stomach in his lap, I was rewarded with my own little epiphany. Fifty feet above the highway, three camels and riders were silhouetted against the noon sky. They moved with a slow, awkward, but strangely hypnotic gait along the railway track. At this point, the right-of-way for the Khyber Steam Train ran parallel to the highway for several hundred yards. Because of political instability in the region, the train was no longer in great demand and did not make regular runs to the border so using the rail lines as a path was safe. However, the train was fired up occasionally when enough bigwigs and wealthy clients made the trip worthwhile. The next run was scheduled for August 26, 2001, at which time I would be either in Afghanistan or heading north over the ancient Silk Road toward China. The three camels might have been transporting wise men, brigands, Asian monks, or nomadic Kuchi returning from the markets of Peshawar. Whatever their mission, these exotic, foul-smelling, and amazingly adaptable beasts were capable of producing a time warp, as if two thousand years had suddenly been peeled away.

We arrived at the checkpoint, as close as we were permitted to the actual border—an unprepossessing clutter of gates, concrete barriers, and bored young soldiers sweltering in the midday sun. We could see, in the distance, the Afghan station and, beyond that, a major settlement, which I took to be the outskirts of Jalalabad. Gudrun and Ikuko passed me their expensive cameras for a photograph, so they'd have a record of their visit to the Khyber Pass. In the process of juggling all this equipment, I managed to crack the viewfinder of my own camera, which struck me as strangely appropriate, considering the anticlimactic nature of the excursion.

We didn't stay long. The heat had sucked up all our energies.

As the border receded behind us, I asked Oazi if he had any children. He told me, with considerable pride and detail, about his sons and their careers, but had nothing at all to say about his daughters. He knew a good deal about history, but nothing about the local flora—stunted trees and flowers struggling among the stones and rocky promontories of the Khyber Pass, nourished only by the spilled blood of legions. The bushes with pink blossoms, he allowed, after consulting the driver, were called *yeti mas*. Nature, like the female sex, was apparently beneath his contempt. He had plenty to say, however, about the politics of the region, insisting that Afghans had defeated the British and the Soviets and would certainly keep the Americans at bay. I suggested that the price for such isolation might be decades of poverty and missed opportunities, especially for women. He regarded me as a lost cause.

"Christians and infidels have always produced chaos in this region. That is why we welcome the Taliban, who guarantee stability and respect for Islam."

I knew this would be my last chance to visit the Peshawar Museum before I headed back to Islamabad for the inevitable bad news about my Afghan visa. If the visa was refused, as I fully expected it to be, I wouldn't be returning to this throbbing, chaotic city, with its huge refugee population, its tribal instabilities, its beggars, its kidnappings, its plethora of aid agencies, and its guns. Three nights earlier, sitting in a Chinese restaurant on the Khyber Road, I had overheard an aid worker negotiating with the owner over some illicit coins unrolled from a white handkerchief and spread out between them on the table. The slightly bloated aid worker, from the American Midwest, was offering advice on how to run the restaurant while speculating on the possible age of the coins. He also related a story about his former boss, who had been kidnapped. According to the driver, who survived the attack, a vanload of armed men intercepted the director's Land Rover, forced it to pull over, beat the driver, then loaded the Land Rover and its owner into the large van and drove off into the night. His boss was never seen again.

"I'll take these coins with me and have them evaluated. They look promising. We'll discuss the price later. Meanwhile, you should think of redoing the decor."

"What's wrong with it?"

"Ceiling's too high. Not intimate enough. Customers don't like to feel exposed while they eat."

That's exactly how I'd been feeling as I ate the local food—exposed—but it had nothing to do with the clever use of space or the interior design, except, of course, the design of my own digestive system. Afghan generosity and Pakistani cuisine had finally laid me low. Unable to refuse the drinks and snacks provided at the Khewa and Jalozai refugee camps or to resist the dubious salads at the Continental Guest House, I had succumbed to Genghis Khan's revenge. Two days earlier, I thought I was going to die. My face had a green, pasty hue, my gums were white, and my toes were red and swollen from the new hiking boots I'd bought a half-size too small in Vancouver, the only ones available that did not look like psychedelic running shoes. All I was running now was a fever; my stomach was so upset, I dared not stray far from the toilet.

My windowless room now felt like a tomb. While the hypnotic theme song of *BBC World* insinuated itself into my brain and the apocalyptic countdown to news time throbbed in my eardrums, I contemplated chucking the whole project and heading home, throwing myself into the arms of anyone willing to care for me in my terminal stages. But my illness passed, more or less. After thirty-six hours, I was able to take a taxi to the Intercontinental Hotel, drift specterlike through its palatial lobby, and feebly sample the famous buffet. I spent several hours in luxury, using the fast-but-expensive Internet hookup and consuming several bowls of puréed carrot-and-asparagus soup.

At the height of my delirium, I'd scratched a few words in my notebook, which I transcribed by e-mail to my friend Martin back home. They made no sense whatsoever, but I thought this narrative remnant might amuse him:

At fourteen I accompanied my mother to a nunnery in Bactria. Marriage will do that to a woman. She tried to enroll earlier, but father insisted on another son. Persecution took us to Purushapura to study the sacred texts, then to Taksashila. Privacy, uncluttered by possessions, appealed to the hermit in her. She'd have been put to death for running off with another man, but not with Buddha. She never understood the texts we pored over, yet committed them to memory, and so astonished her teachers. She also loved the sound of words and might, in more favorable circumstances, have become a poet. On family days, she quoted scripture to birds on the banks of the Indus or traced with rough fingers on my forehead the sacred characters. When I refuted the arguments of heretic monks who mocked my youthfulness, they mounted a campaign against her, and she was caught in the bloody purge that swept the abbess and her nuns from favor.

The museum was an attractive Victorian-style structure which had not been maintained or upgraded in fifty years. The lighting was bad, the display cases awkwardly set up and dust-laden. However, the collection of Buddhist art was stunning. Among the hundreds of large and small sculptures, you could find a Buddha to suit any mood—fierce, benign, enigmatic— or any fashion—plump, skeletal, curly haired, Greek-looking, wearing a topknot, slant-eyed, a sleep. There were Buddhas with intricately woven robes, with disk-shaped halos, a meditating Buddha, a Buddha with an open hand raised in the teaching position, and one with no hands at all. I was particularly taken with a Buddha seated on a wave or surge of water that emanated from his toes. He appeared to be replicating into hundreds of smaller versions of himself. I could not understand the iconography, though I liked the idea of reproducing fragments, psychic cloning. On closer examination, I decided that these were not waves at all, but a throne of lotus leaves. According to Nancy Dupree's *An Historical Guide to Afghanistan*, which I'd been feverishly, if not deliriously, reading, the Kushan were the first to represent Buddha in human form. Before that, Buddha had been depicted symbolically as a wheel, an empty throne, a riderless horse, or a mere footprint, an absence rather than a presence and, therefore, less subject to artistic fashion or politicization.

Overcome by heat and humidity in the museum, I had to sit down every ten minutes. Although several electric fans had been strategically placed, security guards on wooden chairs blocked the passage of cooling air. As I circulated among these images and tried to take advantage of the cross-draft, I had the impression that Huishen might have preferred the more subtle manifestations of Buddha's absence. Although he doubtless studied and practised his religion in Bamiyan, perhaps even in the extensive network of chambers and cells carved into the cliff face behind the two giant Buddhas there, I had a feeling that Huishen would have quietly scorned a dependency on icons. A religion of the heart is, after all, quietly subversive and cannot be so easily targeted.

News was very much on my mind. Given my delicate stomach, I'd missed the Afghan music and national celebrations the previous night at the Jalozzai refugee camp, but I had caught the late-night news and the next morning's photographs of the military parade in Kabul. It was a lackluster affair, to be sure, consisting of armed Taliban in tanks, jeeps, and pickup trucks, guns raised and defiant, but a clear reminder of the continuing dangers of religious fanaticism. There was no talk in the papers yet of releasing the American aid workers from Shelter Now International, accused of illegally promoting Christianity. In fact, international diplomacy had come to naught, and those arrested were expected to remain in detention to await trial. I made a note to put all of my books, Buddhist notes, and anti-Taliban propaganda into storage in Pakistan, on the off chance of my visa being approved. The partisan vitriol, including photographs of corpses and of people maimed and the naming of the perpetrators, standard fare in all RAWA publications, would hardly endear me to my hosts.

» » « «

The museum full of Buddhist art and sculpture, and Huishen's nocturnal "visitation," sent me scurrying back to my notes. Gudrun and Ikuko had asked when the Huishen story first surfaced in the Europe. As early as 1542, the Dutch poet and legal scholar Hugo Grotius had been convinced of an earlier Asian connection with the Americas, based on Spanish reports of the remains of Chinese junks on the Pacific Coast. However, the real breakthrough came in 1761, when French sinologist Joseph de Guignes translated material from Chinese historian Ma Twan-lin's *Antiquarian Researches*, originally published in 1321, that included an account of Huishen's voyage to the east. Ma Twan-lin's version of the Huishen story, though brief—746 characters, about three pages in all—and somewhat less than dramatic, suggests that the monk may, in the original telling, have had a good deal more to say about marriage customs, criminal justice, and domestic politics:

> The Kingdom of Fu-Sang is situated twenty thousand li to the east of the country of Ta-han. It is also east of China. It produces a great number of a species of tree called fu-sang, from which has come the name borne by the country. The leaves of the fu-sang are similar to those of the tree which the Chinese call t'ung. When they first appear, they resemble the shoots of the reeds called bamboo, and the people of the country eat them. The fruit has the form of a pear, and inclines toward red in color; from its bark they make cloth and other stuffs, with which the people clothe themselves, and the boards which are made from it are employed in the construction of their houses.

While devoid of both narrative drive and any vestiges of a real person telling the story, Ma Twan-lin's account does document habits and mores of the peoples of Fusang, some of whom lived peacefully in cities without walls and were said to have a "species of writing." Academic battles raged over specific details—whether the *fusang* tree was actually western red cedar, maguey, or corn, whether there could have been grapes and horses in the countries Huishen visited, and whether Asians had the ships and navigation skills to make such a voyage—but I was more interested in Huishen's reference to writing.

So far as I knew, writing in the Americas began with the Olmec and came to full flower in the Maya codices. Was it independently invented or the result of cultural diffusion from abroad? German sinologist Karl Friedrich Neumann endorsed the idea of Asian diffusion and elected the Mexican maguey as the source of paper and so much else in Fusang: "From its crushed leaves a firm paper is prepared, even up to the present time, as at the time when the Aztec kingdom flourished, and the few hieroglyphic manuscripts that have escaped the barbarity and fanaticism of the Spaniards consist of this paper; and of such manuscripts the Buddhist missionary speaks. The flowing sap is brewed into an intoxicating drink, which is still liked by the people of the country. Its large, stiff leaves serve as firm roots for their low huts, and from the fibers are made all kinds of thread, cordage, and rough cloth. When cooked, the roots form a savory species of food; and the thorns are used as needles and pins."

Ma Twan-lin refers to five monks from Kabul as the principal missionaries. Was Huishen one of them? And why were there five monks? If the written account of the story, as told to the court of Wu-ti in 502 (three years after Huishen's return to

China), were lost or destroyed, how much of the original account survived orally to be set down again in 629, and how reliable was this oral history likely to be? Might the confusion be cleared up by more competent translation? To get some help with these matters, I had talked to my friend Reverend Master Kōten Benson, a former member of the United Church in Newfoundland who was now a priest at the Lions Gate Buddhist Priory in Vancouver, a spiritual trajectory to match the geographical one.

As it had turned out, Kōten was more than ready to have his brains picked on the subject of Buddhism. We were eating vegetable curry at a restaurant in South Vancouver, overlooking the Fraser River. Warehouses and small businesses had replaced the sawmills and their rich cedar aroma. Kōten was wearing a brown robe but did not appear in the least ascetic; in fact, he was very enthusiastic about the meal in front of him and quite capable of doing it justice. The Chinese prefix *hui*, he explained, is a very common honorific given to Japanese, Korean, Indian, and other foreign monks. One obvious example was the Korean monk Hui Ch'ao, who had visited Bamiyan around AD 727 and commented on the devotion of the people to the Three Jewels (Buddhism). It was also common practice, Kōten insisted, for five monks to travel together, as that is the number required for the ordination of new priests. He thought it made perfect sense that the five monks, including Huishen, would all be Afghans, as they would then share not only language but also histories and would have been trained in the same school of Buddhism.

Kōten was familiar with the scholarly debate and with several of the books I'd read about Huishen, including *An Inglorious*

Columbus, by British sinologist Edward P. Vining. Published in 1885, the book provides an exhaustive account of the Huishen story and its bumpy critical reception, the most interesting item being Marquis d'Hervey de Saint-Denys' humorous remarks about a document called the *Liang-sse-kong-ki,* "Memoirs of the Four Lords of the Liang Dynasty." In these pages, Prince Yu-Kie, one of those invited to interrogate the monk, takes great delight in highlighting, and no doubt embellishing, Huishen's quaintly erotic material, particularly his account of the Kingdom of Women, in which the inhabitants were said to have breasts on their backs, to have become pregnant from bathing in a yellow river, to have had short gestation periods, and to have taken snakes as husbands. This latter proclivity, it was recorded, produced loud guffaws at court, perhaps an indication that narrative skill was more highly valued than historical accuracy.

Back at the priory, a modest stucco bungalow on a busy Vancouver thoroughfare, I mentioned these aspects of Huishen's narrative and asked Kōten about the Buddhist rules concerning celibacy and the likelihood that a monk might break his vows. Had the Buddha not advised against looking at women? He erupted with laughter, the brown robe rising and falling around him like a bellows. He reminded me that Zen Buddhist priests in Japan are permitted to marry and that, yes, aside from the usual examples of human weakness, there are always individuals in the faith who take an independent view in such matters, just as there are devout Catholics who practice birth control.

Our discussion of sex led, inevitably, to Henriette Mertz's book *Pale Ink: Two Ancient Records of Chinese Exploration in America,* first published in 1954. Mertz, a copyright lawyer in

Chicago, picking up on a suggestion made by Vining, links Huishen's account to the *Shan Hai Ching*, the four-thousand-year-old Chinese *Classic of Mountains and Seas*, purportedly written by the legendary Emperor Yu. While most scholars view the *Shan Hai Ching* as a work of fiction, Mertz believed that its descriptive mapping corresponds to key elements in Huishen's narrative, both of which could be positively identified with land-marks from Manitoba to Mexico. Huishen's varnished lake, she argues, is none other than the La Brea tar flats in California. And what about those women with breasts on their backs? Mertz puts her legal and investigative skills to work on the problem, asking us to imagine women carrying on their backs infants who sucked at the white ribbons tying up their mothers' hair. It's not difficult to see how the oral transmission of this story during a period of a hundred twenty-five years might result in the white ribbons being mistaken for milk. To put the matter more crudely, if women are described as pulling babies over their shoulders to nurse, after a century of retelling the breasts too might end up on the back. As for women marrying the phallic snakes, Mertz refers us to totem stories of the famous Snake Clan in the American Southwest.

Neither Kōten nor I was a literalist. We were prepared to view the Huishen narrative as a limited gloss on what had been an actual adventure. I was of the opinion that Huishen's story should be judged not on its brevity or possibly garbled details but on its feasibility and suggestiveness. I found my justification in an essay by historian Gwyn Prins on the debate between oral and written history. "We live," Prins says, "in an ocean of written messages" and in a world that "holds the spoken word in contempt." It's an important observation, as

Huishen appears to have left no written record, not even a personal diary, but to have relegated to others the responsibility for setting down his intriguing story. Even as early as AD 502, when the report was made, Chinese culture exhibited a strong bias in favor of written messages, so it's not surprising that a certain skepticism, even disrespect, surrounds the Huishen narrative, a twice-told tale that floated in the ether, subject to the vicissitudes of memory, for more than a century before being permanently recorded. Unlike the personally written chronicles of the traveling monks Fahien and Hsuan Tsang, who made separate journeys west to India to bring back sacred texts of Buddhism, in AD 399 and 629 respectively, the epigrammatic sketch of Huishen's vastly longer and more extended journey eastward is vested with very little authority in the document-driven histories of China and the West.

In such a story, airborne for so long, there is plenty of opportunity for loss, as well as for error and distortion. The abbreviated account of Huishen's travels that we have is the product not only of memory lapses and sloppy recording, but also of periodic scholarly condensations, as imperial librarians, short of space and committed to the glorification of new rulers and new dynasties, set about editing and abbreviating the past. After this kind of major surgery, everything that comes down to us exists in an extreme form of shorthand. If one accepts the unreliability of the Huishen narrative, along with its tenacious persistence through the ages, it is possible to view the furor surrounding its critical reception in the West with a degree of humor and objectivity.

» » « «

Back in Islamabad, I was happy to slip into tourist mode for a few days, reading, sending books and other materials home, catching up on e-mail, checking out the shops, making a day trip to Taxila, and looking for some familiar, reliable food. I spent a few hours in the Jinnah Market, across from the Pearl Guest House, where there were not only a bookstore, a deli, several restaurants, and a host of upscale boutiques, but also a cheap and convenient Internet café, minus the food and drinks. Actually, if you paid the staff, one of them would hop out and buy whatever your thirst required—except, of course, cold beer.

Two young Pakistani males were online beside me in this second-floor hideaway above the Jinnah Market. While I pondered the Silk Road, they surfed the Information Highway. The one on my left was looking at pornography on the Web; the other, on my right, appeared to be constructing a résumé. I spent two hours checking my e-mail and sending rather poorly veiled farewell notes to family and friends, the kind of letter a soldier might write on the night before an impending attack. Without sounding too lugubrious, I told them all—my daughters and close friends—that I loved them and would try to contact them during the coming week, though I had no idea what forms of communication would be available to me. I hoped it was something other than the services of a psychic.

As soon as I checked back into the Pearl, I took a cab to the Afghan embassy to inquire about my visa application. The return ride from Peshawar to Islamabad had been quite different from the ride there, as I indulged myself in a first-class, air-conditioned bus and sat far enough back that I could not see what was happening on the highway. I observed again the conjunction of the Kabul and Indus rivers, trying to identify the exact moment when the muddy Afghan water became indistinguishable in the greater confluence from the north, where I might possibly be heading in one or two days. I felt my own journey had already been muddied by Kabul and its politics. Although sites of political conflict fascinated me, I'd spent more time than I had intended reading and thinking about Afghanistan because Huishen originated there.

Before I left Peshawar, I'd received an e-mail message from my friend and one-time interpreter Wang Ronghua. It was a sign of the changes awaiting me in the new China that Wang, who had once been seconded to the Canadian International Development Agency, had risen in the bureaucratic ranks to become Chinese ambassador to Iceland. I had to restrain myself from asking if the appointment had been a reward or a punishment. Instead, I said that Pakistan in August could use some of that famous ice if there were any to spare. Canadians get a bit crazy in hot places, I explained to Wang, and sentimental when it comes to ice and snow. I told him I expected to be heading north to China right away through the Hindu Kush, the Pamirs, and the Himalayas by way of the Karakoram Highway, the Hunza Valley, and the Kunjerab Pass, traveling across the roof of the world—where glaciers and that other white stuff abounded.

I'd kept my bus window closed because of the air-conditioning. No diesel cosmetics this time. I was wearing sandals and was dressed in a lightweight cotton shirt and slacks, the kind that could be washed and dried overnight. I could have chucked half the clothes I'd packed, but I knew the road north into the high mountains and the weeks of autumn in China would produce some cooler temperatures. I had bread, bananas, and bottled water for the journey. I sat back and enjoyed the views—a water buffalo with a white bird perched on its back and two Asian crows in their gray-brown waistcoats fighting over an empty plastic food carton no doubt tossed from an overloaded truck. In this mood of benign indifference that I was trying to cultivate, it was not difficult to imagine the landscape without its veneer of contemporary civilization, with only farms, animals grazing, the occasional caravan, and a few itinerant monks begging alms.

Before noon, on my way downtown in the taxi, I had rehearsed what I would say when told that the visa had been refused. Although I was beginning to feel secretly relieved by the prospect of avoiding Afghanistan—especially when I could tell my friends I'd genuinely tried to get in—I felt obliged to register some sort of disapproval of the delay and the negative decision. I wanted these suspicious Taliban functionaries to know they were making a big mistake, that in turning me down—because they thought I was too much of a risk or too much of an unknown quantity—a serious injustice had been committed. I wasn't quite sure exactly what this injustice might be, but the idea of myself as the most recent victim of narrow-minded fundamentalism seemed attractive.

I knew where I was going this time and had chosen a local yellow cab, so I arrived at the embassy before completing my Afghan Rejection speech. They were closing the visa office for lunch. Not only would I not find out about the visa, but I'd also have to wait to deliver my rant. I rapped on the door. White Turban opened it slightly and squinted at this intruder, this infidel, this defiler of the sanctity of the lunch hour. I told him my name and he pointed to the chair before closing the door. I could imagine another two-hour wait, part of the game of power politics. While I baked in the hot sun, those petty bureaucrats would be flaked out on carpets, dunking strips of oval-shaped nan into steaming bowls of tea. I wished I were more assertive or at least vaguely important. I should have played my professorial card. Then it occurred to me that the Taliban might have refused my visa precisely *because* of my academic connections. The Center for Canadian-American Studies in Bellingham, Washington, might have sounded to them like some sort of intelligence-gathering agency, though a few of my former colleagues and friends would have shrieked with laughter at the suggestion and joked about the mistake they'd made, in that case, by hiring me. I'm well out of this crap, this diplomatic farce, I was thinking, as the door opened and White Turban announced, with the faintest trace of a smile, "Your visa has been approved. Pay the cashier thirty American dollars and come back at 2:00 p.m."

I signed a written agreement that I would follow the Taliban interpretation of sharia law, not photograph human subjects, not talk to women, and not interview Afghans in their homes.

The news of my visa approval threw me into a tailspin. I would need another visa for re-entry into Pakistan, and there was the matter of eliminating from my luggage any controversial materials. I also had to arrange transportation. Meanwhile, back at the Cyber Pass, the more studious of my fellow Web-surfers had joined his mate in checking out the porn site, with its dazzling array of enhanced breasts, gaping orifices, disgorged organs, and empty, smiling faces. Perhaps he would add this brief moment of rapture, this passport to electronic bliss, to the "relevant experience" section of his résumé.

A Line in the Sand

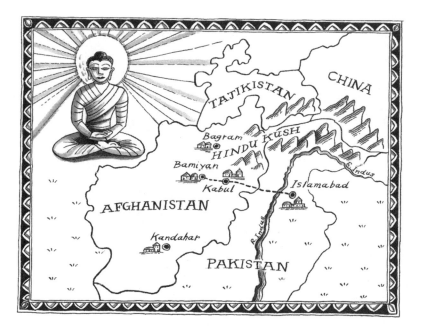

FOUR

WHEN I ARRIVED in Kabul and during the short taxi ride from the compound of the International Committee of the Red Cross (ICRC) to the Taliban's Ministry of Foreign Affairs, my senses were on full alert. I did not know exactly what to expect: perhaps mutilated corpses dangling from lampposts, or roving gangs of armed fanatics dressed in black turbans, carrying severed body parts and beating up women not adhering to the strict dress code. Those were the images dominating Western media, but they were also images reinforced by my interviews with Afghan refugees in Pakistan and from reading the reports of opposition groups speaking out against fundamentalist rule, whether Taliban or mujahideen.

I had, in my knapsack, postcards of Kabul in its heyday, from the 1950s to the 1970s, when it was a thriving modern city, a magnet for young travelers from the West, where they could live cheaply and comfortably and where the drug laws were lax. Theirs was, at root, a genuine, if misguided and short-circuited, spiritual quest, a sort of psycho-narcotic equivalent of the great game, reclaiming old values, old rhythms, old spiritual pathways. The markets were full to bursting. Elegant tribal dresses, much in demand in the hip boutiques of London, Vancouver, and New York, hung in the shop windows, each one a reminder of ancient crafts and current domestic hardship, as Afghan families were not in the habit of selling their heirlooms.

In the oddly tinted photographs of the time, now sold as postcards, the city is a fairyland of unnatural pinks and blues with that forbidding but protective border of mountains in the background.

In one postcard Kabul seems bathed in eternal spring. The moss-green of the riverbanks has seeped upward, as if by osmosis, to stain the houses, pedestrians, and even the *Shah-Do-Shamshira Mosque,*" the Mosque of the King of Two Swords," built in honor of an early Islamic commander who is said to have fought to the death with a sword in each hand, even after he'd lost his head in battle. In another doctored print, the wintry blue sky has permeated the cloak of snow on surrounding mountains and bled into the capital, giving it a cold, spellbound appearance, offset by a few splashes of ocher, setting apart the meeting hall and first cinema in Kabul. In another, you can identify three vintage cars—a jeep, a two-toned Oldsmobile, and a black Pontiac—parked outside a government building, where citizens stroll past in heavy overcoats. My favorite postcard, described on the back as an "Eye-bird view of the city," shows a thriving metropolis with a large and sophisticated commercial center, abundant trees, and green space, rendered even more civilized and inviting by the meandering of the Kabul River.

What I now saw in Kabul bore no resemblance to either the postcards or the media hype. Drought had reduced the river to a trickle. Never properly repaired after the civil war, the potholed avenues were still wide and generous, but few trees remained and there was little traffic. The fleet of ancient, dilapidated taxis, moored and idle, had surrendered the avenues to a smattering of donkey carts, bicycles, relief-agency vehicles, and the occasional jeep or SUV, driven by a merchant or a Taliban official. Collapsed buildings and mounds of rubble remained as monuments to human folly. However, no bodies hung from lampposts, and the only gun I'd seen so far belonged to a bored young Taliban at the airport. A few men in turbans strode purposefully along, but most sat or leaned in the shade watching the smattering of vehicles. Dozens of disabled men, victims of decades of conflict, bent over crutches, and the one woman I noticed rounding a corner wore a headscarf, not a burka, and was not accompanied by the requisite male relative. I was surprised by these contradictions. Either the dress code was more relaxed than I'd been led to believe or the woman was a foreigner. The absence of guns could owe as much to systematic intimidation as to social stability.

I was apprehensive, not only from two weeks of interviews with Afghan refugees in Pakistan, but also from reading three recent books on the Taliban, one of them written by Pakistani journalist Ahmed Rashid, in which the long-entrenched politics of betrayal, revenge, and ruthless foreign intervention is so strikingly delineated. Also, I was reminded of the possibility of danger, thanks to the document I'd signed a few hours earlier, absolving the International Committee of the Red Cross of any responsibility for my safety during or after the flight: "ICRC is taking all possible measures to assure a maximum of security. . . . Nevertheless, it is not possible to guarantee total security. Considering the situation prevailing in the area, anybody is exposed to a certain risk of injuries by bullets, mines, rockets, car bombs or rubble from ruins, explosion of gas or water pipes, etc." A comprehensive list, to be sure, with that explosive and ambivalent *etc.* intended to ignite the overly active imagination.

I'd left my Pakistan notes and what might be considered compromising written materials at the Pearl Guest House in Islamabad, including all my articles and jottings about Buddhism and Huishen. I did have a small camera, however, on the assumption that, living things excluded, I'd be able to photograph buildings and landscapes. I'd also picked up a copy of the Quran, which I'd been reading with great interest to see if I could determine the official position on women's rights, other religions, the arts, and the sacredness of human life. So far I was confused, though definitely intrigued by sections such as Surah 68, which is called "The Pen":

Noon. I swear by the pen and what the angels write,
By the grace of your Lord you are not mad.
And most surely you shall have reward never to be cut off.
And most surely you shall conform to sublime morality.
So you shall see, and they (too) shall see,
Which of you is afflicted with madness.

This poetic invocation was followed by encouragement not to yield to rejecters, defamers, swearers, slanderers, and the usual list of bad influences, with an enigmatic final admonition: "So wait patiently for the judgement of your Lord, and be not like the companion of the fish, when he cried while he was in darkness."

If this was a reference to Jonah in the belly of the whale, I could easily identify with the idea of being at sea, in the dark, out of my element. Secular poets are not given much credit in the Quran for having access to truth and revelation. Surah 26, which is called, surprisingly, "The Poets" and which concerns itself with truth, delusion, signs, and the hoped-for clarity, dismisses bards for having not only gone astray, but also for having taken others with them: "Do you not see that they wander about bewildered in every valley?"

I was bewildered that day in Kabul. Even without such reminders, I was intensely conscious of my ignorance and vulnerability in this alien, fundamentalist milieu. My friends had their own fears on my behalf. Wendy, a poet and neighbor, had given me an ancient Chinese coin, said to bring good luck to those born in the Year of the Dragon. "It has to be carried on your person if it's to work," she insisted. My students, after reading in class John Berger's novel *To the Wedding*, in which a blind Greek seller of medical charms imagines an alternate history for a victim of AIDS, had presented me, as a farewell gift, with the *tamate* of a flaming heart cast in silver. So my tracks were well covered, at least in the charms department.

I'd had three dreams the previous night. In the first, I was at the dock doing a small repair on my boat. I climbed up to a second-floor landing to talk to someone. When I looked down, all the boats had disappeared, sucked under by the collapsing of the concrete platform to which they were tied. In the second dream, I was in a passenger train, derailed by a farm implement that had been placed intentionally on the tracks. There were cries and a lot of scrambling to escape as the coach began to sink in swampy ground. In the third dream, my former wife, Jan, and I were hosting a celebration for the Anglican parents of a Japanese-Canadian friend who as a child during the Second World War had been relocated to an internment camp in central British Columbia. Her mother, whom I had never met, was singing a Christian hymn in a quavering voice—

dignified, serene, and with not a hint of bitterness. A toast was proposed, but I had no glass. Jan handed me a small preserving jar, the kind with threads at the top and the brand name stamped on the side. I was offended enough to complain.

"This is not about you," she grimaced. "It's about them."

The disturbing taste of those dreams was with me all day, though I had tried not to think of them and their significance. At the intersection closest to the foreign ministry compound, my taxi refused to give way to a ramshackle handcart containing vegetables and a man with no legs. The relative or friend pulling the cart jumped out of the way, losing his grip on the shafts. Off balance, it careened into the curb, catapulting its passenger and produce onto the sidewalk. The driver grinned at me in the rearview mirror, displaying a mouthful of broken, discolored teeth. As I turned to look out the back window, I caught the eyes of the disabled man as he raised himself upright on his hands amid the melons and purple cabbages.

His legless torso swung like a pendulum in the midmorning sun, marking time.

I rose early. I'd forgotten to draw the curtains the previous night, and sunlight had washed all sleep from my eyes. Sometime during the night, I had heard the short percussive blasts of mortar fire from the hills, a reminder that I was in a war zone. Ahmad Shah Massoud's Northern Alliance forces sometimes penetrated Taliban defenses near enough to the capital to sow havoc, if not cause serious damage. There had been only drums to signal the approach of that restless Greek, Alexander the Great, making his bloody way east; of Genghis

Khan, who killed every living thing in Bamiyan to avenge the death in battle of his precious grandson; and of that later scourge, Tamerlane. You could outrun a drum (if it was not on horseback) but not a mortar shell.

From the third floor of the Intercontinental Hotel, Kabul had a magical quality, as if the idea of light originated here. I basked in the early-morning rays, which warmed adobe walls, drew colors from the retreating dark, and pooled in the dew of cupped leaves. A more gentle kind of assault was underway: Besieged shadows dug into the ridged hillsides. I felt like a mole surfacing for the first time, weary of cave-Braille, of olfactory navigation. Light burned through the hair on both sides of my snout, two parched regions imagining themselves eyes.

With no one to talk to and with television forbidden by the Taliban, I'd been devouring Andre Dubus III novel *House of Sand and Fog*, a tragedy of manners set in San Francisco that weaves a complicated and deadly tale of cultural blindness and bureaucratic bungling. A distraught young woman, whose husband has just left her, is evicted as a result of a clerical error relating to unpaid taxes from the house she inherited from her father. The house is sold cheaply by auction to an under employed Iranian immigrant, a former officer under the shah, who is morally and financially beleaguered and desperate to succeed in the United States. Their struggle to regain or hold onto the contested house is brilliantly and unrelentingly drawn, even down to the awkwardly formal speech patterns Dubus constructs to convey the colonel's learning, sophistication, and rigidity. As well as being a gripping story, the novel is a powerful rendering of cultural misunderstanding, of crossed signals.

My guide, Hassan, had different reading materials in mind for me. Hoping to educate a poorly informed client, he loaned me his copy of *The Kingdom of Afghanistan* by G. P. Tate, published in 1910 and reprinted in 1970 in response to renewed interest in the region. It was dedicated to "His Excellency Baron Hardinghe of Penshurst, Viceroy and Governor-General of India, by his Obedient Servant the Author." Unfortunately, in describing the emergence of modern Afghanistan, with its parade of leaders, battles, intrigues, and betrayals, the author had been more obedient to his own pre-judices, calling the Afghans "fickle and turbulent" and making a number of racist pronouncements, including the assertion that "the ignorant and arrogant Afghan cannot, however, do without the despised Tajik, whether as agriculturists or administrators." This slur had prompted Hassan to respond in the margin: "This shows the ignorance of the author himself, a ridiculous mistake that discredits the whole book."

I did not point out the irony that the current rulers, the Taliban, consisted largely of Pashtuns whose human rights record was anything but clean and that their principal antagonist was still the "despised Tajik," whose people were the backbone of the Northern Alliance.

That morning we drove south from Kabul past Bala Hissar, ruins of the ancient hill fort occupied for fifteen centuries by a succession of rulers, including the Mogul emperor Babur. It had been destroyed by British forces in retaliation for the massacre of British envoy Sir Louis Cavagnari and his escort in 1879. The road was in bad shape, and we were eventually forced to take a shortcut across a barren stretch of countryside, bouncing in and out of parched stream beds and dodging small groups of children gathering sticks or tending goats. Now that I was actually in Afghanistan, the urgency to interview people at the aid agencies had suddenly diminished, especially as I had spent so much time with refugees and NGO staff in Pakistan. How many more statistics or stories of anguish and atrocity did I need? I'd been discouraged by the Taliban warning not to conduct private interviews; as a result, I'd spent more time alone than was strictly necessary. I asked Hassan if he could organize a meeting with young writers, but this proved impossible. There were merchants and idlers I might have spoken to, but I did not want to put them in the awkward position of answering questions about the lack of food, social services, and individual rights under the current regime, all of which would have had to be translated.

During our rambles in the countryside, we passed a number of small factories in which family members were eking out a living turning junk into furniture, tools, and farm implements. Just off the main road, a group of nomadic Kuchi had pitched their tents and were sitting near an open fire, drying laundry on bushes and drinking tea. Several tethered camels cast a skeptical eye on the sparse grass and brambles. These nomads wore layers of colorful garments. Some of the women's faces were veiled, but none wore the burka. Half a dozen small children chased a mangy dog around the fire; then the dog would chase them. It was a scene so typical it defied time. Behind them, incongruously, was parked a large flatbed trailer and cab. Unlike the Gypsies of Europe, the Kuchi of Afghanistan were apparently not harassed or treated as second-class citizens; in fact, their very mobility made them useful sources of information to the Taliban. Whether they used the truck for transporting goods or piled the whole gang—camels, children, and all—on board to move to their next location was something I might have asked if I'd had the sense to stop. But the seeming aimlessness of the day's outing, not to mention Hassan's likely disapproval of these rambles, was weighing heavily on my mind. My time in Afghanistan was short, there were plenty of other things to see; and here we were, half lost, zigzagging our way through a drought-stricken and probably mined no-man's-land.

I felt somewhat disjointed, having strayed so far from the purpose of my travels, which was to follow Huishen's likely route from Kabul to China. I had thought I would make a quick trip through the region, taking notes on landscape and customs along the way, recording unusual events. I had not expected to spend so much time waiting for an entry visa to Afghanistan. Was I crazy to have imagined I could slip through this troubled territory, with its immense pockets of dislocation and pain, without getting caught up in the politics? In the end, the refugee camps were like magnets, immense vortices of need that could swallow up a life as easily as they consumed the always-inadequate supplies of food from the outside world. Doctors and aid workers alike struggled to resist feelings of hopelessness. The patience they exhibited with naive and ignorant newcomers like myself, to whom everything must be explained in simple, childlike terms, was remarkable, bordering on the heroic.

"No, there's nothing that can be done to change distribution procedures in the camp. The corruption is endemic; it goes with the turf."

This honest response was hardly intended to assuage my outrage at the lack of accountability. At least, I thought, medical efforts will not be crippled by greed, by self-interest.

"This child may not survive. We don't have the variety of medicines we need. Her immunity is low. She'll go back to the same water supply, the same hygiene problems. We just don't have the staff necessary to feed, heal, and educate."

Blame. I wanted to blame someone, to point the finger. As Dr. Qayoom and others had explained to me, blame was not so easy to apportion in Afghanistan. Did it begin with the artificially imposed border called the Durand Line, between Afghanistan and India (or what is now the North-West Frontier Province of Pakistan)? Or with miniskirts in a traditional Muslim society—too much change too fast? The Soviet invasion in 1979 was intended to buttress a tottering secular, Communist regime. The West's arming and training of the regime's unpredictable fundamentalist enemies had backfired in the long-term. In the vacuum of the post-Soviet civil war, Pakistan preferred a strong Sunni Muslim neighbor, as a buffer against the Shiite Muslims of Iran, and the United States favored any regime that might be prepared to ensure a safe pipeline route from the Caspian oil fields. Once you factored in the pan-Arab ambitions of the Saudis to the west and the vested interests of former Soviet republics to the north, the political situation became impossible to read. All of these warring elements had conspired to bring the Taliban to power in Afghanistan and to keep them there.

More vehicles were zigzagging along the potholed road from the north. As I put down my book, I could make out a smattering of donkeys, handcarts, and bicycles, and the occasional camel, as farmers and craftsmen drifted into the city to hock their wares and stock up on essentials. Refugees in flight from drought and from continued fighting in the north used the road. Below my window, there were fruit trees, survivors of an old orchard losing ground steadily—but home nonetheless to a murder or two of Asian crows, second cousins all, decked out in elegant beige-brown vests but with the same raucous cries, the same repertoire of tricks, as those back home.

I'm in avoidance mode, I thought. I'm shirking. I don't know if I can face more injured children and adults, their ghostly limbs irretrievably lost in the countryside we so blithely traversed hours earlier.

Because of the city's elevation, the late August sunlight bathing Kabul seemed almost benign, as if it might heal anything. It poured down on the honey-colored adobe roofs of the old residential district we passed through on our way to the Wazir Orthopaedic Center, funded and operated by the International Committee of the Red Cross. On every rooftop, washing hung out to dry, giving the devastated metropolis a wearily festive air.

I was met at the door of the clinic by Najmuddin, director of operations, a large jovial man with a slight limp. He wore a white smock. Showing me to a chair, he offered tea and asked what I would like to see. Everything, I said. Najmuddin introduced me to various staff members, including Carol, a physiotherapist from Ireland. One of six expatriates in Afghanistan hired to train 260 local workers, thirty-five of them women, Carol spent much of her time engaged in visits outside the clinic, teaching staff and families how to administer home care. I enjoyed the chance to talk with a native English-speaker and was quite prepared to procrastinate, avoiding what lay ahead. However, Najmuddin had taken me at my word about wanting to see it all.

He ushered me into the wheelchair workshop, where six men were making and assembling parts. Only the bicycle wheels came ready-made. Since 1998, the clinic had produced more than five thousand of the simple, sturdy wheelchairs, just a fraction of what was needed. Most of the workers were disabled, Najmuddin explained. He himself had been injured fighting the Soviets and had spent a long time at home, completely dispirited, thinking his life was over. Now he was helping to coordinate a large-scale operation that included centers in Herat, Jalalabad, Gulbahar, Faizabad, and Mazar-i-Sharif.

As I passed several curtained cubicles, I glimpsed a small girl lying on her side on a hospital cot, whimpering in fear or in agony—perhaps both—while two adults held her down and a third bent over her lower body. Her mouth was contorted and her cries were half stifled by gasps for breath. I couldn't tell what was happening, whether she was being fitted for a prosthetic device or having some sort of minor corrective surgery. Too often, operations had to be redone, to remove painful shell and bone fragments or repair a hastily performed amputation, so the stump could be properly fitted with an artificial limb. I wanted to know about her but was too startled and too aware of my own intrusiveness to inquire.

I'm not sure I can do this, I thought. Sickness and injury are bad enough, but when children are involved, my emotional resources quickly evaporate. I could not help recalling my daughter, Bronwen, developing a high fever, when she was just a year old, that no one could diagnose. This happened repeatedly over the course of a year, with frightening trips to emergency rooms and many sleepless nights applying cold compresses to her tiny body. One irresponsible doctor suggested it might be the first signs of rheumatoid arthritis, which had my wife and me poring over ghastly images in medical journals. When, after a year of fear and panic, I finally convinced a surgeon to remove Bronwen's tonsils and adenoids, the problem disappeared, but not before she almost died from postoperative hemorrhaging. A privileged memory, of course, but no less distressing for its context of universal health care and high-tech facilities.

In the second workshop, long strips of recycled pink plastic were being fed into an oven and melted to produce prosthetic devices. The liquid polypropylene was then poured into molds, mostly legs for victims of some of the twenty million land mines left by the Soviets and rival mujahideen forces. A report published as early as 1994 suggested that two hundred thousand Afghans had already died from land mines and another four hundred thousand had been disabled. In any other context, I'd have worried about fumes and proper ventilation, but here I painstakingly followed the stages from making a mold to production and fitting, even refitting, hinges, screws, shafts—my disaster-charged imagination riveted to the tiniest detail.

In the screened courtyard, a dozen disabled people of all ages were "test-driving" their new prostheses or doing exercises, including a small boy named Saeed with legs as twisted as pretzels. To strengthen his body muscles in preparation for corrective surgery, he was being shown how to swing himself along two parallel bars, as if parodying a ballet or a gymnastic display. I could hardly bear to watch, but a broad smile of victory broke out on his face as he made his way, breathless, down the ten feet of bars. Another boy, several years older, marched carefully back and forth on two new artificial legs, anxious to demonstrate his mobility. In a corner, a staffer worked with an older man to determine what adjustment had to be made to his prosthesis so it would bend properly at the knee when he sat.

Hassan came to my rescue, worry beads in hand, to deliver me back to the ghostly precincts of the Intercontinental Hotel, where there would be nothing to distract me—no television, no e-mail, only Iraj and his small bookstore just off the lobby on the main floor. I found myself hoping Iraj had not closed early, so I could check out his books and postcards as a pretext for our having tea together, taking my mind off the Wazir Orthopaedic Center and its maimed children. On the way out, Najmuddin had given me a hug and a brochure explaining that care was now being extended to include nonamputees and the nonwar-wounded. This meant that Saeed might learn to walk again and the nameless girl I had glimpsed earlier could be treated for poliomyelitis. There was something surreal or grotesquely magical about the procedures at the Wazir Orthopaedic Center, this human repair shop with its rows of feet and boxes of joint hinges. In Najmuddin's small clinic, despite those who planted death while claiming to be the people's saviors, a terrible beauty had been born.

Back at the hotel, Iraj was having tea with one of his friends. He fetched a cup and took time to chat with me about books, Canada, and his father's store in Islamabad, where I'd purchased several titles the previous week. There was a small, blue paperback tucked away on the shelf, an English–Afghan Dari dictionary published in 1973, with an introduction that explained why the book was hastily prepared and provided unintentional examples of sloppy editing. I had in my note-book only a small list of Dari words and phrases provided by my

Afghan friends Habib and Gulalai in Vancouver, so I was happy to give Iraj three dollars for the dictionary.

I hadn't a clue about the principles of Dari grammar, so I consulted the notes at the back of the book when I returned after dinner to my spartan room, where the morning's wash of socks, underwear, pants, and shirt was dry and two dimensional on its hangers. The soft colors of the distant hills—brown, green, ocher—had emerged once again in the slant light of early evening. A crow (*yak zaagh*, according to the dictionary) alighted on a branch near my balcony; he had no song today, nothing to crow about (*qaagh qaagh nakard*). I knew the feeling; I couldn't get the day's graphic images out of my mind. The first example in the grammar notes concerned plurals, formed by adding the suffix -*haa*: *dars* (lesson), *darshaa* (lessons); *tefel* (child), *tefel-haa* (children). This was followed by examples of the accusative case: *Tefel raa mebinam* (I see the child), *Tefel khub ast* (the child is good). The third example showed how a word is attached to its modifier by adding *e*: *tefel-e khub* (good child), *dars-e mushkel* (difficult lesson).

The book, it seemed, was reading me.

FIVE

ON THE RED CROSS flight to Kabul, there had been much talk of an American group called Shelter Now International, whose staff had been detained by the Taliban and charged with promoting Christianity. According to the Taliban's strict interpretation of *sharia* law, preaching foreign religions is illegal, and death sentences are handed out to Muslims who convert. Evidence trotted out by the accusers included tapes, pamphlets, and Bibles translated into Dari and Pashto, the local Afghan languages. For some, this was further proof of the rigidity and intolerance of the Taliban. For others, the arrests were a reminder of the vacuum created by twenty years of resistance and civil war that had destroyed the country's infrastructure and left the field open to any group passing itself off as an aid agency.

"Christians, who needs them under the circumstances?"

Emile, who worked for a prominent NGO, wiped the sweat from his forehead as we passed low over the mountains and narrow gorges of the Khyber Pass. He had more pressing problems to worry about than pushy and indiscreet Christians, as food distribution in Afghanistan was out of control. There were only one hundred and fifty thousand internally displaced persons in the camp near Mazar-i-Sharif, he insisted, but aid agencies claimed they needed food for three hundred and fifty thousand. The conclusion was as simple as the math:

Unscrupulous locals and Taliban officials were skimming off and reselling supplies for two hundred thousand invisible refugees.

"Beneficiary identification is the big problem," Emile said. "If you quote me, I'll deny it."

During a lull in the conversation, I could see beyond the bluish-brown ridges of the Hindu Kush to where the land dropped away into the region known as Bamiyan, one of those places, like the Grand Canyon, where nature had wrought something so unusual that it seemed to humans to possess a uniquely spiritual dimension. Once the world's most densely populated center for Buddhist studies, with scores of monasteries and thousands of monks, Bamiyan was once again the site of a profound loss. Other than the desire to score a few political points against the West—which had cut off aid, frozen assets, grounded the national airline, and conducted air strikes against suspected al-Qaeda training camps—there had been no need to destroy the Bamiyan Buddhas; Muslims had lived with the colossal sculptures for twelve hundred years. Even Genghis Khan, who swept through the region like a berserker, had left the Buddhas standing.

The one-hour flight discharged its passengers and cargo in Kabul, then took off for the western Afghan city of Herat. I crossed the airport tarmac with Erhat, who worked for the German aid agency AGFO. He was a tall, gangly, exhausted idealist, a PhD in linguistics and a Dari expert, but he had given up on academia. "It's a nice life if you feel you are part of a tradition, passing on information, knowledge, teaching the occasional interested student. But there was no one standing behind me, waiting to pick up the torch." He talked wistfully about his wife and daughter, now on holiday in Thailand. He was feeling the stress but figured he could last another year, at which time his daughter would need proper schooling.

"And by then I'll need counseling. You either suppress all the horrible things you see here and risk going crazy or you become cynical."

A week earlier I had talked in Peshawar with Nancy Dupree, a walking encyclopedia on Afghanistan and its culture, who was anything but cynical. She had spent most of her adult life poring over every inch of Afghanistan and now, in her mid-seventies, she was not about to stop. In the 1950s, Nancy wrote the first major historical guide to Afghanistan, a lyrical account of a country inexhaustible in its beauties and surprises; then, in 1965, a historical guide to Kabul that had inspired Tony Kushner's play *Homebody/Kabul*. Her office was directly across the lane from the Continental Guest House, where I was staying in the University Town suburb of Peshawar, so I was able to mount a serious campaign to arrange an interview. Nancy was initially unable, or unwilling, to see me, which gave me a chance to pick up a dusty copy of her book downtown.

"Afghanistan," she wrote, "has jagged snow-covered massifs at its heart, softly rounded hills protecting fertile valleys, vast steppelands, forests and a wide variety of deserts—semi, sandy, stony, and salty—each with its own particular charm and fascination. The peoples who inhabit this land are even more varied." Her guidebook is also full of personal anecdotes and tantalizing quotations from the classics, including this telling Turkoman proverb: "The sand of the desert is lightly blown away by a breath. Still more lightly is the fortune of men destroyed."

When we met, I began by quoting this passage back to Nancy and suggesting that she didn't seem that easily blown away, as she was still writing about Afghanistan, attending conferences in Sweden, and running ACBAR, an agency for coordinating Afghan relief. I wondered how much had changed since she described Afghanistan's history as "the perpetuation of tribal disunity alternating with prolonged foreign domination." I commented on the loving detail with which she had described the *Buddhas of Bamiyan* and their surrounding network of elegant, decorated caves; then I alluded to her fascination with the tiny, enigmatic sculptured head from Aq Kupruk, once the pride of the Kabul Museum. This figure, dating from 20,000 BC, might, she had speculated, be one of the earliest representations of man.

Nancy smiled. I'd obviously done my homework, so she was prepared to be charmed, but only for a few minutes, as we had barely begun to talk when the phone started ringing and shadowy figures poked their heads around the door. Nancy had no love for the Taliban and what they and other factions had done to the country and its art, but she had great respect for the egalitarian teachings of Islam, which value resilience, tolerance, obligation, and honor.

"There are moderate elements in the Taliban that should be appealed to," she said, "and a quiet revolution is at work in the countryside, with schools blossoming in places where they never existed before. The family, not the state, is central to this development." Then she described an incident in which the Taliban tried to close a school because they wanted it for their offices. "The locals protested and got it back."

Nancy could identify with this kind of pluck. She had come to Kabul in 1962 with her first husband, a diplomat, but claimed to have had only two great passions in her life: Louis

Dupree, the archaeologist she soon met and married, and Afghanistan itself. Together they explored Afghanistan from stem to stern and wrote about it over most of two decades. After Louis Dupree's death in 1989, Nancy devoted her life to organizations promoting and preserving the country's cultural heritage—not only ACBAR, but also the Afghan Resource and Information Center (ARIC) and the Society for the Preservation of Afghanistan's Cultural History (SPACH). She may have had acronyms coming out her ears, but she was arguably the most knowledgeable person alive on Afghanistan's cultural antiquities.

The phone rang, something about paperwork for the school libraries project, designed to reeducate Afghans in the values and glories of their past. Nancy was not averse to changing directions or changing her mind. She had once obtained a master's degree in Chinese at Columbia University. As she explained to her alma mater, "I started as a musician, but I would have missed so much if I had stubbornly pursued that one career. Keep your eyes on the horizon and see what's coming down the pike."

Few old Afghan hands could claim to have followed that dictum so rigorously. While most scholars and art historians had given up on Afghanistan because of the severity of looting during the civil war, Nancy continued to lobby all sides in the conflict on behalf of the remaining treasures, some of which had been ferreted away for safekeeping in the cellars and vaults of Kabul. She expressed outrage about the political situation but remained— miraculously, it seemed to me—productive and optimistic.

"The essential nature of Afghan society is being undermined by the Taliban, as they allow themselves to be 'Arabized' by Saudi Arabia. There's talk of two thousand and five hundred *madrassas* being funded by the Saudis, with Arabic as the language of instruction. This will destroy all of the old Afghan values."

Nancy's eye was not only on the horizon, but also on the doorway, where a small lineup had formed. I gathered up my notes. Even I could see what was coming down the pike.

When we landed in Kabul I had noticed, skirting the runway, the wreckage of various military support vehicles and a dozen aircraft in various stages of demolition or disrepair, left by the departing Soviets in 1989. Some were stripped to the bone and gutted, others, missing a wing or an engine, grim reminders of the parade of foreign armies that had run roughshod over this country through the centuries, leaving rubble, ordnance, and numberless dead. I could see Erhat loading his suitcases into the trunk of a waiting car. A hundred yards beyond him, shimmering in the intense heat of midday, a father and son were carefully dismantling the tail section of a small Soviet fighter jet, cutting through camouflaged plates with the aid of an acetylene torch, perhaps gathering the materials they'd use to manufacture the jackknives and kitchen utensils on sale at the Saddar Market in Peshawar.

In the offices of the Foreign Ministry, young Taliban were going about their business, or creating the illusion thereof, like seasoned bureaucrats. The difference was that they did not quite look the part; they had not yet developed the requisite glazed or cynical expressions that come with the knowledge that however furiously they plan and pontificate, nothing much will happen—or it will happen in its own good time.

This paralysis was compounded in Afghanistan not only by the shortage of funds, but also by the total collapse of the infrastructure of government. However, unlike the ministries of health and education, which consisted of little more than title and desk, the Foreign Ministry had a modest buzz from having to deal with the daily trickle of journalists and other foreigners with dubious agendas, as well as with sundry spies, arms dealers, aid workers, and drug traffickers.

I was ushered into the office of two young men, one of whom spoke passable English. While he and his colleague examined my documents with great concentration and searched for my name on their admittance list, several interpreters arrived, introducing themselves and talking with me briefly. There seemed to be a problem: My name did not appear to be on the list, although the visa was clearly valid and official. I suggested they try looking under my first name. Meanwhile, tea was served, and a man in his late thirties sidled up to me and began speaking French. "Since you're Canadian," he said, "I assume you understand French. If you work with me, I'll be able to tell you things you won't hear from anyone else, since no one else in this ministry, including the drivers, speaks French." He gave me a complicit smile and lowered his eyes. I thought perhaps I was being set up, so I thanked him for his interest and explained that I had so much to learn about Afghanistan that I did not want to be distracted or inhibited by my modest grasp of the French language.

When my name, "Mr. Gary," was located on the list, the mood in the room shifted. The two officials relaxed and became quite jovial, their task having been successfully completed. I mentioned in passing that I'd met Nancy Dupree, a great friend and student of their country. The young official raised two open hands in praise and hoped that Nancy would get in touch with them, as they needed her advice on important cultural matters.

Formalities completed, I left the Foreign Ministry in the company of Hassan who had been assigned to serve as my official guide. He described himself in perfect English as a recent graduate of Kabul University, where he had studied English and American literature. A tall, graceful youth, who walked with a slight limp, striking in his black turban, Hassan hailed a cab and dropped me and my bags off at the Intercontinental Hotel, the only choice now that aid agencies were no longer allowed to provide lodgings for anyone but their own employees. He wished me a good evening and promised to pick me up the next morning after breakfast.

"I'm doing research here: Following the path of an Afghan Buddhist monk named Huishen, who fled persecution in Kabul, taking the Silk Road to China. According to historical records, he then sailed east to the Americas in AD 458, a thousand years before Columbus."

I told this story to Hassan as we sat amid the ruins of a summer palace north of the capital, eating a melon. He nodded and made some comment to the driver in Dari. I expected him to express surprise or ask if discovering North America gave Afghans an advantage in applying for visas to emigrate to Canada or the United States, but he did not. We had just visited the village of Paghman, where the artillery-shattered skeleton of a victory arch, modeled on the Arc de Triomphe in Paris, presided incongruously over the square, a reminder of better times perhaps, or, a harbinger of worse to come.

Within minutes of our arrival, the local mullah spotted me on my knees with my miniature camera, trying to construct an image that would capture both the beauty and the devastation of this monument. Convinced the future of his village was linked to the fortunes of the victory arch, the mullah posed his question even before introductions were complete.

"You are an architect?"

"No," I apologized, "only a poet." Though it would take both poets and architects to reconstruct Afghanistan after twenty-one years of occupation and war, the mullah could not hide his disappointment. He looked me over, shook his head, and continued on his way to the mosque.

Once a park and playground for the well-to-do, the beautifully terraced valley was now parched; its streams, dry. The reservoir we passed en route, forty feet below normal, contained only a small pond a hundred-and-fifty-feet across, around which two young boys were gathering twigs and amusing themselves by poking holes in the mud. Below us in the valley, little was happening. Half a dozen small gardens had been maintained with great effort, by drawing water from overworked wells; otherwise, the inhabitants seemed afflicted with the same paralysis or sleeping sickness as those in Kabul, as if under a spell. Drought and inaction notwithstanding, the view was breathtaking. Hassan picked up a scrap of mortar from the old palace wall and turned it in his fingers, like Hamlet contemplating the skull of Yorick. He chucked it aside and shook his head. I reminded him that in the old imperial and colonial regimes neither he nor I would have been allowed to sit in this gorgeous spot having a picnic and enjoying the view. He did not rise to my lame proletarian bait but translated it for the benefit of the driver, and they both laughed.

Hassan took another bite of melon and scanned the nearby peaks of the Hindu Kush separating us from Bamiyan. He was faintly Byronic with his black turban and noticeable limp, someone T. E. Lawrence might have ridden with, or at least, written about. The previous day, as we made our way through the rubble of the Garden of Babur, founder of the Mogul Dynasty who had insisted on being buried on this slope in Kabul, Hassan wasted no time informing me that he was not, properly speaking, a Talib, as he had not studied at a *madrassa*. Also, he was neither a fighter nor a fanatic. I took this as an indication that he wanted to distance himself from the current regime. We discussed the destruction of the Buddhas in Bamiyan, which I believed was politically rather than religiously motivated.

"Of course," Hassan said, "but the issue is more complicated. The international community was lobbying on behalf of the Buddhas, but the spokesmen for the Taliban were trying to draw attention to conditions of hunger, brought on by the fighting, the drought, and the monetary freeze. You have to understand how things work here. It's never just a single issue easily resolved. When the UNESCO envoys refused to discuss increased aid, saying it was not their department, the Taliban were put in a difficult position. It looked as if UNESCO, or the West, was more interested in art than in children."

"How do you know this?"

"Everyone knows it, even the UN." Hassan adjusted his turban, then tore off a piece of flatbread and passed it to me. "Besides, I was selected to serve as interpreter at the press conference."

Earlier, we had visited the once-famous national museum in Kabul, which lay in ruins. It had been used as headquarters by more than one of the rival groups of mujahideen fighting for control of the capital and had taken several direct hits. Once the most important museum in Central Asia—holding collections of rare Kushan ivories from the ancient capital in Bagram and double decadrachmas of the Macedonian ruler Amyntas, found in a hoard in Kunduz and considered to be the largest Greek coins ever minted—Kabul Museum had been looted by both soldiers and professional thieves during the ten years of civil war. In 1993, rare Islamic copper and bronze pieces were melted in the fire caused by a rocket attack. Seventy percent of the museum's precious collection disappeared; much of what remained lay damaged in the rubble, though employees, putting their lives in danger valiantly collected pieces of pottery and sculpture in the hope that, with new advances in technology, they might be restored.

As we crept through empty rooms of this shattered building, with patches of corrugated metal keeping out the rain and without heat or electricity, I wondered what was going through Hassan's mind. Anger, embarrassment? The collection had been moved to this location in 1931 in the vicinity of the Darulaman Palace, another contemporary ruin whose name means, ironically, "secure place." I mentioned Nancy Dupree's comment that "if the culture of a nation dies, its soul dies with it," but immediately regretted it.

In *An Historical Guide to Afghanistan,* Dupree mentions with considerable excitement various mounds near Daulatabad in the northerly province of Faryab that were excavated in 1969 by Soviet archaeologists, including Viktor Ivanovich Sarianidi. She lists these and many other treasures followed by a parenthetical note: "(On display, National Museum, Kabul)." I was familiar with this discovery from another source, an article by Viktor Sarianidi in the March 1990 issue of *National Geographic* entitled, "The Golden Hoard of Bactria." Sarianidi describes his work on eight graves at Tillya-tepe, the "golden hill" that delivered twenty thousand artifacts, mostly gold and semiprecious stones. He considered the treasures found in the noblewoman's tomb to be priceless, a major discovery that could be compared to Tutankhamen's tomb in Egypt: "Never has there been an artifact like the chubby little gold Aphrodite, who is Grecian in concept but has the distinctly non-Grecian wings of a Bactrian deity and an Indian forehead mark that indicates marital status."

Sarianidi's article was accompanied by the most amazing photographs of coins, gold plaques, polished mirrors, a glass intaglio, Dionysus fondling Ariadne on a golden steed inlaid with turquoise, a pendant of the goddess Anhita, cupids astride dolphins, a Greco-Bactrian ibex, a gold-and-black ivory necklace, a wonderfully ornate collapsible gold crown that could be disassembled and slipped into a saddlebag, a garment clasp depicting a Greco-Roman warrior, lidded jars, antelope bracelets, signet rings, ivory combs, cosmetic pots, thousands of hollow gold beads, cameos, buckles, intricately designed gold belts, a dagger, and a sword hilt inlaid with turquoise depicting a bear gnawing on grapevines.

Sarianidi and his team saw the Bactrian treasures only once more, when they were allowed to photograph them in Kabul in 1982. In response to rumors that the treasures were being spirited away, even to the Soviet Union, he wrote in 1990, "As leader of the expedition, I can reassure the world that the treasures are still in Kabul. What happens to them now is of concern to the international community. I feel that these artifacts deserve the scrutiny of specialists. They should be seen throughout the world for all the priceless knowledge they reveal. Their story is not just Afghan, not just Soviet or Greek. They write a special chapter of history, and they belong to all humanity."

Ten years later, only devastation was on display in the national museum in Kabul.

Waging war against the past is not a new phenomenon. In ancient times, it was common practice to sack cities, destroying everything you couldn't carry off. The first emperor of China, Qin Shi Huang, not only burned books, but also buried scholars alive. Diego de Landa, a sixteenth-century bishop of Yucatán, acknowledged with scarcely veiled pride that, after the Spanish conquest of the Americas, fanatical Catholic priests burned most of the precious books of the Maya and Aztecs: "These people also made use of certain characters or letters, with which they wrote in their books of ancient matters and their sciences and by these and by drawings and by certain signs in these drawings, they understood their affairs and made others understand them. We found a large number of books in these characters and, as they contained nothing in which there were not to be seen superstition and lies of the devil, we burned them all, which they regretted to an amazing degree, and which caused them much affliction."

Conquest often includes efforts to eradicate written records, thereby destroying the collective memory of the vanquished people. When Huishen left Kabul around AD 450, he left behind one of the most advanced societies of the time. Ideas and art had flourished; debate was encouraged. Bamiyan and its rich agricultural lands had been at the crossroads, the hub of an endlessly exciting traffic of new peoples, goods, and influences moving east and west along the Silk Road. Huishen took nothing with him but memories. The fleeing mendicant would have traveled light, and mostly at night, stopping in monasteries along the way, visiting old friends or co-religionists at Taxila, Bezeklik, and Magao—places I hoped to visit—and dependent always on the charity of strangers. He could hardly have imagined how quickly the religious climate might change, even in China, making yet another departure not just prudent, but necessary.

The melon had been consumed, and it was time to head back to the capital. Only a mountain range and less than sixty miles separated me from the wreckage of the Buddhas of Bamiyan I'd once hoped to visit, but now their ruins might as well be in another galaxy. Successive waves of invaders, repressive ideologies, arbitrarily imposed borders, and self-interest had rendered Afghans impoverished and powerless in the world community. I intended to ask Hassan about tribalism, which had been a vital, and at times nasty part of my own Scottish heritage, and whether he thought it was so different from the corporate tribalism currently thriving under the umbrella of democratic capitalism, the great game of material interests that seemed infinitely capable of reinventing itself. But the moment had passed. Hassan, whose age, origins, and name were not so different from those of my fleeing monk, said to me over his shoulder, "Happily, most of our history is still preserved underground."

The car pulled up to a walled compound, and Hassan stepped out to knock at the gate, his black turban slightly askew from trying to extricate his long body from the vehicle. I'd just come from a meeting with Evaristo, project manager for the Water/Sanitation Program, a special venture sponsored by the International Committee of the Red Cross. Evaristo was in charge of efforts to provide not only clean water, but also safe plumbing to thousands of Kabulis. These involved the drilling of deep wells and the installation of proper latrines and septic tanks, rather than allowing the sewage to run into open ditches. We had driven through what in better days might have been described as suburbs, districts flattened during the civil war and only slowly being reclaimed, reinhabited. Along the way, we passed donkey carts, occasional vehicles, and antiquated trucks, mostly vintage Bedford vans and recycled Soviet transports.

Accompanied by his two assistants, Evaristo explained how they had brought proper sanitation facilities to more than forty thousand homes, an achievement of which he was justly proud, especially as instances of diseases such as cholera and dysentery had diminished as a result. As the four of us wound our way through a honeycomb of adobe houses to the first installation, we gathered a crowd of children and curious inhabitants. By the time we arrived, we might have been mistaken for besieged celebrities rather than a company of sewer rats.

"The main problem," Evaristo explained, "is educating the residents, who have not yet learned to view their sewage ditches as breeding grounds for bacteria. Those bacteria kill one in four children before the age of five. When people realize the dangers, they are more than willing to help with construction, as soon as materials become available." Evaristo beamed. "The idea is catching on."

After the inspection tour, Hassan arrived to take me to a luncheon with the Afghan painter Dr. Yousef Asefi, whom I'd met the previous day. I understood this to be a consolation prize, compensation for the dismal condition at the museum and a reminder that Afghans, in the face of such obstacles, are still creative. Yousef was born in Kabul in 1959 and earned his MD at the Kabul Medical Institute. He also studied with the Afghan painter Nasrullah Sarwari in 1981, combining this new love with his medical practice—that is, until the collapse of the Soviet regime. As the struggle for Kabul intensified, Yousef was faced with the impossible task of providing medical aid to a growing number of civilian and military casualties. He was also waging his own losing battle against mounting debts and his inability to feed and protect his family. Under these conditions, painting became impossible, and he fell into a severe depression that rendered him incapable of carrying on his medical practice.

The property we entered consisted of an elegant residence and walled garden near the center of Kabul that once belonged to foreign oil interests and that had miraculously survived the civil war. We were greeted at the door by the current owner, an entrepreneur named Sabir Latifi. Dressed modestly in *shalwar kameez* and a colorful woven vest, he ushered us for a second time into the large drawing room, where tea and snacks—a variety of nuts and candies—were spread out on a row of coffee tables between facing leather couches. Yousef's paintings lined the walls or were mounted on wooden display frames. They included attractive autumn and winter landscapes, haunting pointillist renderings of the city under siege, and half a dozen starkly realistic views of Kabul burning, flames erupting from mounds of jagged rubble. I found these latter works deeply disturbing and had told Yousef at our first meeting that they made me think of Goya's depictions of poverty and execution in the wake of Napoleon's ravages in Spain.

Popping a candy into my mouth, I fought off the impulse to ask Latifi about his business interests. I'd seen the stacks of Afghan carpets in the corridor and listened to his account of a business trip to Europe and New York to raise money for oil and gas exploration, a promising venture that had collapsed as soon as the United Nations imposed sanctions on Afghanistan. Latifi was not only a survivor, but also a cultured man. Having fallen in love with Yousef Asefi's paintings and gone in search of the artist, he was shocked to find his hero in the grip of a nervous breakdown, looking defeated and aged beyond his years. He paid Yousef's bills, took him under his wing, and nursed him back to health, serving as patron, agent, and promoter. Slowly, Yousef began to paint again. His work had recently been honored overseas, with an exhibition in Prague and a prize in Dubai.

I'd shifted in less than an hour from septic tanks to sepia, from outhouses to oil paintings—not so big a step, after all, when you think of the dadaists displaying an inverted urinal as an art object at one of their exhibitions. As Yousef came into the room, a full black beard framing his handsome face, it pleased me to be reminded that he was not only a professional healer, but also a cultural worker engaged in the task of bearing witness, keeping a record, making a certain kind of sense of our brief passage through time and space. In addition to the white cap favored by devout Muslims, he was dressed in a pale blue *shalwar kameez* and a dark vest.

"I hope you'll forgive me," he confided, "but there is an unexpected guest coming to talk to me and see the paintings. He's from the *New York Times* and is leaving tomorrow morning, so this is the only opportunity."

Barry Bearak, Asia bureau chief for the *New York Times*, was staying at the Intercontinental. As the only foreigners, we'd nodded more than once across the hotel restaurant. The previous morning, I'd asked if I could join him for breakfast.

"Yes, of course, I've been meaning to invite you over," he said. What passed between us for conversation was painfully labored and territorial. Although I mentioned I was a poet not a journalist, we spent an awkward half hour, neither of us willing to give away trade secrets or exchange anecdotes. Happily, his two assistants arrived and the dynamic shifted. During the afternoon, I'd slipped into a shop on Chicken Street, a row of labyrinthine shops specializing in carpets and antiquities, only to learn that Bearak had been there hours earlier. I was about to be scooped again.

Lunch was delayed an hour while Bearak made the rounds of Yousef's paintings, taking photographs, asking questions, making notes. Latifi took me aside to ask if I would mind if he invited the journalist to dine with us. As it happened, the conversation turned out to be very lively, with Latifi telling us that Ahmad Shah Massoud, also known as the Lion of Panjshir, the charismatic leader of the Northern Alliance, had once sat at the same table, discussing art and politics. I did not ask if the Taliban's spiritual leader, Mullah Omar, had also been a houseguest. Bearak posed a question about the possibility of moderate elements eventually altering the hard-line rule of the Taliban, something both Nancy Dupree and Pakistani journalist Ahmed Rashid considered likely. Latifi was on his feet serving us from a huge platter of lamb shish kebabs.

"The Taliban are here to stay since there's no longer a viable alternative," he said, waving several pieces of speared mutton. "Whatever their policies, they have brought stability, an end to the fighting. Relatively speaking, of course. The West will have to either displace them or engage them in dialogue. The present situation, with its suspicions and sanctions, is intolerable. We need aid and foreign investment. Afghanistan cannot heal itself or develop under these circumstances."

Although his grasp of English was limited, Yousef had been paying close attention but saying nothing. In response to a question about his family, translated by Hassan, he smiled broadly and spoke of his young son, how the boy loved to paint and would go through a dozen sheets of drawing paper at a single sitting.

Latifi resumed his place at the table, motioning for the platter to be replenished. He peered over the brim of his cup of tea, eyes intent. He was speaking to Bearak and me, but his gaze remained on Yousef.

"It's for those, the younger ones, that we must begin to rebuild."

When Bearak left, Yousef invited me back to the drawing room, where he had a surprise in store—a painting just completed. It was a small canvas depicting Kabul in flames, fire raging from the ruins and a huge bank of black smoke sweeping left across the canvas, half obliterating a public monument and the shell of a large building. This wall of smoke resembled, in color and shape, the mountain in the background on the right side of the painting, producing, in this theater of dreadful chaos, an unsettling symmetry.

"This is for you."

I was stunned. In response to my earlier praise for his civil-war canvases he had rushed home to finish this one, bringing it in with the oils still wet.

With a bow, he excused himself to join the others in prayer.

SIX

WHEN THE POWER went out at the Intercontinental Hotel there was no panic, no shouting in the hallways. Kerosene lanterns and candles were quickly provided for me and the five other guests by a member of the cleaning staff who lived on my floor and who would, on hearing the sounds of the elevator, be standing at attention in his doorway when I passed. Blackouts were common thanks to periodic attacks by the Northern Alliance, but more often they resulted from incompetence and from funding insufficient to maintain the system.

There was an even more complete blackout in terms of political discussion in the capital.

No one, including people working for nongovernmental organizations, wanted to talk openly about the situation for fear of reprisals. However, there was something else at work, too, a faint residue of loyalty to the Taliban for bringing an end to the civil war, though this was being seriously eroded by fundamentalist abuses. Afghans are fiercely independent; they don't like to be told what to do or what to believe. A refugee in Pakistan whose two brothers had been tortured and killed by fanatical elements within the Taliban put the matter in terms that surprised me: "The Taliban behave like criminals, but at least they are our own criminals. In time, we will educate them, bring them round." He was supervising seven children, three of his own and four belonging to his dead brothers, ranging in ages from four to fourteen, their faces only inches from a wall-sized loom, their small, deft fingers magically transforming a chaos of loose threads. He corrected the work of the youngest, then turned to me.

"Yes, as you would say in the West, we will civilize them."

I had no idea whether this was a realistic assessment of the situation or simply wishful thinking. After all, I am a product of the fast-food, quick-fix, instant-gratification society. I have been trained to expect results. I remember being shocked in 1981 when I asked a Chinese poet in Beijing how long it would take for his country to evolve something resembling democratic institutions, he said, without the slightest dismay or irony, "Perhaps a century." Having interviewed refugees in Peshawar who were tortured and forced to witness the murder of family members, and having read several books on the Taliban, I found the idea of being in Afghanistan as unnerving as my traveling to Chile in 1987, during the military dictatorship.

The feeling of terror in Chile, of being in over my head, had been heightened by my daily interviews with women who belonged to organizations such as Families of the Disappeared, and the Association of the Relatives of the Politically Executed, some of whom had lost as many as five loved ones. I listened with my fellow poets to detailed accounts of torture until I began to have nightmares. During the concerts we attended and the poetry readings we performed, it was not unusual to have trucks of soldiers in full riot gear cruising back and forth outside the buildings; these green vans were known locally, with grim Chilean humor, as "butcher shops."

One of the people I interviewed in Santiago was Jaime Hallas, publisher of the Chilean magazine *Análisis*, which had been closed down repeatedly by the military. The regime had used up its reserves of moral indignation and had no easy excuse for carrying on its deadly games; American support was slipping and an attempt had been made to assassinate Pinochet. The proverbial sticks and stones of the opponents having proved inadequate to oust the general, all that remained were the names, or words, which are not supposed to hurt but which were gaining ground in the struggle to sway international opinion. Hallas, a tall, bearded man, was seated in his makeshift office in front of a poster-sized photograph of his foreign-affairs editor, who had been murdered by Pinochet's thugs months earlier. Seated beside him was his associate editor, who would be arrested and charged with treason shortly thereafter for his editorials. Hallas was trying to explain to me Chile's unusual censorship laws, which did not exactly ban books but which managed to keep a strong lid on dissent just the same.

"Here, your books may survive," Hallas said, running the fingers of one hand through his thick beard, "but you may not."

Terrible things had happened in Afghanistan as well, some the product of tribal and sectarian animosities, some the result of a sustained culture of war, in which few combatants had ever experienced a period in their life in which the decencies were observed. Most of the young Talibs were orphans of war or victims of its legacy of displacement and poverty. All they knew of affection and friendship and sustenance had been learned in the context of a strict religious and ideological code in the *madrassas*, away from the moderating influence of women, of debate, and of compromise. Their only families were their brothers-in-arms, for whom, it is no surprise, they would fight to the death. And yet, in the midst of this chaos, ordinary Afghans had been able to sustain their faith in Allah and, as the Maleka Whiskey joke demonstrated, to find some humor in political events beyond their borders and beyond their control.

In Chile, I had experienced the hospitality and security not only of friends, but also of various organizations, such as the Chilean Writers' Association, that had survived the coup, albeit in somewhat truncated form. Solidarity was a thinner gruel than it had been but still it tasted good. The writers gathered, kept in touch, and watched out for one another's safety and well-being. I was welcomed immediately into the tribe, which gathered around me, offering me at least the illusion of protection. In Kabul, until several days before, when I met Yousef Asefi and Sabir Latifi, I had been on my own. No one to call, no one to visit; no telephones in the rooms, e-mail forbidden. Once Hassan and the driver dropped me off at the Intercontinental Hotel, a high-rise ghost town, and once Iraj closed his bookstore for the day, I disappeared completely from the radar screen. The Western world had forgotten Afghanistan, except for aid and human rights workers, a few feminists outraged by the imposition of the burka, and private oil interests that would prefer to deal with a government more pliable than the Taliban. Canada had no diplomatic relations with the regime in Kabul and posted on its Web site a warning against travel. Unless there was fresh news of an atrocity or an arrest, Afghanistan had become invisible; and for all practical purposes, so had I.

» » « «

Nothing would have been more disagreeable and pathetic to Huishen and his Buddhist cohorts than to listen to this kind of subjective claptrap, especially from someone who ought to know about *wu-wei*, the concept of nonbeing, transcending the ego, emptying the self of desire and the mind of clutter; or more accurately, emptying the mind of thought itself, a process the Daoist Lao-Tzu called "mental fasting." When there was a discussion of the relative merits of action and contemplation, Lao-Tzu came down firmly on the side of the latter: "Without stepping out of one's door one knows the world. Without looking out the window one sees the way of heaven. The further one goes, the less one knows." If I'd read those ancient texts more closely, I might have saved a lot of time and money and been spared a load of discomfort and grief.

Instead of sitting in meditation, head shaved, serenely indifferent to the world and its catastrophes, I was globe-trotting with hair askew and beard rampant, my mind a gridlocked intersection at rush hour, a bustling Asian market, a storage shed filled to bursting with old desires. I'd been asking myself what I was doing halfway around the world. Was there a mystical core to the search I was on, I wondered, or to any of my other turbulent travels, to Chile, Nicaragua, the West Bank, and Gaza? Or was I merely flirting with danger, testing myself, daring the fates? My search for the trail of an ancient Buddhist monk was not without its ludicrous aspect, especially in light of Lao-Tzu's observation, "Cause the people not to treat death lightly and not to wander off to distant places." In this life, which the Chinese call "the kingdom of ten thousand things," it seemed to be my lot to be always on the move.

History has a frightening aspect, as Walter Benjamin so brilliantly dramatizes in *Illuminations*. "A Klee painting named *Angelus Novus* shows an angel looking as though he is about to move away from something he is fixedly contemplating," Benjamin writes. "His eyes are staring, his mouth is open, his wings are spread. This is how one pictures the angel of history. His face is turned toward the past. Where we perceive a chain of events, he sees one single catastrophe which keeps piling wreckage upon wreckage and hurls it in front of his feet. The angel would like to stay, awaken the dead, and make whole what has been smashed. But a storm is blowing from Paradise; it has got caught in his wings with such violence that the angel can no longer close them. This storm irresistibly propels him into the future to which his back is turned, while the pile of debris before him grows skyward. This storm is what we call progress." I understood the helplessness of Benjamin's angel. Once you begin to contemplate the past, there is no turning back, and no end of disturbing vistas. Rilke's definition of poetry, or writing in general, as the past that breaks out in our hearts made perfect sense to me. The healing of art, such as it is, came not from avoiding and certainly not from looking back through the comforting lenses of tranquility or nostalgia, but from confronting and capturing the terror in the cage of form.

Stories, stories, always more stories. A young Afghan father goes through the wreckage of his house after the civil war in Kabul. He finds there a single shoe belonging to his daughter who was killed along with her mother and two brothers in the crossfire that destroyed their home. Although his daughter's body has been immediately recovered and given a proper burial, the father cannot bear the thought of finding only one shoe; he has to have its mate. Before the conflict, he was a translator of Persian literature in the Ministry of Education. He has no money to rebuild and is living with his brother's family in a district of Kabul, the old city, that has escaped serious damage. Each day, after he has sat for hours in the market beside an old blanket spread with useless items for sale, he goes by bicycle to sift through the rubble of his former home, looking for his daughter's matching shoe. Neighbors still camped in the ruins of their former homes bring him tea, ask after his health, and try to convince him to abandon his task. At first the man grows thin and haggard. His brother considers taking him aside to explain that the other shoe will never be found, because the little girl lost a leg during the battle that claimed her life. He shares his concern with his wife, who is wiser in these matters. She stops kneading dough for nan, wipes her hands on her apron, and sits down beside her husband.

"Your brother has found his chosen work," she says. "Soon, there will not be a single pebble, board, or grain of sand on that site of pain and grieving that has not felt the caress of his fingers or been blessed by his loving attention. Give him time."

The man takes his wife's advice. Weeks pass. A marked change comes over his brother, a new determination. When the man rides past the site of the destroyed house, he sees his brother standing in front of a small group of children seated on the ground. Unseen, he observes his brother holding forth with great animation to these ragged orphans of conflict. Beside him, there is a small table assembled from bits of wooden debris. The man can make out three objects on the table: a melon, a fragment of mortar shell, and a child's shoe. The brother has a stick in his hands, with which he has drawn in the dirt an approximate map of Central Asia, without borders. Then, after tying a strip of cotton over his eyes, he proceeds to carve up the map with a series of deeply inscribed lines.

"Now," he says, without removing the blindfold, "repeat after me, slowly, the word *Durand.*" The children repeat the word en masse, then individually, with prompting from their teacher, as yet unaware they are absorbing a lesson on colonial history—*Durand* being the name of the line drawn by the British in 1893 between Afghanistan and India (now Pakistan), effectively dividing the Pashtun peoples. Smiling, the brother compliments each child on his or her pronunciation.

"Very good. After the lesson, we will share this." He taps the melon with his stick. Then, with his right foot, he stirs Central Asia once more into a patch of expressionless dust. *"Baaz goftan—megoyam,"* he says, breaking the stick across his knee.

"Now repeat this phrase."

The time had come to leave. I had permission to stay another week in Kabul, but Bamiyan was out of reach, September at hand, and I had a long journey ahead of me. Also, I needed to take advantage of available space on the ICRC flight. As I checked out, someone whispered to me in the lobby of the Intercontinental that the Taliban's notorious religious police would arrive shortly to destroy a cache of champagne hidden away in the cellar by the hotel's previous management. After three weeks without a drink—not even a beer—I considered offering my assistance in disposing of the champagne, but decided against it.

Rigid fundamentalism in all its forms—Christian, Muslim, Hindu, or Jewish—thrives on ignorance and oppression. So, too, do ideologies of the extreme left and extreme right. The previous night, foreign diplomats, frustrated at being unable to make any progress with the Taliban or to visit the NGO workers arrested for proselytizing, departed for Islamabad to await further orders from their governments. There'd been much talk about these matters between Hassan and me. He was a devout Muslim, but he seemed completely at ease with the existence of other religions and their artifacts. He shared my dismay at the looting of the Kabul Museum and the destruction of the Bamiyan Buddhas. Similar strictures about foreign idols and images of the human form apply across the border, but most Pakistanis, I suggested, are either too sophisticated or too practical to turn their sectarian hatreds against art. While Hassan and I had laughed more than once about the Bamiyan caretaker praying to Allah from atop the Buddha's head, he was not always impressed with my reading of Afghan politics.

A few days earlier, Hassan had left me to wander along the market by the river while he and the driver went into a mosque for Friday prayers. On what had once been a busy riverside thoroughfare, full of shops, traffic, and well-dressed pedestrians, now a few portable stalls were scattered, as well as a dozen sheets covered with domestic junk and sundry throwaway items. I thought of the stories I'd heard in Pakistan and the photographs I'd seen of Kabuli doctors, lawyers, and university professors shining shoes or trying to sell fruit and family heirlooms on the sidewalks. A woman in a faded blue burka sat on the ground next to a wall, one hand slightly extended, her face obscured behind the small window of netting. She might have been a teacher in the old dispensation. I wanted to know about her situation but had to content myself with slipping her a small amount of money as I passed.

I expected to be stopped by overzealous authorities and asked for identification or questioned about my activities; however, no one seemed particularly interested in me, except the few merchants selling food and handicrafts. Most pedestrians were headed to the mosque. On the way back to the car, I passed a "banker," who sat in front of a dozen six-inch stacks of Afghani notes arranged neatly on a small wooden table in the middle of the street. He would, no doubt, have given me a much better exchange rate than I received at the hotel, though I had no intention of getting him or myself into trouble by trading U. S. dollars. After prayers, I was delivered back to the hotel to spend an evening finishing *House of Sand and Fog*. Hassan excused himself early, as he had family visiting from Bagram.

He'd been an excellent guide and companion—generous, informative, not the least bit pushy—and I wanted to show him my appreciation. He'd even taken me to the sports stadium, where a soccer game was in progress, wanting me, I suppose, to witness Kabul at play. The stands were brimming. Vendors, mostly young boys, scurried back and forth with containers of water or tea while the teams contended. A few had nan and popcorn balls for sale. However, the stadium, like its counterpart in Santiago, Chile, reminded me of amputations and public executions. I mentioned this to Hassan and wondered aloud how his fellow citizens were able to dispel such images as they watched a soccer game. Chilean singer and guitarist Victor Jara, before he was killed during the early days of the coup, had his hands smashed in the stadium in Santiago by Pinochet's thugs for daring to lead the prisoners in song. Thereafter, the regime conducted its executions clandestinely.

Kabul's stadium was even more infamous outside the country for its public executions, after one of which a teenager had been photographed parading a severed hand and foot through the streets of the city, grinning all the while. The six images that remained fixed in my mind involved the execution of Zarmeena, accused of killing her husband and shot in front of thousands of spectators. In the first photograph, an enormous mullah, flanked by two diminutive helpers, speaks into a microphone to address the crowd; you can see the chalk lines of the field on either side of him. The next photo shows a bloodred pickup truck driving onto the field with three hooded women in the box, the victim seated in the middle. Then she is on her knees beside the chalk semicircle. Several Taliban stand nearby, one of them with an automatic rifle. According to reports, as Zarmeena's children wept for their condemned mother the husband's family had second thoughts and decided to forgive her, but the Taliban refused to reverse the verdict— permissible under Islamic law—on the grounds that they'd already announced the execution to the crowd. The show must go on. The last three images show Zarmeena being shot in the back of the head, the tip of the rifle barrel nestling in the fabric of the mauve burka, Zarmeena lying prostrate beside a blue and white sports utility vehicle that has been driven onto the field to retrieve the body, and finally, Zarmeena's body being loaded into the SUV by a group of Talibs dressed in brown and black.

Hassan stood listening to me, one hand over his mouth, then turned away. He was clearly disturbed by my comments. As a distraction, I'd purchased a popcorn ball, saturated with honey. As I weighed various strategies for attacking the popcorn without having it stick to my beard, he explained, patiently, that in five years there had been fewer than a dozen public executions but that in the same period there were soccer games in the stadium almost every day, more than a thousand games. I didn't want to argue with him. The Taliban had no monopoly on fundamentalist madness. And I was hardly an apologist for Western justice, in which murderers get off with the aid of clever lawyers, in which fair trials are often subverted by deals and plea bargaining, and in which the jails are over-loaded with members of our black and Native communities. However, the moment was ruined, and we left the stadium shortly after without my ever learning the names of the competing teams.

When we met for breakfast, I gave Hassan a modest sum of money for his services as a guide and told him I planned to send him a continuing barrage of Canadian books when I returned home. I also gave him my copy of *House of Sand and Fog,* wondering what he would make of this devastating portrait of cultural misunderstanding, in which small differences have such dire consequences. The thought had crossed my mind that I might be able to help him gain admission to a university in Canada or the United States for graduate studies, but I decided to leave that possibility until later.

I thanked him again in the ICRC compound for his help. I was somewhat distracted at this stage, upset to be leaving, embarrassed by the paucity of my offering, and fussing unnecessarily about my luggage, which had gone on ahead in another vehicle. I guess, too, I was feeling like somewhat of a failure in my role as journalist and researcher, not having asked enough questions about him and his country. I had plenty of impressions, but I lacked the audacity, the instincts, and the doggedness of a good journalist. Before retreating to the communications office, where one of his old friends worked, Hassan took my hand and held it briefly.

"We'll meet again," I said, without conviction.

"*Inshallah,*" he replied, smiling. Yes, if Allah wills it.

He turned to go, with the small ziplock bag I'd given him— containing a letter, a number of ten-dollar bills, a postcard of killer whales on the British Columbia coast, and the used paperback novel—tucked under his arm. He was tall, elegant in his turban and black vest, as he moved off a short distance with his gentle, rocking motion. After spending so much time with Hassan, I thought, I still don't know the cause of his injury. He stopped and turned to wave a final time, lifting his voice over the sound of the engine.

"It's been an honor."

SEVEN

MY FIRST TASK back at the guest house in Islamabad was to secure another Chinese visa, as there was no way I could make it to the border before my entry date expired. Also, I had to crate and send home by mail my newly acquired reference books and Yousef Asefi's painting of Kabul burning, which was not yet fully dry. With the new visa in hand, I took a cab west to Taksashila—or Taxila, as the Greeks had called it—to escape contemporary politics for a day and immerse myself in the ancient world. Excavations by Sir John Marshall, and later by Pakistani archaeologists, indicate that Taxila was occupied in the late sixth century BC, during the empire of Darius I (518 BC), but the city also figures in the histories of Artaxerxes, Alexander the Great, Chandragupta Maurya, Asoka, Gondophares, and Kanishka. Taxila was offered to Alexander without a fight; and the conqueror remained in the area just long enough to catch his breath for the next prize. While invaders, forty-two Greek kings and queens among them, fought to retain control of the Gandharan Triangle—otherwise known as the Peshawar Plain, a fertile region including Peshawar, Mardan, Swat, and Dir—and left their mark in terms of the art, customs, and gene pool, this confluence of peoples gradually developed into a great center of Buddhist learning and spiritual activity.

My prompt immersion in the ancient past was greatly facilitated by an old man in a white robe, white turban, and flowing white beard who approached me outside the museum, pointing to an attractive rig beyond the gate. This jaunty cart with a canopy and sleepy gray nag—thin but not malnourished—was just what I needed to transport me back through the centuries. After negotiating a price, I climbed aboard this two-wheeled time capsule, and we set out along a tree-lined country road with no fumes and no noise other than the clopping of hooves on pavement. Small children waved to the driver; and, quite unexpectedly, the old gray swerved off the road, drank from a drainage ditch, and resumed its journey. As we turned into the ruins of the Jaulian monastery, site of an ancient university, the horse's tail went up and a bright orange biscuit of dung emerged, stretching the anal membrane until it had achieved a delicate blue transparency.

Halfway up the steps to the monastery, I was besieged by the imperious visages of Darius, Menander, and Kanishka, as ancient coins or clever replicas were thrust in my face.

"Yes, yes, Greek. Very original."

"That is fake, not this. Kanishka. Trust me, Muslim not lie."

I wanted ancient coins even less than I had wanted a jack-knife at Saddar Market in Peshawar. However, the hustlers had blocked my path and the only way I could shake them off was to promise to have a look on the way down, a delaying tactic I knew I'd regret.

Huishen may well have stopped at the Jaulian monastery, or at least joined up with other fleeing refugees there, on his way over the Silk Road to China. It had certainly been a major teaching center, with meeting rooms and an abundance of monkish cells equipped with alcoves for candles, water basins, and statuary. Of course, all such items had disappeared into museums or private collections. The decapitated statues brought to mind Fahien's explanation of the name Taxila, *Chu-cha-shi-lo*, meaning "cut off head." The few remaining stucco reliefs were breathtaking, almost domestic in their depictions of a lounging Bodhisattva, several nude goddesses, and a seated Buddha with a hole in his navel, where the supplicant was supposed to stick his or her finger while praying for a bodily cure. Perhaps it offered a cure for wind. Most of the small shrines or stupas had lost their domes and cylindrical drums. Oazi in Peshawar had called them "umbrellas," but they looked more like many-tiered mushrooms. After I'd given the guide a small tip, he took me aside and offered ancient coins he'd found in the area. I smiled and shook my head. He demurred, then walked me back to the entrance. Unfortunately, the hotshots waiting on the stairs were not so obliging; with their hands thrust in front of me, I could hardly see where to place my feet.

The driver, looking even more like the Archangel Gabriel, came to my rescue, his cart waiting miraculously at the foot of the stairs. I expected the four coin salesmen to clamber in after me, but they understood the protocol. Not a single hand pursued me into the cart, though the voices continued imploring.

"Not expensive. Collector's item."

"What price, then?"

"Take to museum. Verify age. You give money to driver."

These men were trying to make a living, to feed and educate their children. They knew I had enough money to buy one or two coins. They also knew I couldn't distinguish between a fake and the real thing. Still, I was glad when the driver's switch grazed the horse's flanks and we set off at a brisk trot, though

I would not have been surprised if my celestial transport, with "Gabriel" at the reins, had mounted to the heavens.

Having grazed and rested at the Jaulian monastery, the horse repeated its earlier performance, dropping another perfectly minted gold coin onto the dirt road as I retreated down the lane like Kanishka in my chariot.

In Edward Bond's play *Narrow Road to the Deep North*, based on the writings and journeying of Basho, the Japanese poet meets an old acquaintance whom he has not seen in years.

"What did you do in the north?" the man asks.

"I wasted thirty-nine years seated facing a wall," Basho replies.

"I'm so sorry to hear that," his acquaintance says.

"You must be very sad."

"Sad? Not on your life," Basho shouts. I'm a free man; I know I've been wasting my time and will never do it again. How many others can say that?"

As I wended my slow way north along the narrow, sometimes destroyed, roads in Pakistan, I'd have plenty of opportunity to think about time. What did it mean to waste time? I had spent two weeks in Pakistan talking to aid workers and Afghan refugees and another week or so in Kabul witnessing the tragic spectacle of a culture in collapse. During that brief interlude, I had learned nothing about Huishen and only a little about his Buddhist roots, but I had been immersed in exactly the same kind of ideological straitjacket and brutish politics— not only anti-Buddhist, but also anti-art—that drove him and his brethren into exile. I did not get to Bamiyan, but I was seeing decapitated statues and smashed Buddhist icons everywhere.

Now, at least, I was heading north, not yet aware how narrow and dangerous the road ahead would be. My first stop was Abbotabad, a quaint garrison town in the mountains north of Islamabad—once an English colonial enclave with its Presbyterian church, private schools, Lady Garden, and the lackluster Springfield Hotel, but now a refuge for well-to-do military personnel and civil servants from the capital. I spent several hours looking for a bank that would cash traveler's checks or give me a cash advance on my credit card, something I'd neglected to do in the capital before heading north. When this proved impossible, I waited two hours as the bank manager pondered my request. While he phoned associates in other branches, customers and old friends dropped in, each one requiring tea and the time of day in generous doses. I grew frustrated and felt I was being toyed with, tested, the unspoken message being: "Your ancestors kept us waiting for centuries, so we'll see how *you* like waiting." I took refuge in Major Shah, who had recently moved south from Gilgit, a remote and volatile place not fit for his wife and children. Now he was close enough to his own family in Rawalpindi for occasional visits by car. He said he had a brother in New York, driving a limousine and moonlighting as a hotel desk clerk, who wanted him to emigrate. But Major Shah, immaculately turned out, was not impressed. He was not paid properly, but he was rising through the ranks, and military life had its perks.

"I have respect here. If the police stop me and ask for my licence, I tell them I am Major Shah, and they wave me through." However, if he is denied promotion, Major Shah may reconsider his options.

The bank manager, tired of his own waiting game, finally relented. He was willing to cash my traveler's checks as a special favor. While a clerk counted out my bills, the manager explained that he had degrees in political science and business management; then, to my surprise, he asked for my address and said he hoped I would not mind if he contacted me sometime in Canada.

The road north from Abbotabad passes through some of the most spectacular scenery in the world. Once we had left behind the terraced valleys, with their large stands of deodars—an Asian version of the cedar, with camouflage markings on the bark and bursts of long, elegant needles—the Karakoram Highway crossed the Indus several times, climbing steadily until the great river was nothing more than a ribbon, a faintly drawn line scratched on the floor of the valley. The second-class bus, resembling a multicolored lozenge, half-digested, crawled up the steep grades and network of switchbacks, leaving a great plume of black diesel smoke in its wake. Ten rupees for sixty miles was worth the discomfort and the sliced thumb I'd received chucking in my bags through a small window beside the driver and crawling after them. He took little pinches of something, from a plastic bag, chewed them briefly, and spat out the window or onto the floor beside him. Above my head, in an alcove, was mounted a plastic model of a mosque, with red lights on either side that flashed each time he hit the brakes, a gentle warning from Allah to hang on, though it always came too late to be useful.

The bus screeched to a stop to avoid a pile of fallen rock on the road. Then we held our breath as the bus inched forward between a stalled truck and nothingness. The trip left me a nervous wreck and speechless, ironic, given that our first stop was a mountain village called Chattar Plain, a pit stop for prayer, refreshments, topping up the radiator, and, obviously, vocal recovery. On a cement platform in the dirt parking lot, most of the male passengers performed their ablutions and prayed amid the clatter of motorcycles, hawkers, horns, and excited talk. A few miles farther along the Karakoram Highway, construction workers flagged us down and passed around a collection cup for donations to the new mosque they were building on hundred-foot cement pylons over the abyss, a strange choice as there was nowhere for vehicles to park. Presumably, the location was guaranteed to instill the fear of Allah in the most intrepid of travelers.

Not only were the landscape and vegetation constantly changing as we wound our way deeper into the geological tumult, where the Hindu Kush, the Himalayas, and the Karakoram contend, but so were the faces. The influence of Tajiks, Uzbeks, Turks, Mongols, and Chinese began to show in the faces around me. Overall, the blend of races resembled most the Slavs of Eastern Europe. Language was shifting too. Less English was spoken. Urdu and Pashto gave way to unique tribal languages in some of the more remote valleys, where linguists find living echoes of those vast waves of migration and conquest that swept over the region during a period of several thousand years. Seated across from me on the bus were people whose ancestors had been mercenaries in the armies of Darius, Alexander, or Kanishka and who, weary of conquest or in flight for their lives, had found a place to put down roots.

I could feel these languages in the air, like the vibration of bees' wings, though I could not identify a single one. Emily Lorimer, a former Oxford don whose husband had worked in the Indian service of the British government and studied linguistics on the side, returned with him to Gilgit, where he pursued his interest in Burushaski, an ancient language that still has fifty thousand speakers, along the valleys of the Hunza and Yasin rivers, both of which empty into the Gilgit River. With its unique structure and vocabulary, Burushaski has only recently acquired a written form. Although there is considerable debate on the subject, Burushaski shares elements with a language spoken by a small group of people (as few as a hundred) along the Yenisei River in Siberia; it is also said to be related to Apache, Navajo, and other Dene languages of the United States and Canada. Lorimer documented her impressions and her husband's labors in 1939 in a charming and perceptive book called *Language Hunting in the Karakoram*. However, the old written languages, the ancient scripts, were what most intrigued me, particularly the one known as Sogdian, a branch of the middle Persian languages that not only was a principal vehicle for literature and religious communication, but also became the lingua franca of the Silk Road for half a millennium. Ancient letters in Sogdian from the fourth century AD were discovered in Eastern Turkestan, along with documents in Tajikistan and rock inscriptions in the region I was approaching.

Although Sogd was never powerful as a nation, it remained highly influential both culturally and commercially. Merchants, scholars, missionaries, and artists of Sogd, which included Samarkand and modern Tajikistan, established colonies along the Silk Road from the fourth century onward, as far west as Constantinople and as far east as Dunhuang in what is now the Xinjiang Uyghur Autonomous Region in western China, where more of their manuscripts and inscriptions have been found. By the sixth century, they dominated trade and commerce on land much as the Phoenicians once had at sea. Although the Sogdian language was employed for Buddhist, Manichean, and Nestorian Christian scriptures, it was eventually replaced by other languages, and the Sogdian peoples seem to have melted into the various populations along the Silk Road. Once called *the Hu* ("those from away") by the Chinese, they bear resemblances to both the Uyghur and the Hui (Chinese Muslims). And, while one meaning of the word *hui* in Chinese was "go back" (those who returned home regularly), it was impossible for me not to speculate on a possible connection with Huishen.

Another possibility dawned on me. Huishen obviously learned to speak Chinese, but he may not have written it. If he had been trained primarily in the use of Sanskrit, Brahmi, or one of the three Sogdian scripts rather than Chinese, this might explain why he had given an oral version and not written a personal account of his journey.

A night at the Paris Hotel in Besham was enough to make any traveler sick for home and willing to reconsider the dangers and exertions that lay ahead. To call Besham a bleak town with no redeeming characteristics—a cluster of ramshackle businesses, shops, and hotels clinging to the Karakoram Highway for dear life, standing only by the grace of Allah and the current placidity of Earth's plates—would be an act of benevolent understatement. The highway, which doubles as Main Street, was under constant repair, not only from the endless parade of trucks, but also from erosion, so there were no sidewalks, no pavement, only huge piles of dirt and gravel that shifted to and fro like sandbars waiting to be graded. Highway traffic came to a complete standstill as buses and huge trucks navigated— "jockeyed" would be more appropriate—with great difficulty, over and among these archipelagos of earth and stone. The Champs Elysées it was not, despite the Parisian promises of my hotel.

My room looked out onto flat rooftops, on one of which several young men were gathered in the semidarkness around a card game or a skin magazine left by a bored trucker. They waved when I took their picture. They waved again when I returned from a reconnaissance tour through the no-man's-land of road-work with my loot of potato chips, milk, and several oranges. After only four weeks on the road, I was wearing down, running out of books to read, chances for good conversation, and, worst, patience. Still, I was confident that Huishen and his party had passed through here, during a much more arduous trek by donkey, by camel, or on foot, making the kind of epic crossing conjured in T. S. Eliot's "Journey of the Magi," in which hostile towns, rotten weather, and the recalcitrance of camel drivers guarantee for all a cold, hard coming.

Without the consolations of religion, I had only my bookish curiosity and writing obsessions to keep me going. However, I too was on a quest, looking for signs, one or two of which I thought I would find the next day at Chilas, where the river valley was reported to contain thirty thousand petroglyphs and five thousand inscriptions, some of them dating back two thousand years. I had another fitful night, dreaming of dissolving faces, frantic people shouting in languages I could not understand, of earthquakes, landslides, and other less specific threats to my safety. In the morning, a barely decipherable message appeared in my notebook, not in Brahmi or Sogdian, but in an all-too-familiar scrawl:

While he cleans tables and rinses out the bowls, Peng thinks about the gaps in my narrative, gaps large enough for a nation or an eon to fall through. His regulars can count only five distinct phases in my monkish narrative: the People Who Give Everything Away, the Land of Women, the Seal People, the Tomorrow People, and The City That Won't Stop Moving. I was gone forty years yet appear to have stayed only briefly in any of the five places I mention. What kind of history is this? No wonder the emperor and court historians are skeptical, dismissing me as a drunk with an overactive imagination. Peng, however, is not numbered among the skeptics. He is a believer. Something in my telling, some residue of grief, evident even in those moments of self-mockery, convinces him of the truth of my bizarre tales. Of course, detractors will say it's good for business, a monk concealed in every monkey.

The bus that took me north to Chilas had a stenciled message on the window that said "Love to All," but the driver's antics, careening in gravel around sharp curves at breakneck speeds high above the Indus Valley, gave quite a different message:

Death to all, if Allah wills it (or if I blow it). At Shatial, I sat in the shade by a waterfall and nibbled some peanut butter crackers as the driver of the minibus scoured the town for more passengers. Two hours later, he dropped me off in Chilas. After my hair-raising experience, I was ready to take up permanent residence, put down roots and, like the refugees from ancient conflicts, never budge again. However, the town was so bleak and the locals so suspicious and unhelpful that I skipped lunch and hired a man with a Suzuki pickup truck to take me for a quick look at the petroglyphs. I was determined to catch the next bus to Gilgit, the only sizable town between Chilas and China.

The driver, his tiny son in tow, showed me a couple of disappointing rock carvings along the highway, then turned his Suzuki toward the river while I bounced along in the back under a canvas tarpaulin. We crossed a small metal suspension bridge over the Indus, wide enough for one vehicle. A stately gentleman in a white turban stepped from the shade.

"This man is a local hero," the driver explained. "He held this spot against the Indian army and helped drive them back after Partition while the region was still disputed. Now he's the keeper of the bridge and the petroglyphs." He was also, it seemed, a living reminder that this is, and has always been, contested ground.

I was delighted to meet this Central Asian Horatio, at least ten years my senior, and to have him give me a whirlwind tour of the petroglyphs along the banks of the Indus. He strode on ahead and had to wait for me to catch up, while the driver and his son took refuge in the shade of the truck. What, exactly, he enquired, did I want to see? The answer had seemed perfectly obvious until we reached the first wave of rocks, where I was confronted by hundreds of petroglyphs. To my left were rock carvings of Buddhas floating on lotus leaves, Bodhisattvas, temples, elegantly carved stupas with as many as ten umbrellas and a silk banner flying from the top, stick figures, horses, deer, and ibex, with their ridged, curving horns. On the right was a soldier in uniform with a sword in one hand and a mountain goat held by its hind leg in the other. He might have been Greek or Persian. What the slim-waisted hunter and the hapless goat indicated to me was that this ancient campground or watering hole had probably been frequented not only by missionaries, but also by artists, traders, mercenaries, and dignitaries on secular business. It may have been sacred ground to some, but it was a playground to others, especially the countless travelers who, without a shred of talent, had left ignorant graffiti, images of erect *phalloi,* or pathetic imitations of real art in their wake. I saw no evidence of Huishen, but Kilroy was everywhere. In fact, some of the rocks looked as if a class of elementary-school children had been turned loose and told to cover every available surface.

Nearby, to my surprise, I found a detailed panorama of a warrior with headdress and costume that looked decidedly Egyptian, his spear in the throwing position. A yard from the warrior was the half-finished carving of a stupa, the first two levels of the foundation completed before some sudden alteration in weather or security forced the artist to abandon his project and take to the hills or simply press on with an impatient caravan. Most of the rocks were brown, as a result of iron or manganese in the dust, which had coated and protected the images over the centuries.

As I was about to leave, "Horatio" beckoned to me and pointed to a small group of images I had not noticed. I dropped to my knees to study it more carefully. Nestled in the sand was a carving of the Buddha, not even a yard high, surrounded by disciples or students. It did not take an old teacher to recognize this as a classroom scene. So small were the figures, it might have been a kindergarten. Eight students, clustered around a rectangular object I could not identify (a sacred text, a reliquary?), were waiting for words of illumination. The sweet domesticity of the scene on this altar rock, obviously a favorite of my Muslim guide, transformed the moment and the valley, which no longer struck me as oppressive or hostile. When I looked up, Horatio was smiling.

My bottle of water was empty, my film had run out, and my head had begun to bake in the rays of sunlight strafing the valley. I paid my heroic guide and keeper of the bridge for his services. Unimpressed by my stamina, he was at least pleased with the fee. The driver and his son dropped me off at the bus stop for Gilgit. The valley around Chilas had a stark, elemental beauty and had provided generations of travelers not only with artistic inspiration, but also with a welcome break after the steep and treacherous mountain passes of the Silk Road. I considered staying over but had seen no hotels or potential lodgings. Though it must have seemed a blessed respite to Huishen at this stage in his long and impossible journey, on this blisteringly hot afternoon it was not my idea of a good time. Besides, I hadn't eaten properly all day and my mind was set on a decent meal, plenty of tea, a comfortable room, perhaps even a bath.

"Ask for Mr. Babu," Mac Madenwald had advised over dinner in his seaside house in Anacortes, Washington. "Babu runs his own touring business unofficially from the lobby at Green's Hotel in Peshawar. He'll provide guides, porters, vehicle, grub, all at fair prices."

Mac was a surgeon who had done several medical stints in Afghanistan, each followed by a bout of touring in the Hunza region of Pakistan. I couldn't bring myself to tell Mac I was not the mountain-climbing type. I was afraid of heights. Low-altitude hiking was okay, as long as I did not have to inch my way along narrow precipices or try to regulate my breathing and heart rate above vast gulfs of empty space. I'd read Andrew Greig's *Summit Fever*, an account of his participation in Mal Duff's ascent of the Mustagh Tower in the Karakoram Himalayas. I'd even met Andrew when he was a Scottish exchange writer in Canada. He did not seem the mountaineering type; in fact, as a gangly musician and performance poet, he looked as if he'd be more at home in a pub at a table awash with pints of McEwan's ale or Newcastle Brown than struggling through ice fields or dangling from a safety harness over fifteen thousand feet of nothingness.

Mac was wrong. Green's Hotel had been demolished, and Mr. Babu was nowhere to be found. However, he was right about Hunza, its calamitous beauty, its kaleidoscopic variety. Thanks to plate tectonics and the generous support of the Aga Khan, a wealthy native son and spiritual leader of the Ismaili Muslims, the region had rugged natural beauty as well as the benefits of health, education, agriculture, and reforestation. There were terraced gardens, groves of apricots, walnuts, and apples, irrigation canals, and none of the visible signs of the poverty that afflicts so much of Pakistan. Mountains encircled the highway as it wrapped itself almost two hundred degrees around the slopes and valley towns of Karimabad, Hussaini, and Passu. I was never in doubt about the awesome presence of mountains as I traveled north along the Indus River, leaning into hairpin turns, eyeing the overhanging outcrops of granite and shale waiting for the least encouragement to crush the bus and send it plunging into the valley. I held my breath as the patched, bald tires struggled for purchase on washouts and piles of fallen rock. Here in Hunza, however, with the advantage of distance and perspective, the effect was totally different. The roads were excellent. And the traveler's eye was drawn not to the rocks below, but skyward to the towering bulk of Rakaposhi, all twenty-three thousand feet of it, replicating and transforming itself with each new twist of the highway, now obscured in cloud, now resplendent and white against the sky like the fused tips of jib and mainsail, fierce, relentless, the seams of its lower reaches stitched with snow.

One wants to leave a country on a dramatic note, but the border town of Sost at which I'd arrived was hardly the place to do that. I thought I'd exhausted my pejoratives describing Besham, but Sost inspired me to new heights—and not because it was at nine thousand one hundred feet and had an alluvial fan as backdrop. This dreary little outpost—a quarter mile of blight in a wasteland of sand and rock—was a moonscape with a commercial strip and money changers, jerry-built shops and cheap flophouses, an Asian version of the American frontier town, except there were no false fronts; ugliness and impermanence were all hung out for inspection, in your face. Its single redeeming feature was an undersized billiard table somewhat the worse for wear as a result of being kept out of doors. Two young truckers were engaged in guessing which way the ball would veer as it passed over its troubled geography of bumps and warped ridges, a worthy symbol for Central Asia and its geopolitics. No petroglyphs or caravanserai to entertain, instruct, or console the weary pilgrim here, only a huge convoy of semitrailers and decorated trucks bedded down on the open plain.

Caravans would have kept going, seeking shade and protection at the foot of the Kunjerab Pass. Huishen would have kept going, too, given the dangers of the road and the prospect of refuge in China, though I suspect he took respite, as I had, in not-so-distant Gilgit. While there, I had visited the Kargha Buddha on a terraced slope outside town, carved into the cliff face during the seventh century, when Buddhism was once again flourishing and just before Islam swept all other religions from its path. It must have seemed an odd place to find such a well-carved Buddha, until someone discovered stupas and a cave a hundred feet farther up the hill crammed with religious documents on birchbark, all written in Sanskrit. It pleased me to think that somewhere, in Pakistan, China, or the Americas, there might be a remote cave that contained a similar hoard of writings by Huishen, a personal diary of his travels, untouched, unexpurgated, waiting to be discovered.

RIDING THE TIGER

EIGHT

"IN THE LONGING that starts one on the path is a kind of homesickness," Peter Matthiessen writes in *The Snow Leopard*, an account of his journey to the famous monastery at Crystal Mountain deep in the Himalayas. I was thinking of Matthiessen's work because my New Zealand friend Dave Hansford was doing research in Kashgar to see if snow-leopard pelts were still showing up in the markets despite the ban on hunting. Dave was an environmental writer-photographer. He had made various forays into these shops, asking directly, then more surreptitiously dropping hints and glancing in the direction of the back rooms. Like Matthiessen before him, he had found nothing, dead or alive, nor had he heard of sightings. Dave put that down to suspicion of foreigners and his own lack of both the language and contacts.

Although he never saw a snow leopard, Matthiessen claimed to have caught a glimpse of his own true nature as he immersed himself in the breadness and sheepness of his daily routines on the journey. I was prepared for this kind of failure—not finding absolute proof of Huishen's travels to the Americas—but I was not yet prepared for the possibility of finding my own true self. The idea seemed preposterous, if not a little unnerving.

I knew what he meant, though, about travel as a sign of homesickness. I had arrived in Kashgar in the company of four new acquaintances, all writers, who happened to share a bus with me over the Kunjerab Pass, from Sost in Pakistan to Tashkurgan in the Xinjiang Uyghur Autonomous Region of China. After weeks of relative silence, I was ecstatic to be swimming in English conversation and experienced a rapid transformation from near-mute stammering to a severe case of motormouth. Dave and his partner, Marieke Hilhorst, both writing about environmental issues, had hoped to see varieties of wildlife in Hunza and the Kunjerab Pass. Mark Mordue and Lisa Nicol, fiction writers from Sydney, Australia, were stationed in Beijing, where he had a China-Australia scholarship. After we'd gone through the rituals of border crossing, including an officious soldier who wanted to know what was written in each of my ringed notebooks, we celebrated by having our first Commonwealth feast at a Uyghur restaurant in Tashkurgan. We were all so pleased about this unlikely and propitious encounter that we paid little attention to the menu, assenting to whatever the waiter offered, which included platters of mutton kebabs and delicious vegetable and rice dishes. While we joked, talked shop, and belted down large quantities of Chinese beer—my first alcohol in a month—our linguistic and culinary oasis exploded with music; one by one, the Uyghur men rose from their tables to dance, making expressive motions with their hands while the women watched and applauded.

While I rejoiced in the English language as one kind of home-place, the tainted kebabs were making themselves at home and wreaking havoc in the guts of five foreigners. I was the first to collapse, quite delirious on the trip northeast to Kashgar the next morning, so weak I almost disappeared into the ground from the weight of my backpack when it was dropped into my arms from the roof of the bus. I made a zigzag course into the hotel lobby, signed something, staggered down a corridor, and collapsed into bed, emerging thirty-six hours later from an extended bout of fever, hallucinations, liquid bowels, and late-night scrubbing of soiled bedsheets, having experienced, yet again, the romance of the Silk Road. In my notebook, which I found on the floor beside the bed, a few lines had been scribbled that I had no memory of writing. The handwriting was my own, but it was almost illegible and would take me a while to decipher. I wiped the vomit from the cover and crammed the book into my backpack.

By the time I'd recovered, Dave and Marieke, who had been inquiring after me, were sticking close to the hotel, looking askance for accessible toilets. Mark and Lisa had arrived, after two days of trekking at Karakul Lake, with upset stomachs. We all convened at the Caravan Café, run by an American from Seattle who knew just what his saddle-sore and parasite-ridden customers most required. In my case, nothing on the menu was more enticing than muesli, yogurt, and hot chocolate. As my system recovered, I added good coffee, tea, fresh juices, salads made from vegetables rinsed in purified water, cinnamon rolls, and hot apple pie and ice cream. The grins that spread across the faces of five recovering scribblers from Victoria, Sydney, and Wellington would have made a Cheshire cat envious.

"My kids discovered in the guidebook that the name *Gary*, with emphasis on the final syllable, means 'diarrhea' in Japanese." I was telling them about a trip to Asia with my family sixteen years earlier, when my daughters were nine, seventeen, and nineteen. "The kids couldn't keep from staring at the faces of our Japanese hosts whenever I introduced myself, looking for the faintest trace of a smile."

"Natural crap detectors, kids." Mark smiled. His first book, *Dastgah: Diary of a Headtrip*, a collection of traveler's essays, poetry, and journalism, was at his publisher's in Australia. There was an endorsement on the back cover by Wim Wenders. On the strength of this publication and his Chinese fellowship, Mark had chucked his newspaper job to pursue a career as a writer of fiction. He had breakfasted earlier and had been downtown inquiring about local Uyghur musicians.

"When's it due out?" Dave asked through a mouthful of apple pie.

"What?" Marieke looked up from her green salad. "The crap or the book?"

"There's a distinction?" Dave washed down the pie with a glass of milk.

"Publishers may be the shits," Mark said, "but they're not half so forthcoming and prompt as diarrhea."

Lisa, five months pregnant, pushed herself away from the table and rubbed her tummy. She had barely begun to show. "Ever notice how all tourist talk revolves around nutrition and evacuation, the two great poles, or holes, of the quest narrative? Your monk, what's-his-name, probably had the same conversation here fifteen hundred years ago."

"Monks are like the queen." Marieke lined up her knife and fork on the plate. "They don't excrete."

"Not true," I said. "The Buddha died of complications from dysentery, though he'd come to the end . . ."

"The end?" Mark peered over the rim of his coffee cup at Lisa.

"Don't go there," she said.

» » « «

How to buy a camel? Look as if it's the last thing on Earth that could possibly interest you. Keep a straight face, prod here and there for soundness, old injuries, scars. Check the teeth and temperament, how well the camel interacts with other animals, especially horses. Breath? Forget it. Allah created camels with breath to keep you humble and mindful of hell. Oh yes, and don't forget the feet. The more splayed the better. Those spongy leather spatulas will need to take on rock, sand, and bog. Humps? Two are definitely better than one; a valley, sometimes referred to as a "saddle," always takes precedence over a mountaintop. Avoid camels whose previous owner was a schoolteacher. When you kick the shins, jump back fast. Take refuge behind a toothpick and roll it from side to side. Caution: A toothpick lodged in the throat may prove a costly distraction. Pausing to read the newspaper is good, but avoid the classifieds. If someone begins to make a pitch, flare your nostrils and laugh loudly as you turn away. Don't push it to the point of insult.

The only two camels in evidence at the Sunday market in Kashgar were goofy-looking tourist fixtures. Lots of horses, however, as well as donkeys, sheep, goats, and bulls were in evidence. The latter were dangerous, trying to mount or gore one another, so I concentrated on donkeys, of which there were several varieties: large black ones, regulation browns, and miniature grays. Money from a tall Han farmer was being deposited, bill by bill, in the open palm of a bearded Uyghur in a fur-brimmed hat, who betrayed no interest in the transaction. The buyer, on the other hand, was increasingly reluctant to part with his money. Not only was the rhythm of delivery slowing down, but also the bills had changed from 100- to 50-yuan notes. Finally, he stopped, looked up, and extended his empty hand as if to say, this is the last sou you'll get for this four-legged abomination, so consider yourself lucky. Nothing registered on the Uyghur's face. He did not need to count the bills; he knew there were exactly 950 yuan in his hand, a decent price for a five-year-old donkey, but not the price he would extract from this twitchy Han who was already emitting the smell of desperation. The Han grabbed back the fistful of bills, made a few derogatory remarks, and walked away. But he would return; it was all part of the ritual. They'd start over again and he'd part with at least another 150 yuan. Of course, there'd be an intermediary this time, the goat man who smiled with his eyes, a rural diplomat who helped the combatants save face and appear to have gone that extra step.

Aside from the camel market, a faceless modernity was rapidly overtaking Kashgar's ancient culture of minarets, quaint brick-and-adobe shops, and one-man factories with awnings. The vast statue of a waving Mao Zedong downtown conveyed a simple message: farewell to all but the dominant culture. China had crushed revolt, if not nationalist sentiment, among the fiercely proud and independent Uyghur peoples of Xinjiang and was using mandatory migration to increase Han presence in the region. However, despite China's efforts to reduce the Uyghurs to an ethnic minority and their vibrant culture to the status of local color, there was still much to appreciate and enjoy in Kashgar. I spent my last few hours on sensory overload in the crowded markets, amid sheepshearers and boys with ropes of garlic strung like bandoliers across their shoulders, picking my way between mounds of tomatoes, peppers, and bok choy. Sunlight filtered through purple, red, and yellow awnings, a cloud cover of hanging silk scarves. Everything in this ancient caravanserai was spread out for sale on blankets or carpets—used tractor parts, plastic dishes, even kittens. As I stood up, a donkey cart ploughed through the sea of shoppers, transporting driver, two children, their mother, a lamb in a gunnysack, and an ornately carved chest of drawers.

And women, everywhere. Even in the predominantly Muslim Xinjiang—gaudily clad in kerchiefs, moving freely, selling goods; working in hotels, restaurants, and shops; driving taxis, pulling carts along the street. After Afghanistan and Pakistan, where women are seldom seen on the street and are either covered head to foot or heavily veiled, Kashgar might be mistaken for Huishen's Land of Women. The change took some adjustment. Tor Singul stood two feet from me in the Wayfarer's Club Restaurant, pencil in hand. She was a young Uyghur woman with a face to launch a thousand camels or distract the itinerant Buddhist heart. Unlike one of her fellow waitresses, with an unbroken ridge of eyebrow, as fierce and foreign-looking as Frida Kahlo, Tor Singul radiated light; she positively beamed. After basking in this glow for several seconds, I realized with some embarrassment that I was expected to order something to eat. There was no English menus and she did not understand a word I said, but the smile remained. Tor Singul took me by the arm and led me between the rows of tables, pointing to this and that platter. My brain had stopped: All my attention was on the fingertips grazing my elbow.

I pointed to something that looked delicious, which turned out to be spicy chicken: *lazi-jiding*. She repeated the name several times in Chinese, while I tried to figure out how to write it down—a procedure I managed to drag out as I drank in her voice and watched her lips form the words. After sampling the chicken, delicious but deadly for a recovering stomach, I remembered the tiny handwritten Chinese-English menu, folded and tucked into my pocket, which Marieke had photo-copied for me earlier in the day. I waved to Tor Singul, who was stationed by the door to the kitchen. When she was within range, I pronounced, without a moment's hesitation, the Chinese sounds *xi lan hua.*

Xi lan hua. Tor Singul beamed. She was beside herself. She looked as if she had won the lottery. She laughed out loud, nod-ded her head, repeated the word several times to be sure she'd heard it correctly. Steamed broccoli, well I'll be damned. She dis-appeared into the kitchen, transfigured, to share the news of this linguistic miracle with Frida Kahlo and the other waitresses.

"What a great name," Dave said, as he filled all our glasses with beer that evening. "Are you sure you didn't invent it?"

"What do you mean?"

"The last name, Singul. It's a bit obvious, no? Wishful think-ing and all that?" There was a round of laughter at my expense.

Mark and Lisa had found a music store in Kashgar, where they bought three tapes for me and three for Dave and Marieke by their favorite Uyghur musician, Abdurahim Heit (pronounced *heat*) who lived and performed in Urumqi, the next stop on my journey. Judging from Mark's description, the music was a blend of Central Asian and Western styles, an uncharted stylistic hinterland situated between Islamic jazz and Chinese country-and-western. Mark was telling us about the basic musical tem-plates of the form, which allow infinite interpretation and variety, and about the links with Persian *maqam*, which made no sense to me at all, when Alim, the proprietor of the Wayfarer's Club Restaurant, appeared from nowhere, saw the tapes, and came over to the table to inspect them. He was ecstatic with Mark's choice and returned with a bottle of local *mao-tai*, a strong alcoholic beverage that had the potency of vodka or schnapps. Drinks all around.

"To my great friend Gary, from Canada!" I'd been singled out for the simple reason that earlier in the day I had given Alim—he preferred his Western name, Alex—English translations for half a dozen dishes on his menu. He asked me to write them down and repeated the pronunciation meticulously. Short of making me a partner in the business, he was determined to show his appreciation. He brought two musicians from the other room to our table, introduced them, and proceeded to tell us about *datar*, the classical Uyghur music that was once used to guide camels and donkeys through the desert. Uyghur song-lines. My four scribbler friends were all ears—and pens.

"My teachers, who were all Chinese"—Alim was on a roll—"said that people with green eyes and red or yellow hair were bad. Lots of Uyghurs have such features. I went home from school and said, 'Mother, why do you have green eyes and red hair? Are you a capitalist?' My mother immediately dyed her hair and it remained that way for the rest of her life."

The Uyghurs were still under siege by their Chinese landlords, who had managed to secure all the best jobs in Xinjiang. There had been random acts of violence, followed by ruthless suppression of the slightest signs of separatist sentiment among the Muslims. The one small victory for the region was its determination, unlike the rest of China, to ignore Beijing time, running instead on unofficial Xinjiang time, two hours behind the capital. Alim did not speak of such things—he was interested in business, not politics—but before he retired to his table of friends, he shared a Uyghur parable called "The Great Wall and the Lowly Land," clearly intended to assert local virtues. Then he toasted my health, which was in need of all the support it could rally.

September 6, 2001, my last night in Kashgar. I had no desire to leave the refreshing and entertaining company of my newfound friends, but Marieke and Dave had a plane to catch for New Zealand, and Mark and Lisa were flying back to Beijing. I was heading east along the Silk Road, across the Taklamakan Desert to Urumqi, then on to Turpan, Dunhuang, Lanzhou, Xiahe, and Xian. We exchanged e-mail addresses and promised to keep in touch.

Along with friendship, love, and wine, departure is one of the central concerns of poetry in China, a country so vast and sprawling it is rivaled only by Canada and Russia for distance and geographical barriers. Many years ago, I translated, with the help of my friend George Liang, some poems by the Tang poets Li Bai and Du Fu, both of whom were obsessed with departures and farewells. One of Li Bai's poems comes back to me now, so full of his awareness of hills and moving water as constant reminders of distance and loss, of human lives blown hither and thither like tumbleweed, subject to the whim of emperor or bureaucrat. Unwilling to prolong the agony, Li Bai encourages a quick departure:

Even your thoughts are fleeting clouds,
While this friend's heart is sinking like the sun.

Wave to me now and be off,
I hear the impatient whinnying of your horse.

Du Fu's work is riddled with similar moments, similar sentiments. A lover asks: "When will we lean together again / in the empty window, moon drying our tears?" The poet and civil servant, at the crumbling peripheries of empire, finds solace and hope only in the renewal of nature in spring:

In times like these the flowers taste my grief,
birdsong troubles my caged and lonely heart.

Three months or more the warning beacon burns,
news from home is worth ten thousand taels.

If Kashgar was a welcome oasis for travelers along the Silk Road, Huishen included, it had been no less so for me, thanks to these four itinerant scribblers. However, the evening was far from over. Dave was in high gear.

"What is the craziest thing you could imagine doing on a Saturday night in Kashgar?" he asked as we quaffed the last of our beers at Alim's Wayfarer's Club Restaurant. "Other than, say, proposing to Tor Singul." I ignored the rhetorical question, waiting for him to reveal his scheme.

"Why, tenpin bowling, of course." Dave had spotted the newly built lanes a few blocks from the hotel, the first such venture in Xinjiang. "It's something I'd never be caught doing back in New Zealand," he added somewhat sheepishly.

We set off into the warm desert night. Save for a couple of donkey carts hauling produce, the streets were empty. A warm breeze was coming off the distant sand dunes. The manager of the establishment, doubtless questioning his own wisdom for promoting such a little-known game in a remote outpost, couldn't believe his eyes when we burst into the spanking-new bowling alley, boisterous, loud, and surelly reeking of beer. Our enthusiasm filled the place, bounced off the walls.

The largest shoes in stock were size 28, which did not fit, so I was reduced to bowling in white nylon stockings that offered no traction whatsoever. I had bowled fivepin when I was a kid in Vancouver, at Grandview Bowling Alley on Commercial Drive. Those balls were small, slightly larger than a grapefruit, with no finger holes, and the pins were hand-set by a scrawny kid, invisible except for hands and forearms. Now pin-setting is all done by machines. Getting a grip on the huge tenpin balls was the first challenge. The thumbhole was simple enough, but I had no idea which fingers to stick into the remaining two holes. In cartoons, hapless novices sometimes forget to release their grip, or simply can't, and are dragged behind the cannonball speeding down the lane. I was so conscious of the problem that I dropped the ball on the new hardwood floor on my first try. Most of my fellow wordsmiths were as inept as they were competitive. Mark guttered his first ball. Marieke sent down a sleeper that left an impossible split, with only the two outside pins standing. Her second ball, much faster, cruised blithely down the center of the lane for a close encounter with nothingness.

After leaving Muslim Pakistan, Dave's first gesture had been to unzip his pant legs, transforming his trousers into shorts. At least he looked the part—a jock who ought to know what to do in a bowling alley. His wobbly toss took out two pins on the left. Only Lisa, whose pregnant body must have sensed some affinity with the size and girth of the bowling ball, made a strike on her first bowl.

National reputations were definitely at stake. Nothing I did improved my score, all those years of fivepin bowling a wasted apprenticeship. I blamed my paltry performance on the white nylon stockings, which made balance and stopping before the foul line impossible, and on my recent illness, but I knew it had more to do with the quantity of beer consumed. In the morning, quietly and without fanfare, I would hire a taxi to take me to the airport. There would be no last-minute farewells. I would join Li Bai and Du Fu in the long line of poetic mourners, wanting my departure to be as quick and painless as possible.

For the time being, I looked at my four new friends, so vital, so alive, initiates in the tribe, giving off energy and perspiration, radiant with youth and hope, with books and new life waiting to be born, and I was happy to be with them, clumsy in our affection, complicit in our love of words.

NINE

HAVING BEEN SICK twice and traveled on too many cramped buses over nearly impassable roads, I was not anxious to attempt—by camel, jeep, or train—the thousand-mile crossing of the Taklamakan Desert, whose Uyghur name is widely understood to mean "if you go in, you might never come out." I felt guilty about this evasion until I got to the airline ticket office and saw a monk in the line ahead of me, also opting for flight. Buddhists are practical—no point wasting eons learning how to levitate to your destination when you could get there at once by paying a small fee.

The flight from Kashgar tipped me off to the new China. As a delighted escapee from the thirty-one-hour train ride, I sat munching the Chinese equivalent of an Oreo cookie and contented myself with a bird's-eye view of the desert, the Tien Shan range to the north, snow-capped all year, and the burnt-sienna hills to the south, silting over with sand in the half-light, hiding God-knows-how-many ruins and priceless relics. Somewhere below me was the oasis town of Kuche, once an important watering hole on the Silk Road as well as the site of four ancient cities and numerous monasteries. Hsuan Tsang mentioned seeing two large Buddhas at its western gate in AD 644. Most of Kuche's antiquities had been destroyed or stolen, so I decided to pass it by. I'd have to content myself with what remained in the caves at Turpan, Dunhuang, Luoyang, and Datong. Not only was the flight to Urumqi pleasant and uneventful, but the equipment also turned out to be brand-new and state of the art; so, too, were the giveaway treats. During my previous trips within China, I'd flown on aging hand-me-down DC-8s, purchased from Canada, with water dripping from the air-conditioning and with tables that popped open at the slightest turbulence. No more used equipment; China was paying hard cash. Most surprising was the gift of an attractive stainless-steel key chain, a far cry from the dead fly embedded in plastic that had been presented to me in 1985.

Although it lies at the eastern end of the Taklamakan Desert, still well within the borders of Xinjiang Uyghur Autonomous Region, Urumqi, which the Chinese pronounce as *Ulumuchi*, had the trappings of any large Chinese industrial metropolis: smokestacks, congestion, pollution, ugly tile-and-concrete-block architecture, and a cultural vacuum left in the wake of a pathological determination to modernize at any cost. While the streets thronged with Uyghurs, Kazaks, Tajiks, Russians, Han, and other nationalities, nothing else about the capital city of Xinjiang reflected this rich mix of cultures. It had become an important commercial hub, as well as proof of China's determination to fully and permanently occupy the region. Local warlords dominated Urumqi politics until 1949, when the Communist hard-liners took over, driving the Muslim League and other separatist groups underground. There, the separatists had more or less languished except for isolated uprisings, quickly suppressed, including the blowing up of three buses in the city in 1993, which left nine dead and many injured.

Huishen would not have cared that Urumqi is farther from the sea than any other city in the world, 1,350 miles. I doubt he had the slightest inkling either, so early in his journey east, that he would be exchanging camels, those noble and noxious ships of the desert, for a watercraft that would take him even farther over the ocean than he had traveled over land. Afghanistan, including Bactria, had neither coasts nor navy; the region's prosperity was tied up with the Silk Road linking the Mediterranean and the Orient, a route that would thrive until it was eclipsed by oceangoing commerce. With information gleaned from other travelers, Huishen probably chose as his immediate destination the Turpan Basin, where the Bezeklik monastery offered shelter and a chance for discussion and spiritual renewal. In the interim, during an arduous passage through the desert—perhaps along the small trail I could just make out two miles below me, following a dried-up riverbed—his attention would have been focused primarily on the needs of the body, protecting his eyes from blowing sand, nursing the always precarious water supply, avoiding the sun, and keeping a sharp lookout for bandits.

Xi Chuan, a writer in Beijing, had provided me with a list of the names of Chinese poets I might call in various cities. The contact in Kashgar did not pan out. In Urumqi, I phoned Ding Yan, a young poet working at a brokerage, who was purported to understand English. Whatever words she had at her disposal disappeared when she heard my voice on the phone. She had enough presence of mind, though, to get the name of my hotel so she could call back when she had enlisted some help. I met with her and Chung Lizhou, a younger man who was her English teacher, in a restaurant near my hotel. While I ate broccoli and ginger chicken, they poured over my curriculum vitae, several books, and the letter I had obtained from the Chinese cultural attaché in Vancouver, describing the Huishen project and asking that I be given special access to historic sites and cultural relics.

"You want meet Shen Wei?" According to Xi Chuan's notes, Shen Wei was the "most important poet in Urumqi." The word "important" could have meant any number of things, not necessarily literary.

"Only if it's convenient." Ding Yan's lips toyed with this four-syllable word, hoping it might ring a bell. It didn't. Chung Lizhou, who had quit teaching because the pay was so lousy and who now intended to pursue a law degree, explained that Shen Wei had gone for a week to Kashgar. Since Shen Wei spoke no English, his absence did not strike me as a great loss. I said as much to Ding Yan, but she was still trying to decipher my consular letter.

"Who Huishen? I not hear." Ding Yan pointed to the Chinese characters for the monk's name as she spoke. I gave my two companions the same shorthand account of Huishen and his travels that I had given Hassan in Kabul, though I skipped the Afghan connection. Chung Lizhou translated. The name meant nothing to them. Just as the meeting seemed about to dissolve, Ding Yan had an inspiration—or a charitable impulse.

"You like, I show city."

As it turned out, she could not get away from the brokerage firm until Thursday, which gave me plenty of time to explore the city on my own and to organize an excursion to Turpan. I caught an early taxi to the Xinjiang Museum, hoping to examine some important Silk Road artifacts, but it was closed for renovations. As I paused just inside the entrance to the museum grounds, disappointed but reluctant to step into the dust and diesel fumes, I noticed a tiny mimeographed sheet stapled to a noticeboard by the door. It informed me that The Exhibition of Corpses & Relics, housed in a separate building around the back, was still open to the public.

The woman who collected admission fees would not accept any money when she read my consular letter and insisted on hovering nearby in case I needed assistance, though she spoke no English. I did my best to ignore her as I examined a piece of intricate brocade headgear and various swatches of cloth from tombs excavated at the Niya site, a region in southern Xinjiang that is cradled by the Kunlun Mountains. This small gathering of materials included a piece that resembled corduroy, some cotton with a floral design, more cotton with birds and human figures, and, to my surprise, a wall hanging depicting a centaur. A swatch of material from the Tarim Basin was a dead ringer for brown-and-tan Scottish tartan, which the Chinese refer to as a trellis pattern, and it was listed as more than two thousand years old. Even older was a boomerang from Wubao, near Hami, Ding Yan's parental home, where the railway dips away from the Mongolian border in the direction of Gansu Province.

I tried to shake off the attendant, who was more persistent than a boomerang. I was not ungrateful for her attention, but I wanted to examine the corpses carefully and preferred to do it on my own. The Qiemo baby, aged eight-to-twelve months, was bound in red sacking and wore a blue wool hat; he had two flat stones over his eyes and had been found with a feeding device made of ox horn and sheep's nipple. One corpse wore a yellow knitted toque; another, a peaked, brown felt cap. A twenty-year-old girl with brown hair assumed the fetal position, the fingers of her right hand clutching her left wrist. And a bearded Zaghunluq man, tall and decidedly European in appearance, had gone to meet his maker in an elegant knee-length wool coat, a braided red-and-black bracelet, and well-preserved deerskin boots.

These corpses, preserved by the intense desert heat, were important not only for their Caucasian appearance and costume, but also for what they tell us about ancient migrations. How far had they traveled? Perhaps from the Ukraine and the Urals or even farther afield. They had migrated to the Xinjiang region four thousand years ago with their equestrian know-how, including wagons and chariots, and with their weaving and design skills. The discoveries were further evidence that China did not develop in complete isolation. Early traffic between East and West was two-way.

While "The Boomerang" was busy with new customers, I managed to pay my respects to the Loulan Beauty with her chestnut hair, which pushed out from under a felt hat adorned with a goose feather. Her eyes, long lashes still intact, had sunk below the cheekbones. Otherwise, she was well preserved, even handsome. Five feet tall, European, with type O blood and at least 3,800 years of underground experience, she did not look a day over forty-five, her approximate age at the time of death. Since her discovery in 1980, she had achieved special status among corpses. The Uyghurs, arriving much later in the region where the tombs are located, which they call Lop Nur, or Wandering Lake, had nevertheless claimed the Loulan Beauty as the mother of their "nation," and she had been celebrated in song. Unfortunately, the Lop Nur region had been inaccessible to outsiders since 1964, as it was used by China for nuclear testing. None of this notoriety had gone to the Loulan Beauty's head. She appeared serene in her glass case in Urumqi, one shoulder faintly visible through the threadbare weave of her garment, and her lips pressed—in mirth, perhaps—around some truth, some unspeakable enigma.

Turpan is defined by the legends that surround it, some related to its claim to be the hottest spot in China. Turpan's Flaming Mountains, which look as if they are on fire at midday, appear in Wu Cheng'en's *Pilgrimage to the West,* a sixteenth-century tale. Like *Gulliver's Travels,* it's an adult adventure story with characters that appeal to all ages. The monk Tripitaka and his companions Monkey, Pigsy, and Sandy encounter monsters and various obstacles in their journey west in search of the Buddhist scriptures. An old man they meet on the road tells them that Flaming Mountain, which he describes in the singular, is responsible for the heat and drought of the region and is impassable: "Its flames reach out eight hundred *li* so that not a blade of grass can grow round about. A man with a head of copper and a body of iron would melt if he took that road." To put out this fire, they have to get the palm-leaf fan, which is in the possession of the Iron Fan Fairy, who lives at the Mountain of the Emerald Clouds. She turns out to be Princess Rakshasa, wife of the Ox Demon King, with a long-standing grudge against Monkey for capturing and carting off her troublesome son, Red Boy.

An epic battle ensues, after which Rakshasa uses her fan to create a cold wind that drives Monkey fifty thousand *li* off course. Bodhisattva Ling Ji tells Monkey that what he has just experienced is the essence of the Primary Female Principle, created on the heels of Primordial Chaos. This is not good news.

With the aid of a wind-calming pill and a deft transformation into a gnat, Monkey manages to extract the fan, only to discover he has been tricked again and given a fake that fans the flames even higher. The story is too long, and too delightful, to be reduced to a few paragraphs. Suffice it to say, the correct fan is obtained after another epic battle, this time against the forces of the Ox Demon King, and the flames are eventually put out, replaced by healing rains that bring peace and eventual harvest.

The story of the Flaming Mountains, which were appearing ahead on my right as the bus wound south from Urumqi, had a symbolic dimension as well, something to do with uniting the warring elements of fire and water, or passion and reason. I decided it was not safe to speculate on the Primary Female Principle and its power to dampen the flames or to touch the comic potential of the wind-calming pill.

Shortly after the bus arrived in Turpan, I found myself sharing a taxi with three young office workers from Shanghai, who were on vacation and enjoying their experience of China's wild west, that vast and unpredictable region beyond the extremities of the Great Wall. Our first destination was the ancient Han garrison city of Jiaohe, built two millennia earlier and located only a few miles from Turpan on a high ridge of sandstone that forms an island at the confluence of two rivers.

My three companions, working for foreign companies, had acquired Western names. Grace promptly assumed the role of leader of this expedition and did her best to keep track of us as we zigzagged through the ruins of Jiaohe, following the ancient streets, climbing walls, posing for photographs in the cavelike openings of eroded buildings, avoiding large fissures that had opened in the sandstone bluff, and trying to keep from baking in the extreme heat. Although picked clean of artifacts, there was no shortage of magic in this elemental setting, which was happily devoid of signs and souvenir shops. If Thomas Hardy had been Chinese, his fictional Immortals might have finished their play with Tess in this austere place, where one can so easily conjure the gathering of armies and the performance of ancient rituals.

Having been mustered for lunch, the troops were now tipping back some well-earned Chinese intoxicants at Grape Valley, also known as Putao Gou. This vineyard, with vines and trellises overhead and a small irrigation channel beside the table, its open-air restaurant, and its organized market stalls selling fruit, nuts, candy, various trinkets, and souvenirs, required nothing more than the smell of pack animals, shouts of hustlers, and the curses of camel drivers to transform it into the perfect oasis, a welcome refuge from the heat of the desert. While Grace ordered food for the four of us and for the taxi driver, Wallace arranged a group photograph.

After lunch, we drove north to Bezeklik, a series of Buddhist grottoes carved into the sandstone cliffs at the northwest edge of the Flaming Mountains. On the well-maintained and newly paved highway that follows the river valley, we had to slow down for a Uyghur family trotting along at a steady clip ahead of us on two donkey carts. The husband and his brightly clad wife, rigged out in a blue silk dress and gray knit veil, occupied one cart; a boy and his grandfather, the other. I wondered what was on their minds as they moved through a region so rich in history, bodies fanned by their slight passage in the dry desert air. The carts appeared empty of produce, so they were most likely returning from the market in Turpan.

I find myself unnerved by ruins. They exhaust me, render me

mortal, more thin-skinned than usual. Like poetry, language stripped to the essentials, ruins embody a contradiction, a ragged minimalism embracing the whole of life. And the despair that attaches itself to ruins has as its shadowy opposite the fleeting vision of hope. Although they had been looted by Westerners and smashed by Muslims and Red Guards alike, the cave temples of Bezeklik were still impressive. In the early 1900s, German collector Albert von Le Coq removed the best frescoes and shipped them to Berlin, where they were destroyed in the Allied bombings of the Second World War. However, there still remained a number of pale blue and brown images of the Buddha, unforgettable not only because of their unique location, but also because of an unmistakable exuberance and simplicity of line.

Before Bezeklik, we had spent half an hour exploring the ingenious engineering of *karez* in Turpan, a vast network of underground tunnels carrying meltwater hundreds of miles from the mountains to supply the city, irrigate the fields, and defy the insatiable thirst of the desert sun. I was thinking of these cool tunnels as we made our last stop of the day at the ruins of Gaocheng, where not even hat, shades, or bottles of refrigerated drinking water could guarantee survival. This ancient staging post on the Silk Road, built during the Tang Dynasty and then occupied by Uyghurs from Mongolia two centuries later, had had walls thirty feet thick surrounded by a moat as well as an inner city that contained government buildings and a palace. A few fragments of the original walls remained, along with a large mosque, outside of which an eight-year-old girl in a red dress posed for photographs beside a donkey. Her head was shaved and she held a plastic bottle of water. She smiled and raised her right arm, a small gold bracelet flashing on her thin wrist, to give me a peace sign.

Wallace, who had said little all day, was sitting across from me on the donkey cart, his feet dangling over the side as we returned to the car. He had his mouth and nose buried in the crook of his elbow to avoid a cloud of dust from the cart over-taking us. Beyond him, a tall obelisk stood out against the blue sky, the highest point in Gaocheng, a survivor of war and the ravages of time. When the dust settled, Wallace leaned across the donkey cart and tapped me gently on the shoulder. His narrow face, in glasses, had a benign, almost scholarly appearance, accentuated by the worried expression it now assumed. Clearing his throat of dust, he spat into the dirt track, hesitated a moment, then, just above a whisper, asked:

"What do you think of events in New York yesterday?"

Because the television in my cheap hotel room had no English channels, not even CNN or BBC World, I'd watched the attacks and implosions in New York over and over again with only Chinese commentary. Eventually, I located an Internet café and was able to examine the news reports and images on CBC Radio's Web site. When I checked my e-mail, there was a host of messages from concerned family and friends, wanting to make sure I was okay, wondering if I was still in Afghanistan or simply wanting to share their confusion and grief over the attacks. The words *upsetting, very shaken, in shock, paralyzed, horror,* and *dark times ahead,* so pathetic in their inadequacy, leaped from the screen. A message from a friend in Bellingham spoke of borders closing and planes grounded, and advised, "If you have any of those maple-leaf pins left, put them all on." Another, from a professor in Nebraska who mentioned talking to students about hijacking and terrorism, reminded me of being in front of a class the day after the Bay of Pigs invasion in Cuba and of the sense of doom that had hung over us.

I assured family and friends that, aside from being a bit road-weary, I considered myself quite safe in the desert. My stomach had settled down, and I was eating lots of Chinese greens. I felt strangely and disconcertingly removed from what had happened. I wasn't worried about myself. The truth is, I was deeply concerned about my new Afghan friends, Hassan, Sabir, Yousef, and the staff and patients at the Wazir Orthopaedic Clinic, given the inevitable escalation of conflict as shock transformed into rage and a desire for revenge. The thought of Kabul, already devastated from ten years of Soviet occupation and another ten years of tribal and sectarian violence, being "bombed back to the Stone Age," as one commentator suggested, was truly frightening.

Ding Yan's excursion to Tian Chi, or Heavenly Pool, provided a welcome distraction. While not exactly at the right hand of Allah, I felt as close to the gods as is humanly possible as I walked along the shores of this tiny, deep lake high in the mountains outside of Urumqi. Thanks to low-lying clouds, the retreat felt remote and invigorating, with trails winding among pines, small creeks, and waterfalls. Ding Yan, my poet-guide, was silent. There had been bursts of fragmented conversation on the bus as she tried out a few words of English. My own efforts to communicate were no better. Eventually, I resorted to crude drawings of chickens, clouds, or boats on the blank pages in my notebook to explain the simplest idea or observation. It was funny but exhausting, so the gaps in conversation widened and we concentrated on getting a good workout on the elaborate network of stairs, paths, and small bridges.

It was cooler at this altitude, and a number of sightseers at the Heavenly Pool had rented olive-green Chinese army greatcoats with fake-fur collars. Several lumbering tour boats were taking on passengers for a leisurely circumnavigation of the lake. For those with money and short attention spans, a speedboat throttled down, creating a huge wave that followed it into the dock, causing the other boats to bounce and chafe at their moorings. Here and there, along the shore, photo ops were being offered by local Kazaks, whose daughters and small children were dressed in folk costumes for group shots or seated grandly, if a little absurdly, on a horse. Serious business, with not only racks of ethnic costumes for quick changes to appeal to tourists coming and going, but also constantly shifting poses and dramatic gestures to the sound of taped musical accompaniment. The same families rented small round tents called *yurts* up and down the mountainside and at various locations around the lake. Seeing a Chinese woman with an older *lao-wai*—me—a young Kazak man sidled over to ask if we wanted to rent a *yurt* for the day. Ding Yan was furious and gave him a tongue-lashing.

Because it was too late and too miserable, in the intermittent fog and light rain, for a trek around the lake, I suggested we follow the cement steps down a narrow man-made creek and series of waterfalls, which I thought would bring us out somewhere near the cafés and shops where the buses were waiting. Ding Yan was skeptical but willing to try. The scene, with its man-made waterfall wrapped in mist, was breathtaking but familiar. Chinese painting has such a long and vivid history of cloud-socked, torrential mountain landscapes that it was as impossible here not to see nature imitating art as it would have been for a nineteenth-century Englishman not to see a Constable landscape at every twist in the rural road or for a Canadian not to view every blasted pine as a tribute to Tom Thomson's skillful hand and painterly eye. After a winding descent of several hundred feet, we'd left the human race behind and found ourselves enshrouded in so much fog and drizzle that nothing was visible beyond the steps and the handrail. The roar of the cascading water was enough to drown out bird cries and conversation alike. I felt as if I were not so much descending a mountain as going backward in time, to a place where things were basic, elemental, less complicated. And dangerous, of course, because a slip here would mean a broken leg or a broken neck. We stopped on a small concrete platform below the falls. The fine spray that descended on us from a waterfall we could not see felt like the kiss of an angel.

Ding Yan was concerned, correctly, that we had taken the wrong turn and might miss the bus. She was also worried about the safety of her Canadian guest, spry enough but no spring chicken. However, the fog began to clear and a second, narrower series of steps appeared, heading diagonally uphill. By now I was feeling a bit shaky myself, out of breath, no longer the conquering hero of the slopes. Ding Yan, in her black rainproof jacket and tan-colored baseball cap, was ascending the perilous incline a few steps ahead of me when a shout rang out in Chinese. A young man waved from a landing twenty feet above us, a worker from Chengdu, assigned to this remote park in Xinjiang. His brother, he told us, was also assisting with the maintenance of the trails. He showed us the plastic shelter they lived in during the tourist season, with three sides and a mat on the dirt floor. According to Ding Yan's translation, he was no hermit or Chinese Romantic and couldn't wait to get back to the city.

Urumqi, three hours later, was somewhat less hospitable than might have been hoped, even by a young worker from Chengdu, where the uncertain water levels of the Yangtze were a constant concern. The streets of this desert city were awash from the same torrential rains that had flooded more southerly regions of the country—monsoon rains. As I made my way back to the hotel, I got off at the wrong stop and had to walk a couple of miles. The small umbrella I carried in my shoulder bag proved useless and I was soaked in minutes. The tread had vanished on my sandals, so they slipped treacherously on the smooth-tiled sidewalks so much in fashion in the new China. This problem required a slow, flat-footed, and stick-legged gait that amused some of the passersby, one of whom snatched me from the path of a speeding taxi and gestured toward the shelter of a large department-store entranceway. The rain had no intention of stopping, and neither did I. I removed my sandals and set out again, putting them back on only to pick up milk, a banana, an apple, and a few other groceries in a late-night market.

I had arrived in Urumqi expecting a dumpy frontier town that might be worth a day of my time. What I found instead was a throbbing metropolis that couldn't quite decide whether to model itself on New York or Tokyo so was trying both: towering buildings, flyways, pedestrian overpasses, neon everywhere. Like the *Tian Chi* worker from Chengdu, I had to confess I was enjoying the urban buzz. Meanwhile, there was one final pedestrian underpass to negotiate—"navigate" would be a more appropriate term—before I reached the hotel. It was brimming with at least three feet of murky water, at the edge of which several people stood laughing, scratching their heads, and talking in high-pitched voices.

If these had been the waters of Babylon, I would have sat down and wept for those lost in New York and for my endangered friends in Kabul. Instead, groceries held high, I waded right in and strode in slow motion and with water up to my crotch to the other side. There was a burst of applause somewhere in my wake. When I turned to wave, five more intrepid waders—amphibians all—were making their watery way through the dark tunnel, following my dubious, and alien, example.

TEN

MY SEARCH FOR Huishen had taken me more than two thousand miles along the Silk Road from Kabul to Gansu Province, just inside the most westerly extremities of the Great Wall of China. I had left behind the hinterlands, territory of the "barbarians," considered for centuries by the Chinese to be dangerous and beyond the pale. The train from Urumqi dropped me at a tiny desert station not far from Dunhuang in what was known as the Hexi Corridor, or the throat of the Silk Road. Here East and West had once converged. Foreigners arriving by way of the Yangguan Pass to the southwest or the Yumenguan Pass to the northwest merged and were funneled through the Hexi Corridor on their way to the ancient capitals of Chang'an and Luoyang. It was not only a vital staging ground for travel in either direction, but also a vibrant hub and cultural mixing pot. That Buddhists would have chosen this spot to leave a stunning and permanent record of their faith and devotion in man-made grottoes, where neither fire nor water could destroy them, is hardly surprising. In the long run, the principal threat to the survival of murals, sculpture, and written texts turned out to be not fire or war, but religious zealots and thieves, many in the guise of professional archaeologists.

On June 22, 1900, Wang Yuanlu, a Daoist who worshiped and was caretaker at Mogao Shiku, the Thousand Buddha Caves outside Dunhuang, was cleaning sand and dust from the floor of Cave 16 when he noticed something unusual. He brushed aside loose material he'd collected and looked carefully at the portion of wall from which some plaster had fallen. Instead of natural rock underneath, he could detect the outline of a sandstone block, several blocks. His reward for good housekeeping and keen eyesight was the discovery of more than fifty thousand ancient manuscripts in a sealed-off inner cave. In this treasure trove were Buddhist classics, maps, medical texts, and treatises in several languages, including Sanskrit and Tibetan, on subjects as diverse as economics, geography, politics, religion, law, history, art, and literature. The bonanza in the newly numbered Cave 17, which came to be known as the Library Cave, also included priceless paintings on paper and silk, delicate embroidery, and copies of several famous sutras (teachings of the Buddha), done by a process of woodblock printing in AD 868, further proof that the Chinese invented this technology.

A former vagrant and foot soldier in the Qing army, Daoist Wang was not a sophisticated man. In fact, he seems, initially, to have been unaware of the cultural importance or monetary value of this windfall, which he began to dispense piecemeal among local officials in return for certain services. Although he was eventually ordered by the Gansu Department of Administration to seal off and guard the cave, Wang continued to demonstrate his largesse, selling twenty-four boxes of manuscripts and five boxes of silk paintings and other items in 1907 for a pittance to Marc Aurel Stein, a Hungarian scholar who became a British citizen before embarking on his adventures as a collector. Stein's second visit to Mogao Shiku netted a further 570 manuscripts, totaling some twenty thousand items, most of which went to the British Museum, the British Library, and what is now the National Museum of India in Delhi.

Stein's success at Mogao Shiku triggered a cultural gold rush, which brought Paul Pelliot from France in 1908, Zuicho Tachibana from Japan in 1911, Sergei Oldenburg from Russia in 1914, and Langdon Warner from the United States in 1924. While others merely conned Daoist Wang, spiriting away significant portions of China's cultural heritage, Warner managed as well to destroy several murals by trying to peel them off with tape. Fortunately—or perhaps not, depending on how you view the ownership and dispersal of cultural treasures—Paul Pelliot had the decency to show some of his purchases to Chinese scholars in Beijing in 1909, and an order went out from the capital to seal off the Library Cave. A year later the Department of Education of the Qing Dynasty ordered the rest of the hoard to be brought to Beijing, but not before Daoist Wang had ferreted away even more of this material. After local authorities had taken their share, two Beijing officials helped themselves, tearing some items in half in order to keep the inventory numbers consistent. Of the precious motherlode from the Library Cave, only eighteen boxes—8,697 pieces—were delivered to the Beijing Library.

Cave 17 was now out of bounds, with not even an electrical light to satisfy the curious. Beyond the barrier, I could dimly make out the life-sized statue of head monk Hongbian, whose memorial cave had been turned into a library. I mingled with twenty or so curious French tourists in Cave 16, who were listening attentively to their guide while the beams of their flashlights performed a nervous dance in the semigloom of the Library Cave, but I was unable to catch a single glimpse of the forbidden murals.

Samples of *bianwen*, a previously unknown literary form, had also been found among the library documents. As nearly as I could make out, *bianwen* combined prose and poetry, narrative and lyrical elements intended to be read or sung aloud. Although associated primarily with the Tang Dynasty, *bianwen* may have originated earlier, as it seems to have had various unique functions, which included serving as a bridge or script for narrative paintings. This story-song—*chantefable* in French—would sometimes accompany the showing of unscrolled narrative paintings in court. While the viewer's eye moved from one scene to the next, a narrator would read the prose commentary in the vernacular, or common language, and his or another voice would interject a lyrical message in seven-syllable lines.

The Magical Battle between Raudraksa and Sariputra, one of the paintings from the library cave spirited away to France by Paul Pelliot, combines both illustrations and text in *bianwen*. It depicts the struggle between the forces of good and evil, in this case the Buddha and his followers confronting and defeating the six heretical lords, during which figures on both sides undergo metamorphoses. Presiding over this metaphysical battleground is a large white elephant that symbolizes the Buddha. Critics speak of *bianwen* as the origin of the narrative tradition in Chinese literature, a case of the poets finally catching up with the painters. However, narrative elements appear elsewhere in Chinese poetry, particularly in the secular work of Li Bai. *Bianwen* seems more important as a precursor of drama, in which the public presentation of text and visual narrative lead inevitably to character and action on stage. By extension, the function of *bianwen* is not unlike that of the script that accompanied silent film in the early years of the twentieth century.

Bookworm that I am, the Library Cave and the discovery of *bianwen* held a special fascination for me. Much of my own poetic energy had been spent trying to marry epic and lyric, story and song, and I could imagine Huishen, that rare bird of passage, staying long enough at Mogao Shiku to contribute, most likely in Sanskrit, his own version of *bianwen*, spinning his tales of misadventure and flights of fancy in a subversive form. A thorough examination of the contents of Cave 17, now dispersed throughout the world, might even reveal that Huishen was distinguished or eccentric enough to have been mentioned in the lists of nuns and monks in residence at Dunhuang, the ideal location from which to have embarked on his initial studies of Chinese language and culture.

After lunch, I went back to Mogao Shiku to pick up a copy of the commemorative publication for the 2000 centenary, which contained photographs of many of the manuscripts and murals. I considered this volume a gold mine, as the most stunning silk paintings and manuscripts from the Mogao grottoes could be seen only by making a trip to the British Museum in London or the Louvre and *Musée National des Arts Asiatiques Guimet* in Paris. This treasure trove of sold or abducted art includes several commentaries on the Diamond Sutra and a Chinese copy of the Lotus Sutra written in gold ink on silver-lined dark blue paper. One of these, depicting Buddha's subjugation of devils and temptresses, possessed the kind of high energy and maddening detail of a Bosch triptych or the shock and disorientation generated by the minidramas in Brueghel's *Garden of Earthly Delights*. Another of my favorite silk paintings was the subdued ninth-century image of a monk traveling with a tiger. The monk is dwarfed by the huge load of scriptures he is bringing home in a bundle from India. Judging from his docile four-legged companion, the determined look on his own face, and the celestial escort—a small Buddha seated on a cloud—the monk has mastered not only a foreign language, but also the beasts within and without.

I was disappointed to find, revisiting the caves, that the sculptures and murals of the Northern Wei caves, constructed between AD 386 and 534, encompassing the years of Huishen's journey east, were drab, humorless, even puritanical. All the necessary ingredients were there—Bodhisattvas, demons, fierce *vajras* defending the Dharma (or Law), lotus and acanthus, and, of course, *apsaras,* those delightful flying girls more plentiful in Buddhist art than birds. However, there was not enough decadence, chaos, or domestic realism for my taste; Indian sensuality had not yet triumphed over Confucian restraint. I preferred the Tang art, in which it wasn't all serious business, in which there was greater variety of line, extravagant use of color, and more detailed characterization. The most notable exception, for me, was a 54-centimeter bust of a Bodhisattva from the Northern Wei period, which, with eyes cast down, looked like a gentle, demure, dignified, and thoroughly self-contained Renaissance madonna. The mouth was pinched on both sides, giving the lips more than a hint of eros.

Having had my fill of cave art for the day, I spent the afternoon checking out the small city of Dunhuang, which had gone from being a center of international trade and cultural exchange to a regional outpost, when traffic in silk and other precious goods took to the sea. Now it was an oasis of a different sort, a special destination for artists, scholars, and tourists who wanted a unique window to the past. I ordered a latte at Shirley's Café, a local gathering place for anyone traveling on the cheap. Here I met William, an Australian working in Qingdao, who did not have a very high opinion of his Chinese hosts, and Margritte, a nurse from the Netherlands who had been traveling on her own through Vietnam and Cambodia for three months. Plans were afoot for a trip to Crescent Moon Spring, where they would take a fifteen-minute camel ride over the dunes. I'd had enough close encounters of the noxious kind with camels at the Sunday market in Kashgar, and at every other tourist site in Asia, to exempt myself.

I ordered a beer, skimmed several books I'd picked up at Mogao Shiku, and checked my e-mail messages. Someone had sent me a belated report about the assassination of Ahmad Shah Massoud, the charismatic leader of the Northern Alliance who had once been a guest at Sabir Latifi's table in Kabul. The timing of the assassination was too close to the attacks in New York to have been coincidental. There was a cheery note from my middle daughter, Sarcy, saying she understood "you like to challenge your safe life with something that makes you creative and aware, but, for God's sake, be careful." I am glad to have kids who understand me better than I understand myself, though I believed this trip, even with its personal challenges, to be about something deeper, something more evanescent and enduring, even if I could not yet put that into words.

As if in response to these deliberations, there was a message from Joan Skogan, a friend and writer in Vancouver, telling me she was in a swamp of fear about her project, her health, and the international political situation. In response to the wave of anti-Muslim sentiment created by the attacks on the World Trade Center, she was thinking of writing an article about Bosnia and Kosovo, where she had experienced such warmth and kindness. Joan, my age and therefore old enough to have achieved wisdom or to feel its absence acutely, was someone whose writing I admired and with whom I shared an interest in the sea and the history of the Pacific Coast. While I retraced the path of Huishen, she was writing about sightings of the Virgin Mary in Canada. Yes, she'd be glad to discuss our respective writing projects, Joan said, but she had to warn me in advance that she was very cross with Thomas Merton, whose biography she was reading, and would be a "sharp-eared listener" to any religious nonsense I might utter, Buddhist or otherwise. I had no idea what her objection was to Merton, the American poet-priest who challenged the tenets of Catholicism and showed considerable openness to other systems of belief. I was not a great fan of his poetry. I recalled that he had met an untimely death in Asia, electrocuted when he reached up to switch on a light or ceiling fan while standing naked in a shower cubicle at a monastery.

Joan would have appreciated Dunhuang and its attendant miracles, especially the legends surrounding the Mogao Caves and Sand-Sound Mountain, also known as Singing Sands Mountain. I'd been reading about Lotus Girl, born of Deer Mother and raised by a Buddhist monk. She had the unique ability to make a lotus flower pop up wherever she took a step, a talent as potentially troublesome as the Midas touch. In a second story, a young prince named Sadana saw a starving tiger too weak to feed her cubs. He lay down in front of the tiger, offering his body, but she preferred dead meat and refused to touch him. Finally, Sadana cut his own throat, at which point the tiger abandoned her strict rules of etiquette and devoured her expiring donor, presumably sharing the spoils.

The principal Dunhuang legend concerned General X and his army, returning victorious from battle and stopping to bivouac at the place once known as Green Mountain, which was covered by luxurious grass and pine trees. Given a night off to relax, and having set aside their five-colored armor, General X's troops were set upon and massacred by a fierce band of brigands. This dastardly deed angered the gods who, in turn, stirred up an angry wind that buried both victims and victors under a mountain of sand, thus accounting for the faint, residual sound of ghostly drums and gongs and the five colors (red, yellow, green, white, and black) of the grains of sand on what is now called Sand-Sound Mountain.

Before retiring for the night, I peeled off a page from my album of postcards of Dunhuang's Buddhist sculptures, most of them from the Southern and Northern dynasties of AD 220 to 589. They were stunning images, clear evidence that my earlier impressions about the art of the period were wrong-headed or that the best caves were closed to the public. The one I chose showed Sakyamuni in a contemplative moment but with dark shadows around the eyes where the paint had flaked off. He looked as if he'd been in a fight and was not too happy about it. On the other side, my message was brief: "Joan, this is a Buddha, not a bruised Madonna."

» » « «

Although no longer important as a commercial center, Dunhuang is still an oasis for scholars, artists, and tourists. Outside the train heading southeast from Urumqi, sand dunes and scabby patches of parched earth stretched south into infinity, dotted here and there with small islands of red rock and sandstone archipelagos. Nothing grew out there, or so it seemed from my compartment, except the occasional burst of tiny green brush, a succulent whose name I did not know. Although I had a running battle with the stewardess, who kept closing the curtain in the corridor, I managed to spot a string of twenty-two camels moving single file through the sand, against the backdrop of Bogda Feng, a huge snow-covered peak west of Urumqi. Haunting flute music accompanied the sun's demise. I could imagine the excitement building as the caravans approached the westernmost gates of the empire.

In the morning, I shared a cab with William and Margritte to Yumenguan Gate, the westerly terminus of the Great Wall, where Chinese protection ceased and the dubious fortunes of the Silk Road clicked in. The hour of paved and unpaved road, with detours through the sand dunes, led to a bustling construction site where the crumbling gate, now more or less restored, was surrounded by metal scaffolding, its remoteness and mystery completely lost. Only by lying in the sand or dangling by one leg from a metal stanchion was I able to take a couple of cluttered, if indifferent, photographs of the spectacle of this ancient landmark, evidence that the Silk Road—an unparalleled cultural conveyor belt—once passed this way.

A quarter-mile along the dirt track, we would find remnants of the original wall, looking more like a sand fence or snow barrier than something built to discourage invaders. Unlike those sections north of Beijing—huge, well-maintained bulwarks of stone and mortar broad enough on top to drive a chariot—the western remnants of the Great Wall were made of mud, straw, and sand. Bamboo mats rolled around sand, then stacked atop one another, served as containers for whatever might be chucked in the middle of the wall as filler. After centuries of erosion, all that remained was this hundred-yard stretch of adobe fence, skeletal and unimposing in the sand. In the withering heat, it resembled honeycomb.

Little is known about the real life of Buddha. Even the date of his birth is contested, with earlier texts suggesting 483 BC, later ones 368 BC. We do know he was born into a wealthy family, that he walked out on his wife and child and his privileged existence to become a mendicant, a wandering monk, and that he explored a variety of paths, including meditation and fasting, in the search for enlightenment. Even less is known about Huishen, who appears in the Chinese classical records as a monk from Kabul with a strange tale of adventure, a fantastical voyage to, and a forty-year sojourn in, lands beyond the eastern sea. We learn nothing from existing records of his spiritual trials or missionary activities beyond the suggestion that he spread the Word; we don't know if he consistently eschewed politics and the flesh as he made his way through China and more distant lands, giving himself over fully to instructing his hosts in the practice of Buddhism. Most discussion revolves around whether or not he existed and, if so, whether his tale is believable. Presuming he did make a long easterly voyage to a place called Fusang, could he possibly have reached the Americas?

There is something liberating about the absence of such biographical details. In Buddha's case, a vast repertoire of legends filled the gap, legends that, at least among the believers, have assumed the character of fact. When my friend Tony Chan told me he thought the Huishen story was about Immortals, I think he was encouraging me to take the route of fiction and create my own version of the transoceanic and intercontinental journey. Edward Vining resisted the lure of fiction, but his inheritor, Henriette Mertz, did not; she became convinced that Huishen was the original for Quetzalcoatl, the plumed serpent god whose time among the Maya was as unforgettable as it had been brief. So, too, Hendon Mason Harris, a Baptist among the Chinese, found something in Huishen's tale that spoke to his own unfulfilled missionary ambitions.

Without narrative, says Benedetto Croce, there is no history. Croce is not making a case for the historical novel. He is stating the simple fact that history and narrative are intimately linked, that the task of the historian is not to make a list of events, but to interpret and make sense of those events—in other words, to extract meaning from the past. As soon as historians begin to fit together the pieces of the jigsaw, to shape a narrative of the past, they are embarking on a fictional journey, fictional in the sense that there is no original or absolute puzzle to be reassembled, only a template they imagine to exist. And each historian's mental image of the puzzle will be different, subjective, shaped by temperamental and ideological considerations of which the historian may be totally unconscious or only dimly aware.

As I sat in my room in Dunhuang, down the street from Shirley's Café, I picked up my notebook to see if I could decipher the chicken tracks I'd scribbled during my hallucinations in

Kashgar. Breaking the code was not an easy task as my handwriting, at the best and most sober of times, is scarcely legible, a fact constantly confirmed over the years by students and family. For postcards, I had taken to printing my simple messages; otherwise, no one had a clue.

To turn the pages properly, I had to twist the loops of spiral wire back into shape, as they were continually getting squashed in my backpack. After twenty minutes of fiddling, I realized I had in my possession—out of the blue, or the blues, as it were—another tiny chunk of first-person narration:

I've sat on my ass too long waiting for a change of heart or dynasty to give me access to the learned ones at court, those who might derive instruction from my travels, even pleasure. Four decades living among strangers have taught me much, but not patience with my own kind. I've not stepped lightly, but trod with a heavy foot in mud up to my crotch, been rude and belligerent when what was called for was diplomacy and more than a dose of restraint. It's said a wise man conceals his abilities, crams them like precious jewels up his rectum; I have not been wise or practiced rectitude. What you see are rags, not saffron robes, and what you hear will be offensive to your ears. No tips, no shortcuts to nirvana.

I was delighted by the voice, the sarcastic tone, which seemed to me much more intimate and interesting than the rest of my conscious and deliberate jottings. Within an hour I had retrieved another piece from the ether, hardly a sequel, but obviously in the same voice and, this time, perfectly legible.

The usual, Peng. Where is my audience of unsung geniuses and dog butchers this fine morning? Have they no gumption? Did we not make a study of intoxicating beverages when we were young, our diseased brains and livers consulted by experts? Now only old farts with inflamed joints and piles are up and about by noon. I was twenty-five when I shaved my head and abandoned my wife and infant daughter to the charity of friends. I could tell you how heavy books and belongings grew as the miles stretched out behind, but the truth is I took nothing, did not look back. I thought I could write them off as easily as meat and the five grains that author decrepitude. Madness, of course, minds deranged ingesting cinnabar to absorb the essence of gold or jade. What did I know then of the heart's alchemy, maggots of guilt rooted in the bowels? Milky smell of my newborn, her pinched face barely visible among folds of silk, breath more delicate than the supplications of Gautama.

Where was the voice coming from, what deep cave within the self? And why at this particular moment? Though details reflected Buddha's life, this piece was more troubling as it appeared to be coming from a different source, and much closer to home. I folded the notebook and tucked it in my backpack in preparation for an early flight to Lanzhou, an ancient garrison town farther east along the Silk Road.

ELEVEN

WHEN I ARRIVED in Lanzhou, the Huang He, or Yellow River, was swollen from the torrential rains of the previous week but had not yet reached dangerous levels. A number of submerged sandbars could still be identified by the pattern of grassy tufts moving like seaweed in the swift current. Beyond the willows bent mournfully over the muddy water, I could make out the round green dome of a mosque, nestled among the houses and small commercial buildings dotting the north shore of the river, a reminder of the Muslim presence in Gansu Province. In the distance was the usual cluster of office towers, hotels, and apartments of the city center, where I'd find something to eat, eventually. Meanwhile, I contented myself with an ice cream bar from a pushcart with a huge blue umbrella, on which was depicted a gaudy night sky with stars and Chinese characters as well as various images of planets and other flying objects. The orange bar, which had a sugary, psychedelic coating and chalk-white interior, tasted even worse than it looked.

An older Chinese woman in the ice cream lineup pointed to a series of nearby stone sculptures for my benefit, a questioning look on her face which meant, do you know what they represent? I nodded my head. I did not have the Chinese names for Sandy, Pigsy, and Monkey, but I remembered the name of Wu Cheng'en's monk, Tripitaka, whose stone image was mounted on a powerful horse, feet in stirrups and his robe, fastened at the chest by a medallion, flowing out behind. The monk and his horse were facing west, the direct opposite of Huishen's travels and mine. Pigsy, who wore the equivalent of a sailor's hat, had a naked, rotund tummy and pants held up by a rope tied at the waist. He held in his right hand either a loaf of bread or a stone. Monkey, always the troublemaker, raised his fist in defiance or greeting. Sandy stolidly brought up the rear, a string of beads around his neck and a staff in hand. I was surprised and delighted to encounter these mythological acquaintances, even in stone, at this juncture in my quest, and theirs, and wished I could offer them ice cream bars for the scorching heat and limitless desert awaiting them.

"Tripitaka," I said.

I repeated the name to a bevy of smiles and approving nods. Then, to my own surprise and theirs, I dredged up one of Tripitaka's famous locales, Huoyanshan. As soon as I mentioned the Flaming Mountains, my middle-aged interlocutor started to speak to me rapidly in Chinese, but I had to disappoint her with a shrug.

I'd been on the road a little more than a month and this was the halfway point in my travels through Afghanistan, Pakistan, and China. As I made my way along the southern bank of the Huang He, I wondered, not for the first time, what had prompted me to undertake this journey. I am a seasoned, though seldom enthusiastic, traveler. Being on the road heightens my loneliness and, more often than not, prompts unfavorable comparisons with the home place: rocks, forest, the Olympic Mountains in the distance, and the sea lapping or raging at the foot of my property. My ideal version of travel would be to visit exotic places all week long but be back in my own bed on the weekends.

Today, even the thought of travel was exhausting. I leaned for support against Tripitaka's horse, which had neither bridle nor bit. Its head and strong muscular neck strained forward toward the unknown, stone nostrils flared; its mane, like the monk's robe, windblown. Yet the monk himself seemed nonchalant, even blasé, sitting erect on the back of this fierce furlong-munching, clock-stopping nag. Travel, on other occasions, had been known to have a similar effect on me; the heightened pace, the retreating land-scapes, the blurred, numberless faces—even the danger—slowed down time, bringing about a kind of equilibrium that I sometimes lost, or could not find, at home, where the whirl of self in the static world left me dizzy, unsettled. By drawing me out of myself, travel released me once again, into a world so much big-ger, so much more important and, yes, so much more interesting and engaging than my little vortex of subjectivity. I suspected that Huishen's Buddhism, which encouraged a similar escape from— or transcendence of—the self, would make more and more sense to me as this journey progressed.

Gansu Sheng Bowuguan, the provincial museum, was closed, so I could not see the special exhibit called "Cultural Relics of the Silk Road." The sky was overcast and I did not feel like visiting White Pagoda Hill or taking the chairlift to Five Springs Park. Even the nearby Bingling Si, a Buddhist cave-temple complex spectacularly located in cliffs high above the Huang He and dat-ing from AD 420, three decades before Huishen passed through the region, seemed like too much of a production for a visit that would, at best, be cursory. I needed something more at this stage of my journey than devotional art in historic sites. The Labrang Monastery in Xiahe, with its two-mile pilgrim's way consisting of 1,174 prayer wheels, seemed more likely to put me in touch with the practice and spirit of religious inquiry that had motivated and driven the curiously elusive Huishen.

Xiahe lies in long-disputed territory and has known the wrath and reversals of centuries of conflict between Tibetans and Chinese, Buddhists and Muslims. In 1922, Joseph Rock, an Austrian immigrant to the United States who, despite a lack of education and connections, forged successful careers in biology, history, and exploration, claimed to have seen Muslims burned alive in a mosque and Tibetans disemboweled and filled with hot stones. En route to the Labrang Monastery, he found Tibetan heads, including those of young girls, "strung about the walls of the Moslem garrison like a garland of flowers." Nomads of the Golok tribe, descended from seventh-century Mongol warriors, apparently got their revenge: they "charged against the Moslems at full speed on horseback, impaling them on their thirty-foot lances like men spearing frogs." I had no idea whether Rock's accounts were reliable, but they made up in color and graphic detail for what they might have lacked in veracity.

The bus west to Xiahe was a microcosm of Chinese society. Seated across from me were three Tibetan women who were dead ringers for the indigenous women of the Andes. Each wore her hair in two long black braids, and was dressed in a colorful wool or felt blanket coat with embroidered trim at the neck and sleeves, tied at the waist with bright cord and worn off one shoulder. And, to cap it off, an elegant black wool fedora. I have a similar fedora, Italian beaver, that I bought for eight dollars at a yard sale in Toronto but have never worn in public. To my dismay, the eldest of the three was puking into a plastic bag the driver's assistant had given her. She hadn't been on board the bus long enough to have motion sickness and seemed too old to be suffering from the nausea of early pregnancy. She had either the flu or some illness, perhaps a heart problem, that had been exacerbated by having to run two hundred yards to catch the bus. Between bouts of retching, she lay back, her head resting on the chrome tubing of the seat, her face drawn and gray. One earring, which consisted of ten thin silver bars on a silver hoop, could be heard over the roar of the bus, tinkling delicately against the metal tubing as the vehicle pitched and yawed.

The six-hour trip had already stretched to seven-and-a-half, thanks to an overloaded, underpowered bus, frequent stops, mountains, and extensive road construction. There was not enough room for another pair of chopsticks on the roof, already stacked high with luggage, backpacks, boxes, and sacks of grain. Mounted in the middle, like a flying bridge or misplaced figurehead, stood an erect motorcycle, lacking only a human shape among the guy ropes to complete the picture. The driver and his assistant shouted the destinations—*Xiahe-Linxia! Xiahe-Linchia!*—at every opportunity to drum up business, constantly stopping to harass and solicit anyone standing or walking along the road. The enthusiastic young assistant would grab suitcases or bags of produce and haul them off toward the bus while dickering over the always negotiable price. If the potential passenger did not like the amount quoted, he or she would retrieve the bags and wait for the next bus.

In addition to the Tibetan women, we picked up many Hui people, the men wearing white cotton skullcaps, the women with silk scarves over box-shaped headgear. The Hui, China's second largest ethnic group, arrived in China from the seventh to the tenth centuries when Arab and Persian merchants settled in the seaports. Upbeat accounts of the Hui and their contributions to Chinese society list astronomist Jamaluddin, who invented the astroscope, celestial and terrestrial globes, and the planetarium. They also include mention of Admiral Zheng He, who developed China's fleet and made important tribute journeys abroad. What is seldom mentioned in these accounts is that Zheng He's parents were murdered by the Chinese and the boy himself was castrated. Growing numbers and success in trade and other areas led to a racial backlash against the Hui, and they were vigorously persecuted or driven from the country. Those who survived intermarried and adopted the Chinese language and culture.

Clustered around the driver and his assistant was a Dongxiang family—father, mother, and six children—with the characteristic high cheekbones and blue-green eyes. The Dongxiang, who speak a language in the Altaic family, are believed by some to have been brought from the Middle East by Kublai Khan in the thirteenth century. Also thrown into this babble of languages were two distinct voices from the seat behind me, Irish accents, speculating on my nationality, whether it was German or American. Brennan and Anne were headed to the Sangke grasslands, where transplanted Tibetans graze their herds of yaks in summer. Jia-lin, the driver's Han assistant, had been listening too. Suddenly he climbed over a mountain of stuff in the aisle, which was piled high with cardboard boxes, sacks of flour, vegetables, and a trussed piglet that made frantic high-pitched squeals each time the bus moved off in low gear. He jabbed himself in the chest and shouted, "Me *zhongguo*." With equal enthusiasm, he jabbed me. I thought he'd become deranged from the diesel fumes and the rigors of passenger recruitment. Then light dawned. "Me *Jianada*," I said, tapping my chest. He repeated the routine with Brennan and Anne to determine their nationality.

The bus, which might have been called *Streetcar Named Ethnicity*, labored up another hill. Outside, cliff faces were being dismantled to widen the road, the debris of earth and rock trucked farther along to fill small gorges or swampland. Squads of workers moved over the scraped surfaces, using the most primitive equipment. There were no backhoes or earth-movers, only the occasional truck and grader. Shovels, picks, and crowbars were plentiful and labor was cheap. On the right-hand side, a man without a safety rope chipped away at a ledge of sandstone forty feet above the roadway. In a ditch, as the bus inched past, a Hui man with a crowbar struggled to pry loose a rock twice his size and five times his weight. Each time the rock budged an inch, he tried to kick a small stone into place to hold it there, but he lost his advantage, and the rock, like bureaucracy and so much else in China, settled back, complacent, immovable. Yet within a year, regardless of primitive construction methods or human cost, the road to Xiahe would be straighter and wider, bringing in more workers, businesses, and tourists, creating an even greater demand for the crops of corn, rice, yams, chestnuts, and potatoes I'd seen under cultivation along the way.

Tara's Guesthouse, a welcome oasis, was full except for a four-bed dormitory, which I agreed to share with Brennan and Anne—not exactly luck of the Irish for this young couple. There was a common washroom in the corridor that had hot water and a Western toilet with a sign advising not to flush the paper but to put it in the basket provided. The shower was located two floors below, off the courtyard, which contained a table, a motorcycle, and several bicycles for hire. Decorated in the Tibetan style, the dormitory had beds on raised wooden platforms tucked into corners and covered in plump red-and-black embroidered comforters.

"*Tashi dele.*" Tsering Dolma, the Tibetan owner, who spoke fluent English, extended a hand in greeting. She hoped I was satisfied with my accommodations.

I knew I'd be awake half the night from doors opening and closing and from two strange bodies lying less than ten feet away. I also knew I should, like Walt Whitman, rejoice at the prospect of hearing the rhythmic breathing of fellow sleepers rather than grouse about getting up exhausted in the morning. I smiled and repeated the Buddhist greeting, a slow bow with hands clasped at the chest. Tsering Dolma was not only good-natured, but also prescient. She promised a single room the following evening and recommended the nearby Everest Restaurant, where the chicken and vegetable curry, she assured me, was delicious and the prices, despite the name of the establishment, were anything but lofty.

I met Dukar Kayap while exploring the Chinese section of Xiahe, a strip of new buildings and shops a third of a mile long, closed off to all but pedestrian traffic in preparation for paving. He asked if he could talk with me to practice his English. Dukar worked at the local high school, where he taught the Tibetan language. Although the main street was under construction, the two sidewalks teemed with life and color as we walked up one side and down the other. Monks in wine-dark robes with blue trim and hot-pink sashes mingled with farmers, woodcutters in felt boots, schoolchildren, and Tibetans on pilgrimage dressed in high style. The women, like those on the bus, wore black coats, off at one shoulder, with embroidered hem and sleeves; the coats, tied at the waist with red sash, were set off with jewelry and colorful blouses. One sported a tan-colored straw hat with a floral sash that matched the bright yellow sunflowers she had stitched onto her coat. Below her sky-blue pajama-top blouse, festooned with white clouds, were gorgeous pewter medallions attached to a belt and decorative leather flaps on both hips. She had two small children in tow, sucking at strips of candy. After the drab spectacle of Kabul under Taliban rule and the conservative dress of the Muslims and the Han, Xiahe was a veritable banquet for the senses.

Dukar had studied English for two years in India, in Darmsala, an experience he relished. When I asked what was so special about India, he spoke of the individual freedom he had felt and witnessed there. I asked if he thought Tibet would ever be free, but he brushed the question aside. His family, nomads who had emigrated from Tibet a hundred years earlier to the Ganjia grasslands, twenty miles outside Xiahe, raised sheep, horses, and yaks. He was the only family member who was not a farmer. Dukar expressed the hope that some of his students would go on to a university. Away from home and poorly paid, as most teachers are in China, he had a room at the hospital complex in the monastery. He rose every day at 6:00 a.m. for prayers and devotional rituals at the temple. I looked at this young man over lunch, sipping a Coke and toying with an indifferent serving of egg-fried rice, and wondered how typical he was of China's minorities.

Earlier, I'd spent several hours exploring the Labrang complex and climbing to the top of a gilded pagoda, where two young men informed me politely that I was circumnavigating the shrine in the wrong direction. Clockwise, with your right shoulder to the monument, is the correct procedure. The view of the complex, in its setting among the mountains of the Daxia He valley, was even more breathtaking than the sculptural relief of Buddha and his embossed and gilded water lilies. When I emerged in the courtyard below, an elderly monk approached me, raised his hand and whispered, "Dalai Lama best."

He repeated this judgment excitedly three times and waited for my response. When I nodded, he hastened off, looking back once. In addition to making a political statement, I suspect he was hoping for a clandestine photograph of his spiritual leader to be offered. I wished I'd brought along photos of the Dalai Lama, but they might have been seized by the overzealous customs officer in Tashkurgan, causing me no end of trouble.

Motorcycle rickshaws were revving up for business beside the small stream-cum-drainage-ditch that separated Tara's Guesthouse from the Labrang Monastery. Nearby a camel had been gussied up for tourists, with green and red blankets from which tassels hung. Clusters of locals rummaged through sundry items spread out for sale on sheets and plastic tarpaulins. I sat in a doorway, trying to be as inconspicuous as possible in order to photograph passersby. Across from me, recessed into the monastery's east wall, was a passageway containing a plethora of prayer wheels, which pilgrims and the other members of the faithful spun in a clockwise direction as they made their way through the vast complex of temples and shrines. More than a thousand prayer wheels existed in the Labrang Monastery, and they were seldom at rest.

A small boy, not yet ten, led an enormous black yak up the dirt road toward me. It was a wild, fierce-looking creature, a bull with a wide span of horns and shaggy hair all the way down to its split hooves. Yet it followed the boy's prompting without fuss, thanks to the wooden ring in its nose and, perhaps, a promise of grain, the faint memory of which revolved in its tiny brain like a prayer wheel. The boy did not like the idea of being photographed but said nothing and marched stoically on, while his younger brother fell in behind the bull to avoid my invasive eye and camera.

The Labrang Monastery, one of six held by the Gelupka (Yellow Hat) sect, was founded in 1709 by the monk E'angzongzhe, considered a living incarnation of the Buddha. Its golden stupa, eighteen halls, six institutes of learning, and enormous collection of murals, statues, and sutras help to make it the most important such monastery outside Tibet. The monks were to be seen everywhere in Xiahe. I'd watched a number of them hanging about the shops—attractive, wide-eyed young men, as curious about this foreigner as I was about them. These were the novices. None of the self-importance of being part of a glorious and ancient tradition had yet settled upon them.

When I finally located the monastery office in charge of guided tours, I was assigned a young monk in his early thirties who spoke English quite well but seemed bored with his task and more than a little disappointed that he had only one drab tourist in his audience. As a result, he gave me an abridged tour of several shrines, temples, and institutes of learning, including those specializing in the study of medicine, law, theology, and esoteric Buddhism. According to my guide, the population of the monastery had grown to four thousand prior to the persecutions and depredations of the Cultural Revolution (1966–70), when monks were killed, beaten, even forced to marry. Some committed suicide rather than break their vow of chastity. The current population of twelve hundred was more or less stable.

In the monastery's small museum, there were photographs of various lamas, including the old Panchen Lama and the one installed by the Chinese government in the 1990s. I asked my guide about the swords and antique guns in glass cases, as I was under the impression that Buddhists are not supposed to take life. He was of the opinion that Buddhists are permitted to take up arms against an aggressor. I was curious too about the worship of images, because the Buddha had been dismissive of such aids, as well as of religious bureaucracies and hierarchy. I mentioned the ancient practice of representing the Buddha by such evocative symbols as a wheel, a riderless horse, a footprint, or an empty chair, which seemed more in keeping with the spirit of the religion. I wondered aloud if Buddhism had become as icon-laden as Roman Catholicism. The old symbols had the capacity to empty the mind, I suggested, while the elaborate, literal images distract the eye.

"The images of Buddha are not literal," my guide parried.

"Perhaps I should have said 'realistic.'" I was trying to lift him out of his lethargy, not pick a fight. It worked.

"No one knows what Buddha looked like, so how could the images be realistic?" He smiled, pleased with himself.

I told him we had a writer and professor of communications in Canada who argued that television is a cool medium, because the visual images on the screen require nothing from the imagination; they fill all the spaces, with the result that we sit passively in front of the television. Books, on the other hand, are a hot medium, as they require that we work hard to form our own mental pictures from the skimpiest verbal sketches. I suggested that the old symbols for Buddha were like books—they put the mind to work—whereas these ornate statues, sculptures, and paintings complete the picture, leaving the mind passive, inert.

We were entering the main temple, which was currently out of bounds for tourists. The attendant monk challenged us at the door, asking for my special permit, but my guide waved him aside.

"Images of the Buddha are neither literal nor realistic." He was in high gear now. "They share aspects of the human form, but they are idealized. What is your word in English?"

"Archetypes?"

"Yes, exactly. The archetype touches some deeper level in the mind that is not a distraction; rather, it is a penetration. Now, would you describe such penetration as hot or cool?"

I recounted this conversation the next morning to Joe and Marie, a Swiss couple I'd met at the Everest Restaurant, while we waited for the bus to depart. We were heading east again to Lanzhou, where I would catch a train to Xian. Marie was sick and trying to sleep with her head against the window. Joe, his usual boisterous self, has stepped off the bus and was lighting up.

"Congratulations."

"For what?"

"You not only found the visitor's bureau on your own, but also earned a Yellow Hat in the process."

"How so?"

Joe blew a perfect ring of smoke, which settled around his outstretched finger.

"Penetration," he said. "*Yellow Hat* is the Chinese slang for a certain brand of condom."

TWELVE

IN ADDITION TO being the administrative center of the Zhou, Qin, and Han dynasties, Xian (or Chang'an, as it was then known) also served as capital for the Sui and Tang dynasties. During the Tang Dynasty (618–907), Xian boasted a population of two million and was arguably the greatest and most advanced city in the world, rivaling even Rome and Constantinople, with a sophisticated bureaucracy, a large tax base, and an elaborate system of canals and roads linking it to other regions, as well as sizable communities of Arab Muslims, Persian Zoroastrians, and Nestorian Christians from Syria. Twenty years earlier, when I visited Xian with a group of writers, it had seemed small, a dusty backwater. Now, with tourists flocking to see its antiquities, Xian was once again brash and assertive, with flashy new hotels everywhere.

Since this was my third visit to the city, tourism was not a priority and my expectations were modest. I wanted to find someone, an academic probably, who was familiar with the Huishen story. I called a number at Shaanxi Normal University that I'd been given by the consulate. In order to meet some scholars, I found myself agreeing to give a lecture, which seemed a fair exchange at the time. Now that I was in the thick of it, with a hundred students and faculty observing my antics, I was not so sure.

As soon as my lecture was over, two young women approached the podium to protest an unfair statement I'd made, to the effect that China suffers from a dearth of politically engaged writers. My lecture, something thrown together at the last minute to accommodate my new friends in the Faculty of Education, consisted mainly of some thoughts on the role of the writer in society, which, in Canada's case, usually involves the competing demands of history and place. Mackenzie King, I told the assembled students and teachers, claimed that some countries have too much history but that Canada had too much geography. In trying to acclimatize the muses—to give imaginative expression to this vast and sometimes exacting geography—Canadian writers had gone so far in the other direction that they had come under fire for ignoring Canada's position in time—that is, its history. I compared this with the situation in China and suggested that a long history of book-burnings and executions of scholars and literati was not exactly conducive to engaged writing.

After so many weeks on the road, my brain had atrophied. The purpose of my not-quite-coherent introduction was to lead into a discussion of the route I had chosen as a writer, or that had been chosen for me, that was hardly the elegant, lyrical arc of the songbird. The political muse, I suggested, offered a lens, or a navigational procedure, that might bring together history and place and show them to be inextricably allied. It had to do with power politics, with the body. If we learn to love our own bodies and minds—I was stretching here, as all these English-language students leaned into every third word with faint signs of under-standing on their faces—we might learn to love the natural world and each other, to see ourselves as part of a great histori-cal and geographical experiment or continuum. I explained how this vague, never adequately defined vision had taken me not only to Chile, Nicaragua, Palestine, Afghanistan, and China, but also deeper into the history and moral quagmires of my own country and its troubled and troubling neighbor to the south.

"What about Lu Xun?"

Nei-li, my interrogator, couldn't have been more than eighteen. She wore blue jeans and a bulky green cardigan and carried a bundle of books held together with a leather strap that looked like a belt. "No one could be more political than Lu Xun."

I nodded my head in agreement. I had at home the *Complete Works of Lu Xun*, China's leading intellectual figure during the 1920s and 1930s, and also an abbreviated selection of his writings I used more often, edited and translated by Gladys Yang and called *Silent China*. This latter companion contained the Kafkaesque story of Ah Q, a hapless victim of China's moral and political chaos, and two essays on women's rights, entitled "My Views on Chastity" and "What Happens after Nora Leaves Home?" The latter, using Ibsen's *A Doll House* to make a case for social and economic equality for the sexes in China, might have been a companion piece to Virginia Woolf's *A Room of One's Own*. Lu Xun's rhetorical skills and his determination to legitimize the use of the vernacular (*putonhua*) in literature are everywhere present in his writings, even in the simple solution he proposes here: "The crucial thing for Nora is money—or to give it a more high-sounding name—economic resources."

I talked with Nei-li briefly about Lu Xun's contributions to literature and to Chinese social practice, including his membership in the Revolutionary Mutual Aid Society and the China League for Civil Rights, as well as his participation in the founding of the China Freedom League and the China League of Left-Wing Writers. Just when I thought I'd exonerated myself, Lin Baoqi, who was hovering in the background, leapt into the fray.

"And don't forget Li Bai."

This omission was less forgivable, as most educated Chinese knew by heart many poems by the great Tang master. Even I knew ten of those poems intimately, having spent several years trying to come up with passable translations. Li Bai attacked not only social pretension—"Don't put on the dog to tend the garden / or wear your fancy duds to water flowers"—but also the ravages and futility of war:

Casualties strewn on every hand,
cries of dying horses pierce the sky.
Vultures rip and disembowel the dead,
leave intestines hanging from the trees.

Soldiers' bodies fertilize the weeds—
what value have a general's strategies?
The war machine's so violent and cruel,
let saints employ it as a last resort.

I thanked Nei-li and Baoqi for correcting me, clear evidence that they understood what I was saying and were determined to carry on the Maoist tradition of moral development through criticism. I did not make the obvious point that two politically engaged writers in a country the size of China hardly constitute a tradition. I knew how difficult it was to stand up and be counted in China, unlike in Canada, where, as Margaret Atwood has pointed out, you can say anything you want because no one is listening. I was surprised the students had not mentioned

Ding Ling, a brave and gifted woman and lifelong social activist whom I'd first met in 1981. She fell into disfavor after Liberation in 1949 for daring to criticize her male counterparts in the Chinese Communist Party for casting off their wives in favor of younger women.

I was saved by the bell and whisked off to a special banquet with members of the faculty. Nothing is so green as freshly cooked green beans in China—or as delicious, especially with a little garlic and black bean sauce, although tiny pork dumplings, with their delicate, puckered envelopes of pastry, run a close second. The feast also included my two staples by special request: steamed broccoli and spicy chicken. Zhang Zhanghong, who had completed a doctorate on Buddhism in China, confessed to being unfamiliar with the story of Huishen. I was not only disappointing, but also surprising. If he had not heard of my monk, who would have? Zhang promised to look up Huishen in the *Dictionary of Famous Monks* and to consult with his anthropologist friends in Beijing and Wuhan.

Throughout dinner, my mind was abuzz with the students' questions, the relevance of Li Bai's observations about war, and the e-mails I'd received in the morning, all preoccupied with the so-called war on terrorism and with U. S. plans to invade Afghanistan. Mark Mordue was baffled on returning with Lisa to Australia to find that "the world we thought we knew was being smashed to pieces and is now on the brink of war. I really fear for what may eventuate." My eldest daughter, Jenny, reported struggling over the attacks and their aftermath with her students in a class on Holocaust writing at the University of Virginia. In response to their "tears, outbursts of anger, and questions about God's fairness," she was prompted to end the class by "telling them that part of their homework was to find something they could affirm about the world and humanity, or something that brings them joy."

As I exchanged platters and platitudes with my new friends in Xian—that ancient center of trade, capital of dynasties, and perpetual target of warlords and terrorists—I recalled an article I'd read by Israeli novelist Amos Oz, who worried about the rise of "chauvinistic and religious extremism, not only in the domain of Islam, but also in various parts of the Christian world and indeed among the Jewish people." The Great Satan, Oz suggested, is not a particular people or system, but fanaticism and prejudice. Oz's words were comforting, too, the more so because the world seemed to be drifting perilously close to what my monk-guide at the monastery in Xiahe called "the suffer place," the Buddhist term for hell.

After lunch, Liu Libo insisted on taking me on a tour of downtown Xian, now completely modernized, with enormous hotels surrounding the ancient Bell Tower. Liu was an undergraduate. However, as the only fully competent English-speaker, he had been drafted as official shepherd and guardian angel. I suggested I could manage on my own, but he seemed to welcome the chance to practice his English and show me the sights. Having twice seen the Big Goose Pagoda and the Forest of Stele, a library of 2,300 classical poems and drawings carved on massive slabs of stone, I encouraged Liu to show me other sights. The problem was that my feet, clad in undersized hiking boots, were screaming blue murder. We crossed over to Huajue Xiang, an ancient market area restored and full of artisans and shops, many of them selling etchings and personalized stone signature stamps known as "chops." Under Liu's watchful eye, the merchants followed me from table to table, hoping to interest me in carved ink trays, chiming steel balls, jade earrings, and delicate paper cutouts of figures and animals from Chinese history and mythology, a craft I was incapable of appreciating.

Liu Libo was a trooper. When I said I was tired and wanted to return to the hotel for a rest, he insisted on delivering me to my cheap digs by the train station in person. I suggested a bus rather than a taxi, which turned out to be a tactical error, as it dropped us many blocks from the hotel. By the time we reached the Street of Lost Souls near the train station, with its notorious "massage" parlors, I was limping badly and desperate to put my feet up but only after a good, long soak.

All my trips to Asia seemed to involve problems with shoes. In 1985, when I traveled to Japan and China with my wife, Jan, and three daughters, I did not have proper footwear. I'd resurrected an ancient pair of sandals from the '60s and had them resoled, making them so stiff they would not bend. The noise they made on Tokyo streets and in the subway sounded like rifle shots. After a few days on the road the straps began to cut into my feet, which with the application of a couple dozen Band-Aids, were slowly being transformed into abstract works of art. My feet are large, size 12—so big, in fact, that no store in Tokyo could help me. As it was rare for them to stock even size 9, the diminutive clerks looked at my feet with astonishment and mild horror, as if I were the rough beast slouching toward Ginza to be born. One day, after another fruitless search for shoes, I awakened from a nap at the Kimi Ryokan— a quaint hotel in Tokyo with authentic bamboo mats, sliding doors, and movable partitions in the rooms—thinking I would go for a brief walk. As I descended the stairs, I heard giggling noises in the lobby. Peering around the corner, I saw two attractive teenaged girls in the vestibule, one of them standing with her tiny feet in my sandals, which made her look as if she was wearing water skis. Their giggles escalated into gales of hysterical laughter. I waited until they'd left to claim my scandalized footwear.

The search for shoes continued into China, including an entire day cycling around Beijing with my friend Will Goede, who was teaching English and playing saxophone in a jazz-rock band called Beijing Underground. Will had toured the country under the sponsorship of a classical musicians' association, playing to huge crowds of enthusiastic young people, but his mission on this day—less exotic and decidedly out of tune— was to locate shoes for "Big Foot." After weaving in and out of bicycle traffic, those vast schools of two-wheeled human fish sweeping along the avenues, we hauled up in his apartment at the Youyi Binguan (Friendship Hotel) and consumed several bottles of Qingdao beer to console ourselves for the failure— nay, the dissonance—of our enterprise. My feet, at least, were no worse for wear, thanks to the bicycle. Still, I refused to believe there was no one with my foot size in China; there had to have been a run on big sizes, all those visiting Huns, Mongols, and Barbarians cleaning out the stock.

When we reached Xian, the ancient capital, I went for a walk with the family and our interpreter friends from the Chinese Writers Association. Jan and the three girls were ahead of us, checking out bargains at the streetside flea market in progress. I could see their heads—all but nine-year-old Bronwen's—

above the crowd, clearly identifying them as kinswomen of Big Foot. By now, I'd all but given up hope of finding new shoes but was on the lookout for a repairman to fix the sandal straps that had broken under the strain of noncompliant soles. To my surprise, among the blankets and plastic tarpaulins covered with debris for sale was a shoemaker's last, a tiny inverted metal foot used as a base for tacking on new soles and heels. Beside the last, miracle of miracles, lay a small assortment of tools. I pointed to my sandals. The shoemaker nodded his head and grinned.

I was standing there in my bare feet, amid a hundred people, each one staring in amusement and disbelief as my sandal balanced on the tiny last and a new strap was attached, when suddenly the crowd parted, like the Red Sea, and an attractive young woman in a long white dress with black hair to her waist, approached me, pushing a Phoenix bicycle. She stopped in front the shoemaker's last and gave me a thorough once-over, from head to oversized foot. Then, without missing a beat, she said, "Hello."

I gasped. She was trying out her English. Far be it from me to ignore such a friendly gesture.

"Hello."

"How are you?"

"I am fine," I replied. *"Ni hao?"* She did not acknowledge my impeccable Chinese or bother to say how she was, which seemed perfectly obvious: arrestingly beautiful, completely in control.

"What is your name?"

"My name is Gary." I found myself inadvertently mimicking her clipped pronunciation, giving each syllable identical weight. She did not tell me her name and, apparently not offended by my unrepentant size 12 feet, cut right to the quick.

"Are you married?"

My God, I was being propositioned by Mara, Buddha's constant tempter, a demon disguised as the most beautiful woman in China, and half my age. I was not George Washington with his cherry tree and duty to history; I was Canadian and quite capable of telling a lie, especially a small, innocent one just to prolong the moment. I looked around. I could see Jan's and Jenny's heads farther down the street, floating above the stream of shoppers. I thought of my naked and knobbly feet on public display and marveled at their unexpected powers of attraction. How could a barefoot poet enter into such complex and danger-fraught negotiations that might very easily escalate into an international incident? Only then did I notice that I was balancing on one leg like a chicken, the other foot tucked carefully behind, out of sight.

"Yes," I clucked, bobbing my head. "I am married." To my surprise, this felt less an admission of defeat (no pun intended) than an acknowledgment of commitment, a safe haven from the hordes of unattached Asian women likely to be smitten by my irresistible feet and the urge to emigrate. Saved again, this time by the Great Wall of Matrimony.

"Too bad. Bye-bye."

She turned her bicycle around and, with a swish of her long white cotton dress and black rivering hair, moved off from whence she had come, my audience of foot fetishists closing rank behind as if nothing unusual had happened, as if it had all been a dream. Sixteen years later, her final words still hung in the air. I could have reached up and plucked them like apples.

When I first traveled to China in 1981, I was so busy with the bureaucratic end of things—speeches, itineraries, gifts for the hosts—that I despaired of ever writing anything about the people I'd met and the historic sites I'd visited. Two years later, I sat down to a blank page in my horse-barn-cum-office in eastern Ontario and a poem took shape in front of me. It was eighteen lines long, broken into nine couplets; and those two-line stanzas were spoken by one of the soldiers from Qin Shi Huang's terra-cotta army, which had been marking time somewhere in the labyrinths of my subconscious, much as it had marked time under the earth for twenty-two hundred years. The soldier who marched into daylight and stood at attention by my page, ghosts of horses and donkeys hovering nearby, was, appropriately, a charioteer in Qin's bodyguard, whose job was to protect his leader in the imperial afterlife. The charioteer knew exactly what he wanted to say.

He spoke about master potter Lao Bi, who had sculpted him. *Lao* is a Chinese prefix of respect, usually given to elders. While Lao Bi was inclined to crazy behavior and drank a little too much, as I was shortly to learn, he merited respect, for he had insisted on making each of the thousands of pottery figures unique in some small way: a potbelly, the twist of a topknot, the curl of a lip, overarching eyebrows—whatever his tireless eye determined to be of essence. He was also, like Lu Xun, given to using the vernacular and did not hesitate to call a man a layabout and a shirker or to indulge his own propensity for mordant humor and outrageous puns. Having done his reconnaissance and found the terrain safe, even favorable, the charioteer summoned another member of his underground platoon.

The spearman, much younger, was a mere stripling; but he

had pluck. Being sculpted by Master Bi had given him confidence, as he said in his nine couplets—especially the potter's uncanny attention to detail, the way sleeves bunched at the wrist, fleeting emotions caught on the wing and given the permanence of art. He felt better about himself after he'd sat for Lao Bi, his fragile existence somehow justified; if he died in battle now, there'd be something of him left. As a writer, I could appreciate the sentiment about permanence, however deluded it might be. However, I was hardly prepared for the size of the troop that set up camp in my barn that spring: guardsman, minister of war, lieutenant, paymaster, blacksmith, commando, quartermaster, spy. Even less was I prepared for the portrait of Old Bi, potter *extraordinaire*, emerging from these confessions, this trench gossip. Lao Bi, it seemed, was a genius, a drunk, a madman, a fellow traveler, and a saint. But, as the lookout attested, "he told me things about myself that scared me / and some that sent me back thinking I wasn't such a bad / chap, after all. You can't fault a man for that." Even the ghost of the emperor, Qin Shi Huang, puts in his two cents' worth on the subject of Lao Bi: "I joined the potter in his rest; / I broke his ranks but could not break his will."

In 1981, Bingmayong, the name given to the site where the terracotta army was discovered, was still a modest affair, a single structure, a Quonset hut as large as an airline hangar housing some hundreds of reconstructed and only partially unearthed figures of horses and men. Two decades later it had become a circus, a Chinese Disneyland with numerous buildings, shops, restaurants, and an avenue of hawkers. Most surprising was a 360-degree cinema, using film to dramatize not only the creation but also the destruction and looting of Qin Shi

Huang's terra-cotta soldiers by the rebels who overthrew his short-lived and brutal dynasty. Despite the hype, Bingmayong was worth a third visit. Digging continued apace in the surrounding area, and a miniature bronze chariot with horses and driver had been found and placed on display, along with examples of an army of smaller pottery figures. This whirlwind of creativity had taken place at least 650 years before Huishen passed through Xian on his way to Datong or Wuhan. He would have had no idea what lay a few feet beneath his bedroll as he camped outside Xian.

Since my friendly criticism at the hands of Shaanxi Normal University's students, I'd been thinking a good deal about Lu Xun and the precarious nature of creative life in China. Even Li Bai and Du Fu, the two great poets of the Tang Dynasty, had not been immune to the twin specters of destitution and disgrace. Du Fu writes about the hard times that leave him so broke he can't afford cheap wine; he puns on the "taxing work" that keeps him from writing: "What sort of man am I, blown here and there? / One small gull in a vast universe." He knew what it meant to live in civil-service exile, consigned to a remote region. Li Bai, more outspoken and political, was far too critical of management to have ever been completely safe or comfortable in Xian society; he celebrated those who escaped the stench of toadying and compromise, such as his friend Hu Mao Yen:

He gave up fame and fortune in his youth
for the high office of mountain pine and cloud.
He toasted the moon for its beauty

and paid his tax and tribute to the flowers.
Who among us can attain such nobility?
We only breathe its fragrance as we pass.

For Lu Xun, who shared Li Bai's wit and critical disposition, the instability of China's reemergence as an independent nation made mere survival a constant challenge. I'd been reading a book of translated letters between Lu Xun and his student Xu Guangping, who was later to become his wife. It's a delightfully chummy and (in all senses) engaging correspondence, she addressing him as "My Respected Teacher," and he referring to her as "Brother Guangping." But it was also heart wrenching to be so intimate a party to their struggles with bureaucracy, outmoded traditions, financial insecurity, pettiness, and political intrigue. Lu Xun describes how he went from hope during the first year of the Republic (1911), a "time of great brightness," to distress at the later state of corruption and anarchy: "How can the outlook be good when flunkies are allowed to run the household?" A mere change of government was not enough: "The most important task now is to reform the nature of our fellow citizens. Otherwise, no matter whether we have a dictatorship, a republic or whatever, it would still be a matter of selling the same old goods under a different label, which won't do at all."

Lu Xun's attitude to political engagement preoccupied me on my last day in Xian as I struggled with my conflicting reactions to the attacks on the World Trade Center and the military response that was building up. I had been encouraged by friends and by my agent and my publisher back home to write about events in Afghanistan from the perspective of my all-too-brief visit to Kabul in August. Lu Xun had faced similar requests to write about political violence in 1926: "There are a few people who are hoping that I will do something, but I know myself that I can't. Everyone who exercises leadership must in the first place be bold, but I look at things too cautiously—when one starts being cautious one develops too many doubts and is not likely to dash ahead bravely; secondly, he must be ready to sacrifice others without regret, and I am most reluctant to ask others to sacrifice themselves (an attitude I formed in response to events before the revolution), and no major situation can develop. Therefore I end up being limited to publishing books and magazines to air my grievances in empty words."

I was neither historian nor war correspondent. I toyed with the idea of writing a few pieces to show the "human face" of Afghanistan, but this would have meant putting in danger some of my friends and contacts in Kabul and Peshawar. I needed more time; there was so much I did not understand. As I scanned the Web sites of the *Guardian,* the *New York Times,* and the *Globe and Mail,* a familiar nasal voice rang in my ears. It was the chaplain of the terra-cotta army, looking about him at the wreckage of history:

Someone will break us of the habit of war
by taking away our weapons

and we will march against the darkness
(or will it be light?) naked as new-born babes,

tiny fists opening and closing on nothing.

The only certainty, even under the earth, is change,

whether it be cosmetic, paint flaking away
down the muted centuries or

something more violent that destroys the form
itself, icons of public and private selves.

With such thoughts I addressed the potter
on more than one occasion, thinking to shock him.

I'd given up the Tao and had even less time
for the ethics of Confucius in the new dispensation.

Rituals and ancestor worship are as useless to soldiers
as scapulimancy and tortoise-shell prophecy.

Only our vanity is monumental, the potter said,
and that, too, can be broken.

THIRTEEN

ON THE TRAIN east from Xian to Luoyang, in Henan Province, I watched the progress of a large cockroach ascending the wall by the window—it was too dark outside to observe the farm land. As the smokers and spitters plied their grisly trades, I wished I'd cut my trip short. Too late to reserve a berth, I was hanging onto the edge of a thinly padded three-person bench known as a "hard seat." The woman across from me, who was knitting a white cableknit sweater, had made gestures indicating she wanted to exchange seats so she was not facing backward. I had refused and was feeling guilty about it. I looked around me and saw only garbage and a general drabness. Now that the Mao jackets had been chucked, or stashed away for the next purge, the entire population seemed to have resorted to jeans, white socks, and ugly gray or black suit coats of cheap, shiny material. Even the noisy card players, uninterested in the game and discarding randomly, irritated me. The new China seemed as dreary and oppressive as the old.

My hotel did nothing to dispel the mood. My twelfth-floor room looked across at ugly flats that had been built to house those displaced by the commercial boom that was trashing and transforming cities with greater efficiency than the hordes of Genghis Khan. In the canyon between my hotel and these flats were the scattered remains of the former *hutong*, a dozen attached one-story dwellings doomed for demolition. Although they'd been allowed to deteriorate, the houses were still occupied. To enter, residents had to scramble over huge piles of discarded bricks left behind from previous demolitions. Here and there, a small child sat unattended, playing in the dirt, counting rats.

I was in Luoyang, onetime capital of the Northern Wei Dynasty, because of Huishen and my uncertainty about his peregrinations after fleeing Kabul. If he had taken up residence among the Northern Wei, who were at that point more welcoming to Buddhists, he might have left from its northern capital at Datong and returned to the new southern capital established at Luoyang during his absence. The splendors that were Luoyang had not survived the ravages of time. Looking out my window or walking in the streets of the city, it was difficult to imagine anyone choosing to live here, never mind establishing a showcase capital.

As a distraction, I took a bus to Longmen Shiku, the Thousand Buddha Caves along the north banks of the Yi River, once a beehive of religious and cultural activity. The guidebook suggested that vandalism and looting had left the caves, like the city itself, somewhat faceless and down at the heels. The most interesting sculptures and murals dated from the later Sui and Tang dynasties. As much as I tried to imagine what Huishen saw and felt here on his return from the Americas, I suspected he'd been missing its forests, mountains, and rugged Pacific shores as much as I was.

Despite my grumpy disposition, I had to admit there was something unique about these temple caves. The figures were athletic, even theatrical; the Bodhisattvas struck dramatic poses, had more highly developed musculature, and were altogether more whimsical than the ones I'd seen at Turpan and

Dunhuang. A gargoyle peered down at me, covering his stone ears so as not to hear any more of my complaints. Five Bodhisattvas and a headlessBuddha sat on lotus flowers attached to the same plant, wondering whether their missing partner had gone to heaven or, as rumored, to New York or Kansas City. Another headless figure, making an expressive gesture with both arms, had a casual lean to his body, his weight resting on one leg. One of the larger Buddhas, mostly intact, balanced with one foot on the knee and one foot on the head of a diminutive figure, giving a whole new meaning to the phrase "religious supporter."

The sculpture that touched me most profoundly was a nondescript piece, fully exposed to the elements, carved into rock so weathered over the centuries that the contours of the seated, childlike Buddha had softened, almost disappeared. Clothing and gesture were indistinct and almost nothing remained of the head above the nose. Striations in the rock, dating from no particular dynasty but from the beginning of time, now appeared to course uninterrupted through the body and face of the Buddha. As I crawled around on the rocks on my hands and knees, trying to get another perspective on this sacred shape, this apparition—rendered timeless, beyond style, devoid of self—I felt something give way inside of me. My anger subsided and my body began to shake uncontrollably, my eyes watering so that I could no longer see through the viewfinder of my camera. As I sat there, wiping my tears, imagining all the poverty and pain and grime of this world whirl up and disappear into the endless reaches of the universe, I felt a gentle pressure on my knee.

It was a small child, no more than three, whom I'd encountered more than once with her parents as I made the rounds of Longmen Shiku. Lonely, and determined to act the congenial foreign guest, I'd smiled each time and said hello. Eventually the father asked if I could take a photo of him and the little girl, who had short, black bangs and was wearing a pink dress and white tights. Her young parents were immaculately turned out for the occasion, the father in tailored slacks and starched, powder-blue cotton shirt, the mother in a knee-length blue dress and high-heeled boots with cutaway laces. I looked like a tramp or reprobate in comparison. In the photo I'd taken of them, the little girl is sitting between the parents and looking carefully at her own small hand, which she has placed on her mother's knee, as if viewing it for the first time. I did not expect we'd meet again, certainly not in this way. The little girl, startled by my tears, looked worried. I assured her, with hand gestures, that "uncle" was okay, that I had not injured myself climbing over rocks.

I'd been strung out, despite my protests to the contrary, from loneliness, the daily grind of travel, and a sense of the futility of my quest. It wasn't that Huishen and his tracks through history were proving more elusive than I'd expected but that the reality of contemporary politics was weighing heavily upon me. Fortunately, the ancient capital of Luoyang, however dingy and drab, proved capable of more than one redemptive moment. The previous day, finding that the city had more cell phone shops than restaurants, I had surrendered to impulse and slunk into the local Kentucky Fried Chicken franchise, ordering quickly and sitting as far out of sight as I could, in a corner near the washroom. Alas, the waitress had forgotten to give me a spoon and, unless I wanted to stir coffee with my thumb in good Canadian logger fashion, I would have to make a second trip across the crowded restaurant. This proved fatal, as a group of schoolchildren, who had finished their lunches and were now in the play area, spotted me just as I was about to bite into a piece of prefabricated chicken breast. A chorus of hellos overrode the buzz of conversation and the hum of kitchen gadgetry. While my chicken and coffee grew cold, I had to respond to twenty-five separate greetings, not counting repeat performances.

"What is your name?" A daring and precocious boy of ten leaned over the rail of the play area and looked me in the eye, while his friends peered over his shoulder. He was enraptured by his own fearlessness. I told him my name and asked his.

"My name is Luan Zhou," he announced proudly, turning back to his friends, a hero for having addressed the foreign devil, gained face for China, and actually used his English correctly.

By the time I'd finished my cold meal, people were bringing their kids over to have a look at this somewhat disreputable, finger-licking *lao-wai*.

Trying to be inconspicuous is difficult enough in China, never mind doing it in an American fast-food franchise. To the locals, I must have looked, even without the white linen suit, like a taller, skinnier version of the plastic Colonel guarding the entrance. Still, I had to confess that, however cold and reconstituted, the food was delicious and no more deadly than the deep-fried egg pancakes I'd been devouring at street stalls.

The Chinese are like Texans. They do everything—whether communism or capitalism, making art or destroying art—in a big way. There's nothing like a new idea to take possession of the Chinese soul. The current idea is private enterprise. For better or for worse, the coming generation will wear Western clothes and speak fluent English, though the signs posted at Longmen Shiku suggested there was still a distance to go. A billboard on the destruction of religious artifacts declared that the caves had been "damaged by natural or factitious erossion." Nothing, however, not even "progress" or bad translation, could kill the poetic impulse in this always surprising country. On the stretch of lawn below the Thousand Buddha Caves and the tiny meditation cells carved into rock was a sign saying, "Preserve the green grass, retain the green color." This sign, quaintly rhetorical and making use of alliteration and repetitive syntax, could not compete with the euphony and personification of a more inspired poet-gardener, whose message adorned a sign farther along:

"The little grass is smiling, please use the pavement."

Before heading on to Beijing, I made a quick detour south to Wuhan, in the province of Hubei, another possible port of departure for Huishen. I hoped to talk to monks at the Guiyuan Si monastery and to see the contents of Marquis Yi's tomb, now on display at the provincial museum. Wuhan, halfway between Beijing and Hong Kong, straddles the Yangtze and offers three cities for the price of one: Hankou, modern, brash, and bustling; Hanyang, grubby, over-crowded, and industrial; and Wuchang, almost pastoral by comparison, with a lake, tree-lined streets, and an abundance of modest older buildings. My first activity was to find the ferry terminal and set out across the Yangtze, the infamous watercourse that has aided and abetted generals, drowned an inordinate number of ordinary citizens with its regular flooding, and captured the attention of painters and poets, including Du Fu.

Du Fu was particularly attuned to rivers, lakes, and waterways, but one of his most engaging and endearing poems is about receiving news that the imperial forces have recaptured Hunan and Hubei, which means he can return home:

I thought of my wife—where was sorrow now?
Half crazy, I chucked my poetry books together

and spent the whole day drinking and singing.
I'll set out pronto from Pa to Wu Gorge,

down to Hsiang Yan in the direction of Lo Yang.
Green spring will be a good companion.

Du Fu was heading home via Wuxia, one of the Three Gorges on the Yangtze. I had less than two weeks remaining in China before heading home myself. Watching the dark waters of the Yangtze eddying around the pilings of the ferry terminal and feeling the engine's vibrations through the soles of my feet, I was beginning to share Du Fu's excitement.

As China's greatest river at approximately 3,800 miles and the third longest in the world, the Yangtze originates in the snow-clad mountains of Qinghai Province and traverses eight more provinces, including Tibet, before it empties into the East China Sea north of Shanghai. Today, overcast, the river was black and impressive, with lots of low-slung barges heading downstream, loaded to the gunwales with chemicals, sawdust, iron, and other cargoes. A helmsman returned my wave from his wheelhouse perched above the double-decked cabin at the stern of one of the smaller barges, now empty and riding high in the water. With a long steering oar and with sails instead of a diesel engine, he could have been the young Huishen setting out on his journey into the unknown, or little-known, eastern seas, a trip that would take him forty-one years—a lifetime— to complete.

Although Huishen is reported to have returned from the Americas in AD 499 to nearby Jingzhou, there is no official record of his having set sail from that capital. While he was abroad, the Liu Sung Dynasty (AD 420–479) was replaced by the Southern Ch'i (479–502), a dynasty both short-lived and hostile to Buddhism. Huishen is also reported to have been buried in Jingzhou after spending his final eighteen years as head of Buddhist missions in the northern territories. As I did not have time to visit Jingzhou, I was anxious to find someone in Wuhan who had heard of Huishen. Guiyuan Si is not an ancient monastery—it was built in the seventeenth century during the late Ming and early Qing dynasties—but it seemed the most likely place to find information about Huishen, one of Buddhism's most widely traveled pioneers.

I disembarked in Hanyang and walked to the monastery, situated at the north end of the Wuhan Changjiang Daqiao, the Yangtze River Big Bridge. At the opposite end of the bridge stood a statue of Sun Yat-sen, beside a building that had been headquarters for the Wuchang uprising of October 10, 1911, which marked the end of the Qing Dynasty and the beginning of the Republic. Sun Yat-sen, who would become the Republic's new leader, was fund-raising in Vancouver and the United States when the rebellion started. There was something poetic about a bridge with a monastery at one end and a rebel headquarters at the other. Like poetry, Buddhism had been, at the best of times, a profoundly subversive force in society, undermining not only political and military hierarchies, but also the greed and materialism on which they thrived. The monasteries, as might be expected, were also a refuge for misfits, scoundrels, and layabouts, which made them easy targets for their religious or political opponents.

I was greeted at the entrance by a laughing Buddha in painted brown plaster, with a white frog peering out from his sleeve. The monk I spoke to had never heard of Huishen. I showed him my letter in Chinese from the consulate, which described my project in greater detail, in case I had not made myself clear, but he continued to shake his head. He even consulted one of his superiors, to no avail. Huishen was definitely not a local hero. If the Buddhists of Wuhan had not heard of him, what were my chances of finding someone who had? His bones might be interred beneath a video shop or a lotto vendor's stall next door and no one would know the difference.

Although staid and bucolic, with its trees, lake, and old buildings, and brimming with contemporary history, Wuchang was not my principal interest. I skipped the Mao Zedong Museum and Wuhan University, where students involved in the Cultural Revolution in 1967 had fought pitched battles with the People's Liberation Army, with machine guns mounted on the roof of the library and tunnels dug into the hillside. I wanted to concentrate on ancient history—present and recent past already too much with me. The United States was assembling its coalition against terrorism while it sorted through bits and pieces of the World Trade Center, and news from home was full of little else. My friends Desmond and Barbara, with whom I planned to rendezvous in London, had written to say they would prefer to meet in Oxford, a less likely "terrorist target." A friend in Bellingham, responding to my comment about feeling remote from events back home, told me he had felt the same way in July 1968, when he took an "overseas separation" from the U. S. Army in Germany in order to explore Europe. While he had his first taste of yogurt in a small café in Amsterdam, he saw, flashed on the television, scenes of the police riot at the Democratic Convention in Chicago: "I was shocked, didn't know what was going on, and I was not so sure that I even wanted to return home." Although he confessed to being "rocked to the core" by recent events, my friend was not blind to history or his country's shortcomings.

"We were so ethnocentric in those days," he added, "that events in the United States were described as 'back in the Real World.'"

Marquis Yi, having had excellent taste and visions of grandeur, was buried in high style. The Zhenghouyi Tomb, unearthed in 1978 on the outskirts of the more northerly city of Suizhou, had been unintentionally submerged in water, which preserved most of its contents, including burial boxes, gold, jade, tack, harness, weapons, bronze ceremonial vessels, and musical instruments. In addition to stringed instruments and bamboo flutes, there was a set of sixty-four bronze bells with a two-tone, seven-note scale, proving that a musical scale had existed in China at least since the Warring States Period around 433 BC. In the adjoining auditorium, several musicians played an exact replica, striking the bells with poles and padded wooden hammers and ending their performance with the popular Scottish tune "Loch Lomond." Marquis Yi's seven thousand favorite items included an elaborate bronze refrigerator—a central container surrounded by ice—and a long-necked, gold-plated phoenix with antlers, symbolizing long life and prosperity. In addition to a bronze vase covered with Medusa-like gold locks inlaid with jade, the ambitious Marquis Yi was accompanied into the afterlife by nine ritual bronze tripod vessels, a number usually restricted to emperors. Lest he be lonely in death, twenty-three retainers, including young women, had been blessed with the privilege of accompanying him.

Lights came on in the shops and odors of cooking triumphed over the pollution of passing vehicles in the teeming backstreets of Wuhan. A woman in an open doorway, pegging a brassiere and a turquoise blouse to her clothesline, might have taken me for a peeping Tom. Instead of cursing or giving me the finger, she laughed and waved the brassiere. A card-player called me over, showed me the three of hearts in his hand, and offered to sell me the wrench, solder gun, and small red propane tank in a basket at his feet. I felt at home here among the working poor people and so close to the river. The dwellings with patched roofs had a beleaguered look, outstripped by the crass, new, skinny apartments with ugly pink or white tiles that were cropping up in their midst. At one of the stalls, I ordered *shuangdong doupi*, a local snack of bean-curd pancake wrapped around meat, rice, and vegetables, apparently a favorite of Mao, the Great Helmsman.

Unlike Mao, whose body was perfectly preserved and on

exhibit in Beijing, Huishen, even after a return journey of twenty thousand miles, remained an unfathomable enigma, though one that might yet be solved by scholars in Beijing. Whereas Mao and Marquis Yi represented history from the top, Huishen, like my neighbors in the pancake line, represented history from the bottom, microhistory, so much of which falls through the cracks and is lost. I wanted the story of this obscure monk, a little-known Afghan refugee, to seem not just possible, but *probable*. I'd made a few wrong turns in my navigation, but I was still at the helm. I dipped my bean-curd pancake into the dish of chili sauce and sat down to see how the card game would end.

Before I left Wuhan, my ghostly companion Huishen provided yet another piece to the puzzle. Like me, he was tired of intrigue, warring states, and hegemony and was ready for a change:

I was taken with stories of Buddhist Fahien and his pilgrimage to India in 399, how he traversed the desert of bones and snowy mountains to reach the holy place, then Ceylon. He returned by sea, storms driving the ship off course to Java, then all the way to the Shantung peninsula. All that for the Vinaya, a set of rules of conduct he faithfully copied and brought back for his followers. Though I made myself useful reciting sutras privately in the capital, I was no longer satisfied with my station, even when the new emperor, Wen-ch'eng-ti, issued a decree granting, once more, freedom of practice. I persuaded Shih-hsien, instead of pouring money into the restoration of stupas, to stake a mission to the outer islands beyond Fu Sang. He'd survived the purge by posing as a doctor and was duly put in charge of the Office to Oversee Merit. I suggested the operative word was over-look, *not* oversee. Later, when the capital shifted to Luoyang, they renamed his department the Office to Illumine Mysteries. By then, in the company of my seasick brethren, I was twenty thousand li removed, a mystery not even Shih-hsien could fathom.

FOURTEEN

CONSIDERING THE bibliographic deserts I'd traversed since leaving Kabul, the Foreign Language Bookstore in Beijing was a glorious oasis, a spiritual watering hole. While not exactly abundant, English-language books were readily available there, plus many excellent translations of famous Chinese texts. Browsing the shelves with me, though not quite as voraciously, was Alice, who'd chucked her job and connections in England and resurfaced in Perth, Australia, in order to pursue her love of painting. She must have seemed, to her English mates, quite exotic, a sort of female Gaugin, although Perth was no Tahiti. Bright and attractive—another kind of oasis—she was also staying at the Lu Song Yuan Hotel. Now that her friend and traveling companion had returned to Hong Kong, Alice had latched on to me for the sole purpose of sightseeing. I was grateful for the companionship, though after two solitary months on the road, I might be forgiven for wishing her intentions were more inclusive.

With her finely tuned antennae, Alice was several jumps ahead of me. She held up a paperback called *100 Chinese Two-Part Allegorical Sayings,* open to a page with an illustration of a tiger looking over its shoulder at a man straining to touch its hindquarters. The accompanying text included the Chinese phrase *lao-hu de pigu — mo bu de,* which meant nothing to me. Alice read the translation aloud.

"The tiger's buttocks—cannot be touched."

Alice smiled, added the slim volume to the pile of books under her arm, and sauntered over to the cash register. After we'd visited a couple of museums and sampled the dishes at the evening street market, a 200-yard strip of food vendors where you could ski on the patina of discarded food littering the street, we headed back to the hotel and went our separate ways. Feeling somewhat ridiculous and antiquated, I pondered the wisdom of the monkish life. I'd arrived at the heart of the Middle Kingdom in search of a notoriously unknown Buddhist missionary, but I seemed to have learned little in the process about the management of desire. Even more disconcerting, I'd just looked up the quotation about the tiger's buttocks in my own copy of the book of *100 Sayings*, only to discover it had less to do with Venus than with Mars. According to the commentary on the following page, the saying was applied not to erotic hopefuls, but to those who ride roughshod over individuals or groups.

Back in my room, I dozed off briefly in front of the television, dreaming of caves, white rabbits, a broken bicycle, a pigeon nesting on the Buddha's head, and some lines by Yeats about the paltriness of growing old. I awoke with a start at the sound of loud voices in the corridor and wrote down another message from Huishen, this time about love and politics in fifth-century China:

Discovering women, I gave up meditation and tried to regulate my breathing. Each one was breathtaking and inspired me to lie about in mute adoration of the eccentric stupa of blood erected in her honor. Alas, the machinations of Ts'ui Hao and Kou Ch'ien-chih, one a racist and Confucian throwback, the other a Daoist, brought my dalliances to an end.

Ts'ui's appointment as chancellor opened the door to a period of integration, during which foreigners were encouraged to marry into good Chinese families; he also convinced the Wei court to wage a successful war against the Pei-Liang kingdom. Nothing seemed likely to stop him controlling the predominantly Han bureaucracy and turning the emperor against the religion of the barbarians. Ko Wu's abortive rebellion, which led to the discovery of stores of arms and wine plus cells of subterranean debauchery on the monastery grounds, brought down the final decree. I watched friends butchered after being forced to smash their own temples, set fire to sutras they'd spent years copying. In due course, I got revenge, reporting details of the uncomplimentary history of the Northern Wei inscribed on stone tablets Ts'ui Hao's lackies carted through the streets on route to the Temple of Heaven. He and 127 clansmen put to death. Not even his wife was spared, who'd opened more than her heart to the new religion.

I propped several pillows around me and sat up to read in the small alcove that contained my bed at the Lu Song Yuan Hotel, built two centuries earlier by a Mongolian general and, judging from the stone sculpture in the courtyard, once the Beijing residence of Lu Xun, the radical thinker who had been so much on my mind. It felt good to be here, to be alive, to be still searching. I had much to answer for in my life—where anger and insecurity often masqueraded as love—and even more to be grateful for. As I skimmed the three companion volumes of Chinese parables, lore, and witticisms, there was no shortage of wisdom to imbibe. In fact, everything seemed strangely applicable to my life at this stage, even *ma ge guo shi,* which meant "horsehide shroud" and referred to the idea of dying in battle with your boots on rather than surrounded by the comforts of home. What about *lao ma shi tu*—"an old horse knows the way"? Could it be referring to that other way, the Dao? Or *shou bu shi juan*— "always with a book in hand"? As I prepared to put aside the fourth volume, *100 Common Chinese Idioms and Set Phrases,* my attention was caught by the line drawing of a man and a woman, elegant and privileged from the looks of their costumes and from their two delicately patterned ceramic vases. She was saying:

Qi hu nan xia—"When one rides a tiger it is difficult to dismount."

Friday afternoon, September 28, 2001. A sunny day at the heart of the Middle Kingdom. I felt like Marco Polo, arriving here after an arduous journey more than seven hundred years ago to meet and do business with the Mongol emperor, Kublai Khan. Marco's description of his exploits, modestly titled *Description of the World,* would open the eyes and excite the curiosity and greed of generations of Europeans. My friend He Zhixiong, studying in Boston, had given me a list of names of scholars in Beijing who knew the Huishen story and had written about it, so I was anxious to make contact. Chinese interest in Huishen's journey to the Americas goes back to the early twentieth century, when scholars, freed from the deadly insularity of the Ming and Qing dynasties and inspired by pro-democracy sentiments, began once again to look outward. Two early names are Zhang Taiyan and Liang Qichao, author of

Voyage to the New Continent. Close on their heels were Chen Ziliang, whose article "The Chinese First Explored America" appeared in *Words Monthly* in 1940, and Zhu Qianshi, whose "Discussions on the Discovery of America by the Chinese Buddhist Monks 1,000 Years before Columbus" appeared a year later. Hardly a decade has gone by without the subject resurfacing. Ma Nantun, a historian and former mayor of Beijing known as Geng Tuo, wrote three articles on the Huishen story in the early 1960s for the *Beijing Evening Newspaper*. In 1969, Wei Juxian completed his three-volume *Chinese Discovery of America*, which was published in Hong Kong and Taiwan. A decade later, Fang Zhongpu, a historian specializing in navigation, published "Sailing to America for 3,000 Years: Preliminary Discussion of the Trans-Pacific Voyage of the Yin People" in the *People's Daily.*

It's not clear why all this scholarly and journalistic interest in Huishen and his travels, written and published in the Chinese language, has not attracted a wider audience to the story. The Bamboo Curtain and the Cultural Revolution are partly to blame; so, too, is Confucian xenophobia.

Without coming across as a lugubrious whim-wham, I intended to remind the scholars that these five missionaries, while availing themselves of Chinese ships and navigational skills, were monks from Kabul. Such thoughts, like white rabbits, were hopping about my gray matter as I strolled along Di'anmen Dongdajie toward the Chinese Academy of Social Sciences (CASS). To reach CASS, you had to enter the gates of a walled compound. The academy was tucked away in the grounds of what appeared to be a former medical facility, a labyrinth of wooden, two-story colonial-type structures with verandas and high ceilings. As the gatekeeper spoke no English, I showed him my list of professors' names in Chinese. He didn't seem familiar with any of them but indicated that I was welcome to go hunting on my own. I went through the same procedure in the Border Studies Center, where I was hoping to locate Ma Dazhong. No luck. Perhaps the Institute of Latin American Studies would recognize the names of two of its scholars, Li Xiangchun and Yang Dianqui. A young man, a junior professor wearing a Grateful Dead T-shirt, went out of his way to examine my list of names, my consular letter, and a couple of books I'd brought along to convince my hosts that I wasn't a total charlatan. He offered me a seat and disappeared for ten minutes.

"One die, one move other place. Nobody know where."

He handed back my materials, explaining that this was the last day of classes before the week of national holidays and that most faculty had already gone home, which meant there was no point looking for the Institute of Ethnic Studies at the China National University. As I'd be leaving in less than a week, this was definitely not good news and my face showed it. I must have looked either ungrateful or dead, as the young man apologized profusely for the inconvenience caused by China's national holidays. Privately, he must have wondered what kind of dolt I was for not knowing this in advance.

To overcome my disappointment, I spent the afternoon by a lake, not far from the Lu Song Yuan Hotel, dallying on the promenade as the paddleboats went by with their scalloped blue awnings. In the shade of a willow, I made a few notes but was easily distracted by the fishermen, mah-jong players, lovers cuddling on a park bench, and a skiff half-submerged among the lily pads. A display of flaming red flowers, 625 pots in all, bordered the lake, and the late-afternoon sun striking the metal fence had laid down shadows on the path that resembled the wooden ties and parallel lines of a railway track. It was not difficult to imagine this spot as the playground of emperors. In response to this idle fancy, a large skiff with a dozen passengers under a pink awning passed in front of me, the man in the stern working the oar that both propels and steers the boat, while a goddess, her hair in a bun, sat in the bow in a wicker chair facing the passengers, playing a lute and singing.

Slipping away from Beijing for three days to visit the ancient Northern Wei capital of Datong, even with its reputation for having the finest cave art in China, was not easy, especially after spending some time with the family and friends of Xi Chuan, one of China's finest young poets. They had included me in a private celebration of the national holiday and moon festival at a retreat in the Badaling Mountains north of Beijing. I relaxed, letting the sounds of domestic solidarity and laughter wash over me, while Xi Chuan's two-year-old son Man Yi, who wore a red headband, greeted me continually across the table.

"*Lao-wai yi-yi.*" I was delighted with my new name, which meant "foreign grandpa."

The idea of packing again, giving up my room at the Lu Song Yuan Hotel, looking for new lodgings during a week of national holidays, and spending two days on the train getting there and back had little appeal. Yet here I was tramping through Yungang Shiku, a vast honeycomb of grottoes containing 5,100 statues carved into the cliffs of Wuzhou Shan about ten miles west of

Datong. Pingcheng, as Datong was once called, has been around since the Warring States Period (475–221 BC) and was of strategic significance to several governments. When the Toba tribe, after a long series of victories, eventually unified Northern China in AD 439 under the Northern Wei Dynasty, they established their capital here and began construction of the caves.

The point of my visit was to see the city and environs and try to imagine them as they were during the period between Huishen's arrival in China, approximately AD 450, and his departure in 458. There was no way of knowing for sure whether he visited Datong or sailed east under the patronage of the Northern Wei, but he may well have spent time in the capital and been on hand to experience uncertainty and aftershock from the purges of Tai Wu Di, who, fearing the power and insularity of the monasteries, and at the prompting of his Taoist minister Cui Hao, ordered widespread persecutions of the Buddhists in 446. Monasteries were burned, nuns and monks murdered. A similar wave of persecutions would also rock the Southern Ch'i Dynasty around the time of Huishen's return in AD 499, requiring that he sit on his heels waiting for a change of heart or a change of leader. I was inclined to believe that his travels abroad were prompted as much by a desire to escape the downturns of Buddhist fortunes in China—more sporadic but no less severe than what he had experienced in Kabul and Bamiyan—as by any driving missionary impulse.

When it came to discerning foreign and local influences, including the feature called "looking up at the mountain"— which involves building a colossus so close to a facing wall that the viewer can admire or worship it only from below—I felt quite inept, though I noted the parallel with contemporary urban architecture. Even more than the colossal Buddha and the enduring color of the murals—a deep, rich, exuberant red that teemed with Bodhisattvas, dancers, gymnasts, archers, and *apsaras*—what impressed this jaded pilgrim were the hands: bruised hands, deformed hands, chubby hands clutching a lotus bud; hands of Shiva, holding a bow, an arrow, and a small bird; Buddha's hand stroking the head of Rahula in a "fear not" gesture; preaching hands; the enormous damaged hand of Maitreya supported by a tiny warrior; a healing hand; a hand held close to the chest as in cards; a vast hand, the thumbnail as large as my head, resting on the round blue ball of a knee in lotus posture; even the missing hand of a Buddha, who stands there like a war veteran or the victim of a land mine in Afghanistan. What do you need more in times of trouble than a hand, offering food, assistance, or tenderness? Hands reaching out from the past, in the form of poems, paintings, sculpture, symbols of greeting, of solidarity, revealing the mind in its most generous moments, closest to achieving what we think of as divine.

As the city of Datong had no redeeming characteristics, I did not dally downtown, except to check my e-mail before heading back to the hotel. My cheap room, in a cut-rate annex to one of the larger hotels, had no heat, so I grabbed a quick snack nearby and crawled into bed to make some notes, most of them related to the train I'd catch again in the morning for the return trip to Beijing. I'd "borrowed" a menu from the train for its literary, rather than culinary, merits. In addition to "shimp," the menu offered "friend eggs" and special service for "newly-weeds." I was pleased to learn that the dishes, which promised to be meticulously prepared if not edited or proofread, had four significant features: color, fragrance, taste, and shape. Beijing, I was informed, had been the capital of Yuan, Ming, and Qing dynasties since 1953. In that fair city, wonder of wonders, "there are many huge buildings on both sides of the smooth street." All this came in the brochure after the official Welcome Speech, which said, "Considering the visual sense and psychology mentality, the designer focus on the harmonious effect of color arrangements. The chosen of the material of curtains, tables, sleeping carpets, the arrangement of the food ware and frame with calligraphy and paintings and service slogens are all show the character of the time and intension." What concerned me most was the caveat, "vacant sleepers will be sold in public." Must I stay awake and alert or risk ending up in a caravan, in chains, heading back across the Taklamakan Desert to the Sunday market in Kashgar, where they once sold slaves along with camels, donkeys, and snow-leopard pelts?

As my plane descended toward Heathrow Airport, I was still thinking about Beijing. The Chinese capital was beginning to have the same appeal to North Americans that Paris once had. It was an attractive city, mysterious, exotic, full of artistic and architectural wonders, its rhythms charged with a different kind of energy than that which is found in Europe, and still affordable. However, it shared with Paris and Rome the self-satisfaction and arrogance of the ancient capital, arbiter of fashion, broker of destinies. The previous night Xi Chuan had picked me up for supper with some of his literary friends. Fall rains had descended on the capital. Streets were awash, the cyclists trying to navigate under umbrellas. It was a relief, and a far cry from the intense heat of my arrival in Kabul or the withering aridity of the desert. I'd spent the afternoon packing and sitting in the lobby of the Lu Song Yuan Hotel, watching water in the courtyard splash off the stone face and moustache of Lu Xun.

A small man, tubercular, badgered for his beliefs and caustic satire, Lu Xun nevertheless struggled to the end of his life trying to initiate reforms in China. He carried on a vigorous debate with the past, arguing not only for a return to the vernacular in literature, but also for a rejection of outmoded values, corrupt politicians, and "the aphorisms of those gentlemen [in public office] who have justice on their lips but self-interest in their hearts." He knew that the struggle against apathy and despair would have to be as great in the emerging nation as it was in himself if political rights were ever to be achieved.

Lu Xun's solution, in part, involved the cultivation of what he called "good memory," the kind that requires not only keeping the past constantly in mind, but also clearly in focus. This difficulty was not lost on me as I trekked through Asia, following the route and inquiring about the origins and spiritual coordinates of Huishen. Bad memory involved idealizing or sentimentalizing the past, ignoring its negative aspects. Good memory demanded that we learn from the past, which had the potential to liberate us, to make the present bearable, humane. I suspected that Lu Xun, China's preeminent social critic, would have laughed at the Huishen story, dismissing it as a fairy tale irrelevant to the present. Ironically, I had come to view Huishen as a clerical version of Lu Xun, an outsider, a critic of his time, someone who, like James Joyce or Henry James, was more comfortable commenting on his country from a distance. Lu Xun had gone to Japan as a young man in order to get some perspective on his homeland, to consider other social and political systems; he had planned to travel next to Germany, but responsibilities took him back to China to care for his mother. Huishen had come to China hoping to escape the religious persecution he experienced in Kabul; what he found here, despite a highly developed social and economic infrastructure and intellectual sophistication, were two despotic regimes that might, on a whim, devour their own.

I considered myself a practitioner of good memory, though I was not unaware of my biases, my distorting lenses—or, for that matter, the extent of my own ignorance. If I forget those limitations, there is no shortage of friends and family members ready to remind me. Before starting my journey, I had phoned Knut Fladmark, a professor of archaeology at Simon Fraser University in Vancouver, a pioneer in coastal migration theory, who argued that the west coast, with its glacier-free patches and rich food supply during the last Ice Age, was a more likely route for peopling the Americas than the Bering land bridge and the so-called Ice-Free Corridor east of the Rockies. I thought he might lend a sympathetic ear to my quest.

When I called to ask if we could meet to discuss the question of pre-Columbian Asian contact with the Americas, he said, "What question?" I was taken aback by the abruptness of his dismissal. "There is absolutely nothing," he told me flatly, "in more recent Native culture in North America that requires pre-Columbian Asian contact as an explanation."

I made a few feeble remarks about Asian-looking artifacts, linguistic parallels, and comparative iconography, but he dismissed these notions as pure speculation. His reference to the scientific principle of Occam's Razor sent me scurrying to my *Oxford*

English Dictionary, where I read that Occam's Razor, or the Law of Parsimony, asserts "the logical principle that no more causes or forces should be assumed than are necessary to account for the facts." According to Occam and Fladmark, my search for Huishen had already taken me too far out along the razor's edge—fifteen thousand miles, to be exact—placing me in an extremely precarious, if not untenable, position. Yet there were not only historical records referring to my monk and his travels to the east, but also a growing body of "evidence" for cultural diffusion from Asia that was increasingly difficult to ignore.

I'd made inquiries about ocean passage from China to the west coast of Canada or the United States so I could replicate the next leg of Huishen's travels across the North Pacific, but that would have to wait. There were affairs to attend to back home, including plans for my youngest daughter's wedding, and money to be earned. Besides, I needed time to reflect on what I'd seen and done so far and, alas, to dislodge the livestock—rabbits, deer, raccoons, rats, cougars, and bears—that would have repossessed the house and property in my absence.

As the British Airways jet approached Heathrow, I noticed that a steeper bank and altered flight path had been introduced to avoid passing over London—yet another reminder of the events of September 11. I expected security to be tight; in fact, I was worried about my passport, which contained one Afghan, two Pakistani, and two Chinese visas. Under the circumstances, this would likely mean some questioning by security personnel. I don't like to be interrogated, having an irrational fear of uniformed authority figures. I debated whether to go into the whole story about my book on Huishen and pre-Columbian

Asian contact in North America—I could already see the officials' eyes glazing over—or to say, simply, that I was a journalist and flash the letters from the *Vancouver Sun* and the *Edmonton Journal* that I'd used to get into Afghanistan.

Because they'd upgraded my ticket to business class in Beijing, I was among the first off the plane, but there were only two customs agents on duty. Fourteen passengers were ahead of me, negotiating the circuitous network of plastic barriers and stainless-steel posts. I looked carefully at the two agents, as if intense scrutiny might warn me in advance of their hang-ups and powers of intuition. Which one had slept more soundly the night before—bills paid, children in good health—the man or the woman? Hair pulled tightly into a bun, the female agent looked tired, severe, not one to be easily charmed. I decided I'd be better off with the man. I rearranged my face and slid my glasses down my nose to look more professorial, an image to which my slovenly dress and shaggy beard would lend support. Maybe I'd be better off playing the smiling, innocuous tourist, dazed, exhausted, compliant, clutching a guidebook and a few souvenirs.

"Number 5, please." The light was flashing, and I found myself directed toward neither original agent, but one of several who had emerged late from an extended coffee break in the staff room. The face confronting me looked mean and caffeine-deprived. I knew my orientation was wrong. I should be properly shaved, wearing an old school tie and a Harris tweed sports jacket. I placed my passport on the counter, customs form inserted discreetly to make it fall open at my photograph and personal details, while I constructed a benign expression.

The agent, his clipped moustache bristling, flipped quickly

through the pages of the passport and looked as if he would apply the entry stamp and wave me through. Then, he put down the stamp, opened the passport again and passed his eyes slowly up and down the pages, his mouth half open, as if reading a gripping novel or the last will and testament of a wealthy relative recently deceased. Without raising his head, he looked at me over the rim of his reading glasses.

"Would you mind stepping over to that door with the red light for a few moments?" He gathered up my papers and marched ahead of me to a small office, where two men in plain clothes told me to make myself comfortable. There were no torture racks on the walls or brass knuckles, just a couple of plain wooden chairs by the desk, a green-vomit–colored vinyl couch with cracks in the upholstery, and a picture of the queen.

"Your passport contains two Pakistani and two Chinese visas. Why did you need duplicates?"

The visa issued by the Islamic Emirate of Afghanistan, which was obviously what interested them, was not mentioned. I decided to play along. "I hadn't expected to leave and reenter Pakistan, so I needed two visas."

"And China?"

"I spent more time in Pakistan than I'd expected and missed the entry date on the original Chinese visa. Rather unfair, I thought, as I'd already paid the full fee in Vancouver."

"What was the purpose of your trip?"

"Gathering information."

"Information?"

"Yes, people, sites, history. The sort of things travelers notice."

"And what did you notice in Afghanistan?"

During five days in Kabul, I noticed women on the streets in high heels, unaccompanied by male relatives and not wearing the obligatory burka. I noticed kites flying in some districts of Kabul. I noticed hunger, begging, small children injured by land mines. I noticed a city still devastated from a civil war we had supported then abandoned. Oh yes, and one more thing: the only gun in evidence was at the airport, in the lap of a bored young Taliban.

"Not much. I was too busy interviewing aid workers."

"We've had your luggage brought over for a routine inspection. Would you mind stepping outside to open it?"

I unzipped all the pockets and laid back the flap of Bronwen's backpack, knowing I'd never get all that stuff in a second time. The other man, the one who had remained silent, began to unfold the shirts and underwear, making small, neat piles on the table. The camel bone with a frieze of carved Buddhas was next, then the folding knife from Peshawar, the blouses made by Afghan refugees.

"And this?" he asked, immensely pleased with himself, as if his unasked questions had finally been answered. He was holding a clear ziplock bag full of white powder. I suppose he expected me to deny all knowledge of the bag and its contents or break down and confess. I made a deliberate attempt to swallow guiltily.

"Why don't you taste it? Chinese laundry soap is lemon-flavored."

Inside a pile of unwashed clothes was a small brown Jiffy bag. He dumped out the thirty-odd Canadian maple-leaf pins given to me years ago by Foreign Affairs in Ottawa that I had thought might be fun to pass out to the kids I met on the road. Then he reached inside and pulled out a huge wad of foreign currency, each note worth 5,000 afghanis. I'd forgotten I had them.

"Nigel, look at this," he said excitedly, counting the bills. The seconds ticked past in slow motion. "Two hundred and sixty thousand afghanis!"

Before I had time to explain that I'd forgotten to exchange the bills in Kabul because the whole wad was worth only three dollars, my interrogator reached into the bottom of my pack and pulled out a dozen or so magazines and pamphlets from various NGOs, which he dropped on the table. On top was the glossy brochure from the offices of RAWA, the Revolutionary Association of Women of Afghanistan.

"I think you'll have to come with us."

Of course, none of this happened. Heightened British security did not even notice my Afghan and Pakistani visas, and I was sent on my nefarious way without a hitch. Canadian customs officials were equally efficient, so concerned with my trip to England that they never even noticed I'd been to Afghanistan. Before waving me through, however, they did give me a white sheet of paper that contained information and warnings about hoof-and-mouth disease.

CONVEYANCE BY WATER

FIFTEEN

THERE WAS A bright full moon over the boom of the loading crane; and the greased cables, impatient to be done, smacked against the orange girders. Containers rose and descended on the strings of their engines as neatly as drugged marionettes until the locking nuts clicked into place. Below the bridge, with shouts and much clanking, longshoremen anchored the bottom two containers in each row to the top deck, using galvanized diagonal support bars. Above it all, the crane operator watched godlike, silent in his sliding bug-eyed-cage, lives and profits at his fingertips. As the containers were lifted and lowered into place, the black electric cable over the clamping apparatus coiled and uncoiled in its greased cone like a cobra. Off the starboard bow, the pilot boat waited, drifting in and out of the quavering shafts of reflected light from the far shore of the harbor.

I was back in Asia, after a hiatus of several months, to continue my search for Huishen. I was convinced that he stopped in Korea during his outgoing voyage in AD 458 to whatever lay beyond the eastern sea. Pusan would be my last port of call before Seattle and Vancouver, but Huishen would have sailed from port to port, landfall to landfall, including the Kuril and Aleutian islands, renewing his supplies of food and water, spreading the word, and gathering information from the locals. Korea has played a significant role in the history of Buddhism, with monks such as Hyeryun and Sok Hyeop making arduous pilgrimages to India and to the rich monasteries of the Ghandara region of Afghanistan, where score of pilgrims gathered the honeyed wisdom of Buddha and from which Huishen had once fled.

After Taiwan and Korea, our itinerary included a direct and unwavering course of 54 degrees to Tsugaru Kaikyo, the strait that runs between Japan's main island of Honshu and its largest northerly island of Hokkaido. Then we would follow the great circle route to Juan de Fuca Strait, where the container ship *Pohang Senator* would pass between my house on the southern tip of Vancouver Island and the mountainous Olympic Peninsula in the state of Washington. Huishen and his compatriots would have preferred the more protected Sea of Japan, following the northwest coast of Hokkaido and stopping in fishing villages such as Sapporo before passing into the Sea of Okhotsk by way of La Perouse Strait. Only then would they have begun to island-hop, using the two great chains that lie like stepping stones between Asia and the Americas.

My return to China had taken me from Hong Kong to Chongqing and down the Yangtze River to Jingzhou, once an ancient capital and purported to be the burial place of Huishen. A watery route, to be sure, but guaranteed, along with my trip from Kabul to Kashgar and along the Silk Road to Xian and Datong, to give me as close an approximation as possible of Huishen's pilgrimage from birth to the grave. Since the *Liang Shu* indicates that he told his story to the emperor and court historians in Jingzhou, it's a reasonable assumption that his nautical departure had taken place nearby on the Yangtze, following its course downstream to Shanghai and the South China Sea. I had seen Wuhan, Shanghai, and the lower reaches of the Yangtze and the Whangpoo already, so I chose the doomed Three Gorges section as my river sampler.

The twelve-and-a-half-hour flight from Vancouver to Hong Kong was late, so I missed the connection to Chongqing and had to spend another eleven hours in the new airport, where bevies of well-dressed school kids doing surveys kept zeroing in to ask what I thought of the new Hong Kong. When I finally arrived at the Shin Pin Hotel in Chongqing, I was too wrecked to think about dinner, though not too tired to feel the excitement of being in a large and famous city at the junction of two rivers, the Yangtze and the Jialing Jiang. I awoke early, arranged a boat ticket for the next day, and spent my time checking out bridges and cable cars and walking between the downtown and the waterfront. Low-slung barges advanced almost imperceptibly against the current, and a calamity of small craft jockeyed for position as they raced downstream, dodging the cumbersome ferries and tour boats that appeared to hang helpless in midriver as they swung broadside in order to dock with their bows facing upstream.

Chongqing is an important river port and played a significant political role during and after the anti-Japanese war, as it was first the wartime capital of the Kuomintang, then a staging post and headquarters for Mao Zedong and the Communists. Japanese pilots based downriver in Hankou followed the silvery course of the Yangtze at night to bomb and strafe the city where the two rivers meet, a relatively safe evening's outing. For their part, the Chinese were doing their best to finish the job years later, turning the ancient city with its labyrinthine passages and its warrens of low-rise apartments into a crass and faceless metropolis of high office towers, cell phone boutiques, and one-way streets. Because of the hills, there are almost no cyclists in Chongqing but, despite its forced modernity, the city is still full of stick-stick men with their thick bamboo poles, staggering under the weight of heavy loads suspended from both ends or lounging in small, noisy groups waiting for business. Outside the Xinhua Bookstore, the complete staff of forty clerks and the warehouse staff were doing their light morning calisthenics in military formation in unison to music and under the direction of the floor manager.

Having seen enough grottoes and murals for two lifetimes, I skipped Dazu, but I managed a visit to Luohan Si, the small temple in Chongqing that was home to some strikingly realistic sculptures of *arhats* (enlightened ones), including several of African descent. I liked the whimsy involved in the creation of these religious figures who, except for their uniformly distended earlobes, seemed to represent every human mood and type. Like Snow White's seven dwarfs multiplied by seven, there were the usual sleepy ones, the grumps, the dazed or dopey figures, the arrogant, the shy, and the afflicted types. There was even a Buddhist cowboy astride a roped steer and an enlightened one with a pronounced forehead who was using a stick to clean his ear. A Buddhist version of Rubber Man grinned maniacally, his left arm stretching to twice its normal length as he pointed heavenward. The self-mocking humor, it seemed, was a by-product of cultural maturity and political stability, both in short supply in China in recent centuries.

Buddhist humor was equally scarce during my trip downriver on a tour boat. The first stop of the Yangtze River ferry at Fengdu included a trip to the Palace of the King of Hell, which involved passing through a not-so-pearly gate into the netherworld. This particular temple complex, high atop a hill, was an amalgam of all the tortures and perversities imagined by great Western artists—Bosch, Brueghel, and the fire-and-brimstone medieval painters—as well as some innovations you might expect from a comic-strip hell such as Hatlo's *Inferno*. After the chairlift to the top, I was expecting something special and was not disappointed. In a room at the apex of the temple complex, I encountered a sculptural rendering of a sinner being tossed under spiked wagon wheels. There were demonic animals in attendance as well, including a psychotic ape and a crazed blue donkey. At the nearby tea station, with no irony intended, a tape was playing a version of "Smoke Gets in Your Eyes."

My shipmate Colin, who ran a gas station near Perth in Scotland, had been having trouble with Miss Jang, the pushy tour guide, who seemed less than enamored of the fact that she had a couple of *waiguoren* under her care. To prove to himself and his girlfriend back home that he could rough it with the best of them, Colin had booked a third-class berth on the Chinese tour boat *Eastern Prince* of the Don Yang Wang Line and was wedged into a cabin he shared with seven people, including a young married couple. Because he had the decency to do his smoking on deck, he thought the least he could expect was some consideration from the others when he was trying to sleep. No such luck. When he asked if she'd be giving any explanations in English, Miss Jang responded with perfect enunciation and gleeful maliciousness, "No way!"

Toward the top of the four hundred steps leading to the Zhang Fei Temple, where another hellish display awaited us, the old woman in front of me started tapping her chest cavity to give her overworked heart a little encouragement. The message was simple: I know you're in there, doing a terrific job, but don't stop now, just a few more yards to go, you can do it. The temple, wonderfully located on a ridge overlooking the Yangtze, was in a bad state of disrepair. I remarked on its condition to Pieter, a Dutchman, and he told me it would be submerged or relocated when the Three Gorges were flooded. I couldn't say I was disappointed. My thoughts were on all that effort the old lady had expended getting up the hill and on the small, boiled fresh potatoes roasted in garlic and red peppers that I was planning to sample from one of the street vendors on my downhill run to the boat.

"Which do you recommend," Pieter asked, as he steadied his camera to capture the curl of the crumbling eaves, "drowning or removal?" He had trained as a scientist but was currently working in the field of curriculum development in Amsterdam.

The choice seemed simple enough to me. "Drowning." I offered him a section of my orange, which he graciously refused. "Then it could be turned into an underwater exhibit for scuba divers or for tourists to visit by way of a watertight elevator or a submersible. You could call the exhibit 'Through Hell and High Water.'"

Pieter groaned appreciatively.

The damming of the Yangtze River for hydroelectric generation seemed as inevitable in China as the return to capitalism. Not only did Mao Zedong once swim across the river and write a poem on the subject, envisaging a future dam, but also China's first republican leader, Sun Yat-sen, had predicted the project. The dam was a contemporary equivalent of the Great Wall, the system of canals, the imperial navy, and the Great Leap Forward, those colossal undertakings by which earlier rulers had left their mark on the country and its history—dangers, inefficiency, lives lost, and sheer folly be damned—or had distracted the populace from their other failings. As in the case of the Scottish Highland clearances, "progress" could prove more devastating than war. Along the hillsides of the Yangtze, wherever there was a small town or village, could be found large white signs—175 meters— indicating the level to which the new lake would eventually rise, as if this were a fact to celebrate rather than a grim uprooting for millions of displaced families. If seismic activity did not cause it to burst or silting render it useless, the Gezhouba Dam would certainly put an end to a long and colorful chapter in China's history, as well as to archaeological studies of prehistoric settlement in the region, now thought to be a much earlier site for Asia's primitive forebears than the Huang He, or Yellow River.

The Yangtze River spoke its own language, in case anyone was listening—the low humming noise of water on the move, passing over sand, rocks, the hulls of sunken vessels. At other times, the boils, whirlpools, and surges emitted a deeper, distinctively guttural sound, a muted roar like the noise of bees swarming. Small watertight metal skiffs, mounted with a slatted white pyramid and a green or red navigation light, marked the navigable channel, though only the Yangtze tour boats paid much attention to them. The other craft—three-log sampans and five-log *wupans,* along with shallow barges and hydrofoils—skirted reefs and sandbars, ignoring all the rules of the road. Here and there, as from time immemorial, a boy stood silent on a rock, fishing, drawing what seemed like an overlarge butterfly net through the water, always in the direction of the current. Striations from glacial gouging and plate tectonics formed an elemental backdrop.

The Lesser Three Gorges—fast, narrow, and very intimate when seen from the perspective of a small boat—were more dramatic. The rock walls of the canyons were the color of my favorite ice cream, tiger-blend: licorice-orange with swaths of caramel and molasses. I was taking notes madly, trying to get it all down, while the boat leaped and twisted in the current. Granite and limestone cliffs, menacing overhangs, cave mouths with stalactite fangs, a brown female monkey and her two babies on a rocky outcrop, a yellow butterfly adrift on the warm air, Horse Returning Mountain, inaccessible ledge where an ancient lord was installed (God knows how) in his coffin, shrub, moss, purple gentian, layers of broken shale like stacks of unshelved books, Tang poetic graffiti. And the ubiquitous square holes punched at regular intervals in the cliff face twenty feet above water level to anchor the tracking platforms that once ran the length of the gorges, where men in bare feet hauled junks and barges upstream, as nearly suicidal an occupation as might be imagined.

The small metal boats we were transferred to, forty feet long and priced at 30,000 yuan ($4,000), carried twenty-five of us slowly against the current. At the narrows, the light craft could navigate the rapids only by dumping us ashore. The helmsman stood in the cabin, a metal pipe attached to the rudder post nestled in the small of his back, and leaned forward. Along the portage, as we watched him and his mate fight the current, the inevitable vendors lined the way with food, drinks, antiques, and trifles for sale. Among them I managed to find an ancient bronze tripod pot and the folded copy of a handscroll depicting a cross-section and day-in-the-life of an ancient city with commerce, barges contending in the river, and a plethora of scenes of entertainment and leisure. I was so excited with my purchases I almost missed the boat. Downriver again, the crew using a long secondary steering oar mounted like a lance on the bow, crew and passengers taking turns singing. All this—caverns and outcrops, pines and poplars hurtling past—soon to be underwater.

I'd been reading Simon Winchester's *The River at the Center of the World: A Journey up the Yangtze and Back in Chinese Time,* an account of traveling with the indomitable "Lily," fixer extraordinaire, from the river's mouth in the South China Sea near Shanghai to its headwaters in Tibet. It gave me a better sense of the importance of the Yangtze in Chinese history—not only its nautical importance, as a site of clashing armadas and impertinent British gunboats, but also its role as an appropriate jumping-off point for Huishen on his travels to the Americas. In a few short hours, I would disembark from the *Eastern Prince* in Yichang, forgoing the opportunity to see the colossal dam under construction. A short passage in Winchester's book summed up the megaproject in a nutshell: "Mao's poem 'Swimming' envisaged the structure in two lines of verse, lines that helped invest the project with an almost mythic importance. Building a dam across the Yangtze was in many ways like swimming across the Yangtze—it was a means of demonstrating man's supremacy, and Mao's supremacy, and the Party's supremacy, over the Chinese landscape, as well as being the realisation of the worthiest of ambitions."

Such collisions of mythic power and fanatical ambition were often the best incentive needed for departure, for seeking refuge in foreign lands—that is, if you did not want to die constructing a wall or from some other imperial folly. Huishen and his four companions from Kabul were by no means the first to opt for the Great Leap Abroad in fifth-century China, cooking up a scheme to justify their voluntary exile. Why Huishen came back to tell his story to the court historians and to deposit his bones in Jingzhou, a place hardly less foreign to an Afghan than the as-yet-unnamed British Columbia, California, or Mexico, was something I had yet to fathom.

As I disembarked in Yichang along with the two Dutchmen, Colin gave me a hearty wave from the boat's lower depths, his burning cigarette inscribing an arc in the cool night air. Even Miss Jang, having divested herself of yet another bothersome *waiguoren* in her tour group, managed a thin smile.

"The furtive leopard accessed the deer. Abruptly the leopard fell on the deer fiendishly. But the deer dodged flexibly."

The sign in the Jingzhou Museum describing the scene on the lacquerware wine container was an excellent reminder of the dangers of the wayward adverb, if not a good advertisement for local translation skills. In contrast, I struck gold by finding Sunny Suyu to translate for me. She was a middle-school teacher of English and had responded to my call for assistance in tracking down information about Huishen. She had not heard of the monk but was determined to exhaust every avenue on my behalf, even to the point of enlisting her father. Our first stop was the East Gate Tower, which had a mural celebrating an unusual collaboration, in which the Han emperor "borrowed" the city of Jingzhou from its ruler in order to stage a battle against one of his enemies. This made sense at the time because Jingzhou was walled. It now has the distinction of being the only fully walled city in northern China.

I questioned the use of the verb *borrow*, on the grounds that emperors don't usually return things they find useful, but Sunny assured me that that is exactly what happened. Like the city of York in England or Italy's Siena, Jingzhou represented security, sound sleep at night. It was a quaint reminder of ancient times, when city walls could still protect, however briefly. The only thing modern man has that compares with a walled city is the gated community, though only petty thieves would be deterred by a wire fence, a video camera, and a single armed guard.

From the East Gate, we took a taxi to the Zhanghua Temple in Shashi, the nondescript, down-at-the-heels industrial town with which Jingzhou had recently been amalgamated, much to its dismay. A group of Buddhist monks were saying prayers and chanting with a small congregation of believers, so we took refuge in an adjoining room. Sunny wasted no time explaining my mission to the young monk at the desk. He in turn called in an associate, who was dispatched to the library to look for Huishen's name in the temple's dictionary of famous monks, one of only three copies in China. We followed close behind, pausing to examine the series of ceremonial lances that had been presented by Zhixi, a Qing empress. The pewterwork was intricate and included a dragon, a monkey, a macelike ball, and an elegant hand emerging from a crown. Zhixi's hand had a gem at the wrist and inch-long fingernails and was holding a brush pen.

From the set of large rosewood cabinets, the monk had removed several narrow wooden boxes, each containing folded sections of the dictionary.

I knew Huishen was listed in this dictionary, as I had seen an English translation of his entry. It mentioned his burial in Jingzhou after his eighteen years of service as head of missions in the north, an appointment that must have followed his audience with the new emperor, Wu-ti. But try as he might, using "Huishen," "Hwei Shan," "Hoey Shin," and any alternative spellings I could muster, the monk could not find his name. I could see I would have to take lessons from the lacquerware deer in the Bowuguan and learn to dodge more flexibly if I hoped to find anything useful in Jingzhou.

"Hubei food is the best in China," Sunny announced as yet another dish was delivered to the table by her sister.

Sunny and her husband had purchased a small building outside the city gates, using the main floor as a restaurant and the rest as living quarters. Her sister, who ran the restaurant, had encouraged me to use her laptop computer on the counter to check my e-mail before dinner. Liu-Jin, another English teacher who had been Sunny's classmate in college, joined us: and we planned our strategy for the next day, which included trips to the museum, the National Religious Bureau of the Jiangling Local Government, and the File Office for dignitaries past and present. I was certainly not going to argue with Sunny about Hubei food, as the dishes served were all tasty and completely new to me. Spicy Yangtze mussels, deep-fried potato cakes, and lotus roots were followed by "floating flowers," a sort of thin gourmet dumpling in broth, and a wonderful dish consisting of little cylinders of pork wrapped in fish slices.

The pork wraps were arranged on a platter with a rooster carved from a huge turnip with a red-pepper comb, all set on a bed of thin cucumber slices.

When we arrived at the museum the following day, Sunny's friend on the archaeological team at the Jingzhou Bowuguan had no knowledge of Huishen but was keen to show me the museum's holdings, especially the contents from Tomb Number 168 at Fenghuangshan, about three miles north of Jingzhou. Recent excavations of a Chu grave site had unearthed 563 artifacts and the corpse of Mr. Sui, so well preserved the skin was still supple. The internal organs, on display beside the body, were intact, and all the body joints functioned perfectly. In addition to gorgeous lacquer objects, a stone ink tablet, and a jade seal, the tomb contained strips of writing, including a bamboo tablet with the message, "It is Gengchen date, May in Thirteenth Year. The Head of the Jiangling County is reverently reporting to Lord of the Underground, 'Sui, the Fifth Daifu in Shiyang, claims by himself that he is going to underground, accompanied with twenty-eight slaves such as Liang, eighteen servants such as Yi, two chariots, one ox chariot, four horses in one set, other two horses, and four riding horses.' You may order your men to register them. I reverently report it to you, Lord." Registering for the afterlife—it made sense to me. Fortunately, on this occasion the deceased had the decency to insist only on symbolic companions in the afterlife, contenting himself with beautifully carved wooden figurines, a model ceramic stove, and a ceramic house. His only recourse to realism was in the choice of socks and slippers, both of which showed signs of having been worn while he was still alive.

Although she was not keen to view the corpse of Mr. Sui, whose perfectly preserved genitals were discreetly covered by a white strip of cotton, Sunny Suyu shared my interest in the lacquer objects and a jade mask with stylized moustache that had been found on a female corpse in Tomb Number 2. She even blushed at the English version of the commentary—"Yet it is very intriguing that one can deduce a lot of imaginative stories from the male mask covering the female face"—which was about as close as Chinese officialdom ever came to hinting at androgyny or gender bending in the Middle Kingdom.

Sunny went off on a personal errand and I made my way by foot back to the hotel, promising to meet her at 3:00 p.m., when she would say good-bye and pass the baton (me) on to Liu-Jin. I purchased an airline ticket from Wuhan to Hong Kong for the next afternoon and cashed some traveler's checks so I could give her 500 yuan, about a hundred dollars. I knew this was a substantial sum in Chinese terms, as her monthly salary at the middle school was only 1,500 yuan; but it seemed quite modest for the help she'd given me, not to mention the spectacular dinner I had not been allowed to pay for. I put the five 100-yuan notes in a copy of one of my poetry books and, after many thanks and an extended farewell, gave her the envelope and suggested she not open it until she arrived home.

The young man at the National Religious Bureau was asleep in his chair when Liu-Jin, blue scarf flying, rapped on his door. He rallied quickly but could not muster much enthusiasm for our search for Huishen, whose name, yet again, drew a complete blank. He located in his book the poet Quyuan in connection with the date AD 299 and another literary type named Sung Yu, who figured prominently around AD 380, but there was a 220-

year gap before the next entry, which turned out to be a Daoist monk with the same surname, Hui Wei. I asked the young man if he was religious; he shook his head. As a member of the Communist Party, he was expected to be above mere superstition. To show he was not prejudiced, however, he decided to accompany us to the Daoist temple next door, now in private hands; and a dispute erupted at the entrance when he insisted we be admitted without charge. I don't know you, the doorkeeper said. Liu-Jin showed him my consular letter in Chinese. The man was not impressed. I offered money, but he could no longer accept it without losing face. Reluctantly, he stepped aside.

At the inner temple, a troubled caretaker in her mid-forties launched into a lament about her bad luck, which had begun with her son defaulting on a loan, having to withdraw from school, and abandoning his dream of becoming an interpreter. Through the charity of the temple, she had been given a job handling joss sticks, dusting the statues, all of which looked faintly bohemian, and putting the squeeze on visitors. Because I'd been too distracted by the abortive library search at Zhanghua Temple to think of burning joss sticks for Huishen, I decided he would not mind being remembered and celebrated among the Daoists. Three joss sticks and three loud rings of the gong earned the temple a ten-yuan donation, which went into the mournful mother's pocket rather than the collection box. I decided this exit fee was a fair exchange for our free admission.

Liu-Jin checked the time, then wiped her forehead with the tip of her blue silk scarf. As a teacher, she was not used to being out-foxed. When she marched me into the municipal File Office, introducing me and presenting both my case and my consular letter, it was already 5:15, time to lock the filing cabinets, dust off your coat, and prepare to make a dash for freedom. At least that's how most offices and all bureaucracies functioned at home. Mr. Jan He, however, was an exception to the rule. Despite the fidgeting of his junior colleagues, he was in no hurry. He opened a hefty gray volume and ran a thin index finger slowly down several pages of famous persons, stopping at a monk named Fazi, whose date (AD 580–636) placed him at the end of the Sui Dynasty and the beginning of the Tang. Fazi had mastered all the religious writings by age eight, was teaching at age twelve, and could outshine all his superiors in debate. He went on to write eight books, among them *Zhong Lun*, which concerned theories of harmony and balance. This was interesting information indeed, but going nowhere. Liu-Jin glanced at her watch again, then at me. Death certificates were not issued in ancient China, a practice that continues today; only births merit being recorded.

Jan He's finger, still scanning, stopped at another name; Hui Min—close, but not close enough.

We got up to leave. But Jan He was intrigued by this curious case. He had another hunch and asked us to wait for a few minutes, disappearing briefly upstairs. Liu-Jin fanned herself with a brochure from his desk. Jan He returned shaking his head—another dead end—but recommended that I contact the local File Office in Wuhan and the Buddhist Association in Beijing, writing both names out for me in elegant Chinese script on a piece of official paper.

I thanked Liu-Jin and made my way by taxi back to the hotel, to pack and prepare for an early-morning departure by bus to the airport in Wuhan. An hour later, there was a knock on my door. Sunny Suyu stood there with a plastic bag in one hand, clutching the tiny fingers of her two-year-old son with the other.

"In the book is too much money. I have bought small gifts— jade bracelets for your daughters and a traditional wall hanging for the wedding of the youngest. It's the symbol for harmony."

Sixteen

WITH THE PORT-BOW thruster engaged and tugboats at both ends, the container ship inched away from the dock in Kaohsiung. From the bridge it seemed, however implausibly, that the island of Taiwan had chosen to separate itself from this hulking tribute to marine technology by inching a few yards closer to mainland China. Built by Hyundai Heavy Industries in Korea to German specifications, MV *Pohang Senator* was a triumph of utility over aesthetics. At close to a 1,000 feet in length, 107 feet in width, with a height from keel to top of 187 feet, it was neither sleek nor elegant. With its 55,000 horsepower diesel engine vibrating in readiness and a nearly full capacity of two thousand 40-foot containers aboard, its closest modern relative would not be the sailing ship or even the coastal steamer, but rather that strange anomaly the aircraft carrier, which resembles a stretch of paved highway dropped diagonally atop a floating mountain. For better or for worse, the *Pohang Senator* would be my watery residence for the next two weeks, so it behooved me to look on the positive side, not making the mistake of imagining it unsinkable but nursing the illusion that all this bulk should at least make for a reasonably smooth ride.

"Poison?" Igor held up a coffee cup.

Now that we'd cleared the harbor and dropped the pilot, Third Mate Igor Bol'shakov was on watch. No samovars for Igor; this gangling Muscovite loved his coffee. I shook my head and continued copying down the ship's coordinates from the rectangular box at the right side of the radar screen. The bridge was quiet now, a few muffled voices coming in on the VHF from other ships, requesting information about pilots, anchorage, loading schedules. I'd brought my own GPS along, but it gave me incorrect readings; it was either kaput or unwilling to believe it was not still on the British Columbia coast at N 48.43, W 123.07, rather than in the South China Sea at N 27.04, E 122.29. I admit there were moments I had the same resistance to reality, having stayed in a flophouse in a slum high-rise called the Mirador on Nathan Road in Kowloon and now embarking on an excursion into that great absence known as the North Pacific.

The three other passengers on board were also drifting in and out of the bridge, watching our progress through the gap in the breakwater and out into the shipping lanes. Udo Tietz, from Karl-Marx-Stadt in Germany, had calmed down considerably since our first encounter in Hong Kong, where he learned that shore leave had suddenly been reduced from twenty-four hours to a measly three. Udo was a nurse who worked with neurological disorders. At that moment, he seemed in need of medication himself: "I shocked," he said, hanging his head. "Sorry, tomorrow I better." While Udo had boarded the ship in Hamburg, Jeanne and Bob Cox, from Oakland, California, were on the return portion of an epic voyage, not quite around the world, but done in eighty days, more or less, depending on wind, weather, port traffic, and the whims of the marketplace, as Hanjin Shipping, the charterer, could change the *Pohang Senator*'s itinerary at a moment's notice. They had traveled from Oakland to Hamburg via the Suez Canal and were now doing the return trip to Seattle. Jeanne was already an old hand on board, having gone through two cooks and two captains, digested all of the admiralty charts, kept track of every passing ship, and maintained her daily supply of homemade yogurt, thanks to a portable yogurt-maker, several dozen small amounts of skim-milk powder stowed in ziplock bags, and a healthy starter batch.

"How many pages?"

Igor made a small steering correction to accommodate another vessel that had the right-of-way. He was a gauntly attractive man who had the disconcerting habit of twisting his face into strange, vaguely demented shapes. When I did not answer promptly, he glanced up at me from his calculations, the light from the radar screen giving him a slightly green hue. I'd been crazy enough to bring along my laptop computer, carting it up and down ramps, gangways, and portages on the Yangtze and its tributaries, as well as lots of reading material to fill the hours at sea, but I realized now my biggest mistake was telling Igor I was working on a book.

"Lots of blank ones."

"Take poison. Like magic, you many pages write."

Udo Teitze was sunning himself at the fo'c'sle when I reached the halfway point of my afternoon circumnavigation of the ship, the only exercise available. Despite its size, the *Pohang Senator* rose and fell perceptibly in the ocean swell. Udo had melted into a deck chair he'd scrounged from the forward equipment locker. I could not tell whether he was sleeping or not.

"Ahoy, mate," I whispered. "Time to splice the main brace."

He smiled, though his eyes remained closed. I had a devil of a time trying to explain that this was a nautical expression used by sailors and pirates for cracking open the rum rations. I had asked Udo earlier what he thought about the possibility of ocean crossings in small boats, and he had been thinking about the subject.

"Gary, Gary, I cannot imagine this doing on a—how you say, raft? Even not a small boat."

I loved the way he spoke, especially the huge intake of air as he geared up to make himself understood in English. I sat on one of the bollards, bolstering the congregation of sun worshipers by a hundred percent.

One of the difficulties skeptics have had accepting the idea of pre-Columbian Asian contact with the Americas, according to anthropologist Paul Tolstoy, is visualizing how it might have happened. Little has been known in the West until recent years about Chinese nautical history, navigational skills, or shipbuilding capabilities. We have heard about watertight compartments, magnetic needles, and the sailing junk, which to the inexperienced Western eye, seems suitable enough for river and coastal traffic but a quite unlikely vessel for crossing the ocean. In addition there has been, as yet, no intact ancient Chinese wreck or ship burial found in Mexico, California, or British Columbia—no Asian equivalent of the Viking site at L'Anse aux Meadows in Newfoundland—to provide visual and material evidence for trans-Pacific Asian voyaging. On the other hand, there are countless articles and books dealing with isolated evidence of pre-Columbian voyages, such as coins, Chinese anchors made from millstones, Asian melanotic chickens, bark-beating and papermaking technologies, wheeled toys, and ceramic funereal figures on swings, not to mention icons, images, and concepts appearing in sculpture, murals, codices, and calendars that appear to owe something to Asian influences.

David Kelley, a noted scholar and professor emeritus from the University of Calgary who helped to decipher the Maya glyphs, has no trouble envisaging regular exchange between Asia and the Americas. When I interviewed him at his house in Calgary, he showed me an article he had prepared for publication that described an important early experience in his hometown of Coeymans, New York, on the Hudson River: "One morning, to the surprise and interest of most people in the town, a small Chinese junk tied up at the pier. The owner had sailed his boat from China and was picking up some money for supplies by selling admissions and postcards. It is my recollection that he had sailed part of the time alone and part of the time with a companion. The quarters, though tiny, seemed unimaginably luxurious and utterly foreign, in the poverty-ridden thirties." Kelley went on to study the Maya calendar, convinced that it had Eurasian roots or was invented by a Chuh Maya "who had acquired a broad knowledge of Eurasian calendars, astrology and astronomy." His PhD thesis at Harvard was equally controversial, arguing that Uto-Aztecans from Mexico had reached the South Pacific, influencing Polynesian language, mythology, and calendrics. David is a believer.

"Demonstration, at an impressionable age," he insisted, in connection with his youthful encounter with the Chinese junk, "is far more effective than any theory. The idea of the oceans as barriers has never, thereafter, seemed as important to me as the idea of the oceans as conveyor-belts."

Off the port bow, sunlight reflected off the myriad surfaces of this vast conveyor belt which, I hoped, would convey me safely home. A few small vessels could be seen in the distance, fishing boats returning to ports in the Sea of Japan. I recalled an exchange I'd read between two Europeans, anthropologist Robert Heine-Geldern and his friend Karl Mauss. The task, Mauss had suggested, was to show that the Pacific was nothing more than a Mediterranean Sea to Chinese and Asian navigators. Heine-Geldern took his friend's advice to heart on more than one occasion: "Those who believe the ancient peoples of Asia were incapable of crossing the ocean have completely lost sight of what the literary sources tell us concerning their ships and their navigation. . . . The influences of the Hindu-Buddhist culture of southeast Asia in Mexico, and particularly among the Maya, are incredibly strong, and they have already disturbed some Americanists who don't like to see them but cannot deny them."

But what kind of vessels would have been used? Sailing rafts made of giant bamboo are still in use after thousands of years, equipped with daggerboards and deckhouses and capable of carrying three persons and up to seven tons of cargo. They are virtually unsinkable and can be easily repaired at sea.

Tim Severin's expedition, described in *The China Voyage: Across the Pacific by Bamboo Raft,* was an attempt to replicate what might have been the Hsü Fu voyage of around 220 BC. Having brought China's warring factions into line and connected most pieces of the Great Wall, Qin Shi Huang, the first emperor of China, was on a roll. In order to prolong his life and his run of good fortune, he dispatched Hsü Fu to sail off in search of elixirs that would guarantee immortality, magic ingredients purported to exist among the eastern islands along with mountains of gold and caves of jade. The first trip produced no results, but Hsü Fu returned and cooked up a good story to suggest that progress had been made.

The following account appears in Joseph Needham's *Shorter History of Science and Civilisation in China*. It begins with the storyteller quoting Hsü Fu's words to the emperor:

In the midst of the ocean I met a great Mage who said to me, "Are you the envoy of the Emperor of the West?" to which I replied that I was. "What have you come for?" said he, and I answered that I sought for those drugs which lengthen life and promote longevity. "The offers of your Qin King," he said, "are but poor; you may see these drugs but you may not take them away." Then going south-east we came to Pheng-Lai, and I saw the gates of the Chih-Chheng palace. In front was a guardian of brazen hue and dragon form lighting the skies with his radiance. In this place I did obeisance to the Sea Mage twice, and asked him what offerings we should present to him. "Bring me young men," he said, "of good birth and breeding, together with apt virgins, and workmen of all trades: Then you will get your drugs."

The account ends with some droll remarks by the storyteller: "Qin Shihuang, very pleased, set three thousand young men and girls at Hsü Fu's disposal, gave him the seeds of the five grains, and artisans of every sort, after which he set sail. Hsü Fu found some calm fertile plain, with broad forests and rich marshes, where he made himself king—at least he never came back to China."

Though it's doubtful that Hsü Fu would have made his journey to the islands of Japan or beyond in bamboo rafts, especially given the armada he would have needed to transport three to four thousand people, Tim Severin's was a valuable and instructive expedition. He and his intrepid crew—fighting time, weather, human frailty, and ship-eating worms—had put the theory of a slow-moving raft-crossing to the test, coming within a thousand miles of the coast of California before having to abandon ship. Had they started from Tokyo rather than Vietnam, or chosen a coastal route, the bamboo raft might have survived the Pacific's wear and tear, as the structure of the craft was such that it absorbed and dispersed rather than resisted the action of the waves. What finished them in the end was the chafing of the bindings that held the bamboo poles together. In a somber moment, while convalescing from the breaking of three ribs, Severin mulls over the evidence for pre-Columbian Asian contact and the opposing arguments and comes to this conclusion: "I felt I had a foot in each camp. I could appreciate the doubts of the so-called isolationists who believe there had been no contact, and equally I was beginning to accept that trans-Pacific voyages were possible in the most ancient of vessels."

The junk, which so impressed David Kelley as a young man, is another story. According to anthropologist Gunnar Thompson, Chinese junks traveled as far afield as India, Indonesia, and Siberia long before the birth of Christ: "By the third century BC, shipyards had the capacity for building merchant vessels as long as eighty feet and weighing up to sixty tons." Naval historian Peter Caley concurs: "Although the Chinese junk may appear cumbersome and clumsy in its above-water lines, it was actually the safest and most efficient ship in the history of sail." A similar conclusion is reached in Robert Temple's *The Genius of China:* "Four-masted, oceangoing vessels were equipped with fore-and-aft lug sails by the second century AD," and such vessels "reportedly carried up to 700 people along with 260 tons of cargo." Chinese merchant vessels, with stern rudder, three masts, and fore and aft lug sails with battens, were considered much more seaworthy than the square-rigged European vessels, especially as they had a greater capacity to sail into the wind.

Udo had dozed off. I returned to my cabin to do the same. With evidence of Polynesians in New Zealand, Caucasian mummies in the Taklamakan Desert of China, and Vikings in Newfoundland, it's difficult to avoid the conclusion that where a journey, however distant and arduous, is shown to have been possible, the chances are that ancient peoples attempted it.

Along with his colleagues and coauthors Wang Ling, Lu Gwei-Djen, and Ho Ping-Yü, and others, the great Cambridge sinologist Joseph Needham has made an exhaustive study of nautical technology in the Middle Kingdom and discussed at length, in *Science and Civilisation in China*, not only the range and nature of smaller Chinese vessels, but also the floating fortresses and castled battleships that were instrumental in Yangtze River engagements and that helped bring about the overthrow of dynasties. As evidence, he lists bulkheads, watertight compartments, the vertical rudder post, the fenestrated rudder, leeboards and centerboards and, once again, the aerodynamically efficient mat-and-batten sails: "Such sails were never used in the West during the period of importance of the sailing-ship, but modern research has demonstrated their value, and present-day racing yachts have adopted important elements of Chinese rig, including battens for tautening the sails, and the system of multiple sheets." According to Jeremy Green, head of the Department of Maritime Archaeology at the Western Australia Maritime Museum in Fremantle, with whom I had corresponded, recent underwater explorations in Thailand, the Philippines, China, and Korea of wrecks dating from as early as AD 1270 indicate that Chinese oceangoing ships often employed three wooden beams at the base of the hull and that these pre-European "dragon spines" were indeed keels in the conventional sense. The evidence of Needham, Green, and many other scholars makes an impressive case for the stability and oceangoing potential of early Asian craft.

While I was preparing for this second leg of my journey in search of Huishen, I visited an exhibit at the Maritime Museum in Vancouver called "The Watery Kingdom," put together by the museum director and maritime archaeologist James Delgado. It was an instructive exhibit, quoting various ancient Chinese sources on the subject of ships and navigation. The king of Wu (514–496 BC), for example, talks of naval tactics, comparing the various ships available to the heavy and light chariots, battering rams, and light cavalry available to him on land. The Song Dynasty, which succeeded the Tang in AD 960, built up its navy to ward off invaders from the north. Within two hundred years, it boasted a navy of seven hundred vessels, some of them a hundred feet long, with catapults, incendiary devices, and trebuchets used to toss gunpowder bombs. I talked to Delgado about the abortive Mongol invasions of Japan in 1274 and 1281, and he grew quite excited, as he was slated to participate the following August in an underwater excavation with Japanese maritime archaeologists in the

Hakata/ Takashima area (not far from Nagasaki), where most of the three thousand or more invading ships of Kublai Khan, some of the biggest in the world at that time, were sunk at anchor in eighty feet of water during a freak storm in 1284.

Just prior to my departure, I heard on the radio that British historian and former submariner Gavin Menzies had completed research for a book on Chinese admiral Zheng He, a Muslim eunuch, whom he believed had been charged with the task of circumnavigating and mapping the world from AD 1421 to 1423, seven decades before Columbus. Zheng's travels were not exactly news to me. Louise Levathes had published a book about Zheng He a few years earlier, called *When China Ruled the Seas*. Delgado's exhibit also included a quotation from Emperor Zhu Di (AD 1409) that describes what would be the dynasty's nautical policy for the next twenty-odd years: "Of late we have dispatched missions to announce our Mandate to foreign nations and during their journeys over the oceans they have . . . escaped disaster and misfortune, journeying in safety to and fro." According to available Chinese records, this vast navy boasted 1,350 warships and smaller craft, 3,000 merchant ships, 400 grain-transport ships, and 250 "treasure ships," some of which were 440 feet long and 180 feet wide, half the length of the *Pohang Senator* but almost twice as wide. Zheng He's circumnavigation fleet consisted of about 106 vessels, including the flagship, the smallest being five times the length of Columbus's *Santa Maria*. These ships, many armed with guns, cannon, and incendiary rockets, were not quite so lucky with the weather, many of them sinking en route. In his lecture to the Royal Geographical Society in London on March 15, 2002, Menzies claimed that he knew the location of several Chinese wrecks in the Caribbean from this expedition but was withholding that information pending the publication of his book.

What was most interesting to me about Menzies' account was the question of maps. He had encountered a planisphere (a circular map of the world) in Venice, dated 1459, showing southern Africa and the Cape of Good Hope, which was not supposed to have been discovered until 1497, by Vasco da Gama. An unusual place name on the map, as well as notes suggesting a journey around the cape and a drawing of a Chinese junk, tripped a switch in Menzies' brain. Using the computer program Starry Night and his own knowledge of astronavigation, this former submariner worked out the route of Zheng He's fleets, which had used the bright star Canopus to help chart their course. Menzies was convinced that some of Zheng He's charts had been copied and smuggled back to Venice by the merchant Niccolò da Conti, who had accompanied Zheng He's fleet in India. These copies, Menzies argued, were subsequently incorporated into European *mappa mundi*, which explains why Cook, Magellan, and da Gama seemed to have been in possession of maps of the very places they were setting out to "discover."

The Chinese were not always inward-looking. Like the Arabs and Phoenicians, two other great navigators of the ancient world, they were curious, daring, and well informed about ships and the sea. However, thanks to court politics, we do not know the full extent of their travels. What is known is that a group of xenophobic mandarins, not only jealous of the power of the court eunuchs, but also anti-maritime in sentiment, encouraged the next two emperors, Hongxi (1425) and Xuande (1426–1435), to abandon these costly and sometimes ill-fated expeditions, to drastically reduce Zheng He's fleet, and to destroy many of the maritime records and charts. Remaining historical accounts of the period do not mention a 1421 voyage to Europe or the Americas. However, I thought, if Menzies manages to locate and positively identify the wrecks of ancient Chinese vessels in the Caribbean, he could well provide the kind of physical evidence demanded by archaeologists who have hitherto dismissed the possibility of pre-Columbian Asian contact with the Americas.

Making the same journey by container ship was not exactly romantic, but it had its advantages. At twenty-two knots and in ideal weather conditions, the journey would take less than three weeks, and that included stops in Taiwan and Korea. At dinner the second evening, in the Officers' Mess on A-deck, I tried to explain my project to Bob and Jeanne, who were working their way through servings of boiled potatoes, frozen peas, and turkey in beef gravy, washing it down with copious quantities of weak tea. Given the prevailing winds and currents, I said, it seemed inevitable that Asian mariners would have made it to the American continent, even by accident. If you lost your rudder or sail, you could end up in the Queen Charlotte Islands, Oregon, California, or Ecuador. I also mentioned, by way of example, that in the coastal city of Prince Rupert, overlooking the harbor, there is, on public display, a thirty-foot Japanese fishing boat called the *Kazu Maru*. It had drifted from Owase, Japan, all the way to the Charlottes, where it was found overturned near the rocks of Skidegate Inlet by a patrol vessel of the Department of Fisheries and Oceans. The *Kazu Maru*, lost September 25, 1985, was found in March 1987 and brought to

Prince Rupert, where it was restored and placed on exhibit. The body of its owner, retired civil servant Kazukio Sakamoto, was never recovered. In an ironic twist, Prince Rupert and Owase had become sister cities twenty-five years earlier, not only giving substance to the Confucian adage "Men within four seas are brothers," but also confirming the exceptional delivery skills of Japan's Kuroshio Current.

Drift stories, as Bob and Jeanne knew, abound in British Columbia, the Pacific Northwest, and California, from the glass fishing floats we all picked up on the beach as kids to legends and newspaper accounts of Chinese and Japanese vessels found drifting off Vancouver Island with either no survivors or a few who had resorted to cannibalism. The Makah people near Cape Flattery, at the entrance to Juan de Fuca Strait, rescued Japanese survivors of one of these wrecked drifters late in the nineteenth century and held them as slaves until the Hudson's Bay Company intervened to repatriate the unwitting migrants.

The reputation of the Kuroshio Current for faithfully depositing Asian people and objects on our shores is celebrated even in children's books, such as the recent *Ducky*. This brief, illustrated book, based on a real incident, is the story of a rubber ducky, one of 29,000 toys originating in Hong Kong, set adrift when a container bound for Tacoma, Washington, was washed overboard in a storm. Some of Ducky's companions were to end up in the Arctic; others would wash up here and there on the West Coast from Alaska to California. The good news is that Ducky eventually gets to exchange the uncertainties and terrors of the big, shark-infested ocean for the soapy refuge of a bathtub, which it shares with the young boy who found it washed up on the beach in Washington. *Ducky* is a charming, if innocuous, little book, but of some value from an educational point of view because it reminds us of how cultural exchange can take place, even by accident. If people, rubber ducks, and glass fishing floats can be transported thousands of miles by accident, why can't pottery, art, weapons, food products, tools, agricultural methods, architectural designs, religion, and ideas be transported these same distances intentionally?

When I returned from Afghanistan, Pakistan, and China, a friend showed me two interesting articles in *The Smithsonian.* One described a scientist who studied "floatables" in the North Pacific, tracking their distribution by ocean currents. The other proposed that most early migrations to North America were conducted by sea rather than by land, as there is now considerable doubt that the Ice-Free Corridor east of the Rockies was habitable, that it contained sufficient animal and plant life to sustain humans, even in transit. As I explained rather clumsily to Bob and Jeanne while the dessert was served, there has also been a dearth of archaeological evidence in northern regions to substantiate such a transit along this corridor. Both of these articles indicated a shift in thinking about marine links between the two continents. Coastal migration was beginning to seem a more and more plausible explanation for the peopling of the Americas.

"Mahlzeit!" The chief officer, Mr. Braüer, clutching a salad and a glass of orange juice, took his place at the next table with the captain and chief engineer. Everyone repeated his greeting.

Jeanne, her meal finished, was pouring some of her powdered skim milk into a glass. Bob replenished his tea and mine from a large white plastic container on the table. Udo, who always arrived late for meals, was just tucking into his main course by the time I'd wolfed down my dessert. Jeanne smiled as I finished my Huishen saga. She had her own story to tell about currents and inflatables. On the first leg of their journey on the *Pohang Senator,* the Puget Sound pilot learned there were Americans aboard and asked if they would do him a favor. His mother had passed away the previous year, and the family wanted to do something special in her memory for the anniversary of her death. He arrived the next morning, when the ship was leaving port in Seattle, with a dozen empty wine bottles, each corked and containing a message, a photograph, and something that a member of the family had chosen as a way of remembering the deceased, who had always wanted to travel. In addition to the mementos, each bottle included a note and telephone number. Bob and Jeanne had agreed to drop one of these containers, which the Germans called "bottle mail," overboard in each of the oceans or major bodies of water they crossed. With as much ceremony as possible, and with the blessing of the ship's captain and crew, they tossed their floatables overboard one-by-one into the North Pacific Ocean, the Bering Sea, the Sea of Okhotsk, the Sea of Japan, the South China Sea, the Indian Ocean, the Bay of Bengal, the Red Sea, the Mediterranean, the Atlantic, the English Channel, and the North Sea.

I told Jeanne, who claimed to be a teetotaller for health reasons, that I thought this story an ingenious, if convoluted, way of covering up a nasty drinking habit.

SEVENTEEN

THE PITCH AND ROLL of the *Pohang Senator* in a following sea swell while seldom reaching beyond ten degrees from the perpendicular, were sufficient to keep me from sleeping soundly for several days. When I'd jammed enough blankets and pillows around my body to keep from rolling off the bed or crashing into the wall, there were still those strange, corrosive sounds in the night (and day) to disrupt the sleeping mechanism. If I took a leisurely walk forward during the morning or afternoon, the grating sounds of metal on metal from the shifting containers produced such symphonic variety that I would stop to see if I could identify the instrument or what part of the floating orchestra the sound was coming from. A hellish growling noise from the bowels of the ship would be followed by the bellow of the last surviving mammoth or the high-pitched squeal of a pig about to be slaughtered. At least when I reached the bow, I could surrender myself to a well-earned tranquillity, and there, if I managed to resist the temptation to fling myself overboard, wind and water would soothe the fevered psyche. Not so amidships, where metal doth murder sleep.

In daytime, I could distract myself with the porthole drama of an unduly visible ocean disappearing completely while a deluge of menacing gray sky poured into the torture chamber. Night offered no such distraction. When I was not being flung onto the floor or dashed against the wall or the sharp corners

of the bedroom furniture, my ragged and rattled consciousness would be raked by the shriek of grinding metal, like
fingernails across a chalkboard or a shovel scraping snow from
a concrete driveway. Then there were the rattles: Get up, lift
the stopper chain on the sink, add a bit of water. Back to bed.
Get up, close the cupboard door. Bed. Up again to jam paper or
dirty clothes under one corner of the creaking coffee table.
Damn, the toilet seat cover should be down. And so it went,
transforming my body from bruised banana to mush, from
wheat to porridge, from steak to ground beef—and I had
thought the perverse Buddhist imagination had concocted
every possible punishment for that ghastly inferno they
called the "suffer place."

Never missing an opportune moment, Huishen was delivered
of yet another enigmatic, if nocturnal, emission, which surprised
me not only with its martial imagery and prophetic aspect, but
also with the leap that seemed to have been taken from China to
the Americas. Was Huishen stoned?

*Armored dragons. Machines of war I'd not imagined, visions
put to sleep with legendary Yu. The innocuous shaman, with
his spurs and amulets, his sack of potions. Animate rocks,
trees that protested human usage. I was not immune to his
magic. Mushrooms, tiny buttons pricking from earth black-
ened the sky with their obscene desires. Flight, conflagra-
tion, creatures entering and rising from the surface of the
lake, the mirrored crater. Residue dissolving on the tongue,
a bitter aftertaste. A noose of silk, another world I did not
wish to know or enter.*

Other than noise, movement, and such disturbing nightly visitations, the *Pohang Senator* was a treat. The cabin was spacious and well appointed, with radio, television, VCR, couch, bedroom, bathroom, and a desk equipped with no-slip rubber matting, much more comfortable and attractive, in fact, than any of the hotel rooms I'd rented in Asia. I found a washer and a dryer down the corridor, plus a lounge with library and video selections, most of which were in German, though there was one erotic delight called *Voyage to Thailand* that consisted of two attractive young Asian women masturbating each other for forty minutes, sometimes with the use of a rubber dildo that could be strapped on like a gun and holster. I don't recall there being any comprehensible words on the soundtrack of that film; it was thereafter constantly in use, so I could not check. I mentioned the infernal rolling of the ship to Igor on the bridge as I scanned the horizon in vain for whales or passing traffic. Be grateful, he said; smaller ships are much worse—they roll every twelve seconds and more than twenty degrees from the perpendicular.

I am grateful, I thought, replacing the binoculars. I could have been on a Chinese junk or a bamboo raft for five times as long, with no contemporary navigational equipment, no refrigeration, no laundry, no detailed charts, sharing a floor covered with damp matting and, when they're not praying, four snoring, grumbling, farting companions. Weather aside, running out of food and water would be the major concern on a small boat, though fishing was always an option. By comparison, I was living in a luxurious cocoon. Alas, this large-ship consolation is not shared by experts such as anthropologist Stephen Jett, who argues that a vessel's "seaworthiness is not proportionate to size; on the contrary, the larger the size the greater the stresses set up by wind and wave as they encounter the inertia of the heavy craft and thus the greater the possibility of breaking up. A fairly small craft, if well constructed, is more likely to survive a long sea voyage, especially if it is of flexible construction, as are lashed-log rafts and seven-plank boats."

This sounded plausible enough, though I doubted I would ever opt for a small boat in a storm-bound Pacific. What it did suggest was that Huishen and his compatriots probably had a better chance of making it safely to the west coast of North America than I did. Jett concurs with C. R. Edwards that mainland-to-mainland crossing is no great challenge and repeats the much-quoted comment of Pedro de Quiros (1597) that even "the most stupid can go in their embarcations . . . to seek a large country—since if they do not hit one part they will hit another." Jett attributes much of the resistance to the idea of pre-Columbian Asian contact to nautical ignorance, even thalassophobia, a morbid fear of the sea: "There is a tendency for non-seafaring, machine-dependent, deadline-dominated scholars to over-estimate the dangers of transoceanic voyaging, particularly raft voyaging, and to underestimate the willingness of many poor or primitive peoples, especially desperate ones, to take the time and risks that would be involved in transoceanic voyaging." Huishen, voluntarily poor, was no primitive, but he may, given political instability and shifting religious allegiances, have been as keen to leave China as he was to spread the Buddhist message.

Before heading back to China, I made a brief trip to New York. The previous year I had written to the American Museum of

Natural History in New York, where there is an excellent collection of artifacts from Mexico and Central America, to inquire as to the whereabouts of Gordon Ekholm, a proponent of pre-Columbian Asian influence in the Americas. Ekholm, alas, had died, but my letter was passed on to a Dr. Spencer, who instructed his scientific assistant, Christina M. Elson, to reply. "Dr. Spencer asked me to respond to your inquiry dated March 9, 2001. The consensus among anthropologists and archaeologists working in Mexico and Central America is that there is no body of evidence supporting pre-Columbian contacts between Mexico and Asia. Most objects suggested as evidence for such contacts either have been found to be fakes or have been misdated or can easily be explained within the cultural context of native society."

Ms. Elson, speaking on behalf of Dr. Spencer, the museum, and presumably the whole camp of funding-conscious academics, wanted nothing to do with such heresies. "The American Museum of Natural History," she concluded, "believes that pre-Columbian society and all its wonderful achievements is [*sic*] an indigenous development and cannot be explained through a model purporting the influence of Asians over indigenous people." How, I wondered, had Ekholm, with his doctorate from Harvard and in his position as curator of Mexican archaeology, managed to function in such a closed environment? He considered the question of pre-Columbian Asian contact to be "one of the most challenging and important problems of American archaeology," but his colleagues or successors apparently did not consider it at all. Ekholm was well aware of the strong opposition to his views. He attributed this resistance not only to the amount of rubbish being perpetrated by the "lunatic fringe," who insist that every idea and invention must have come from abroad, but also to the "archaeocentrism" (thinking their own patch of study is the world) that sometimes accompanies the slow and hard-won efforts of digging for proof.

Writing in 1964, Ekholm admitted to having accepted the "diffusionist" label and went on to argue the case for moderate Asiatic influence in the Americas, offering the example of wheeled toys found at sites in Huasteca and Tres Zapotes in Mexico, items he had initially considered an invention of the Americas. Not so much toys as funeral objects, these artifacts closely resemble the miniature wheeled animals so often used ceremonially in China, India, and Japan. In the Americas, their presence is sufficiently rare as to suggest foreign influence. While admitting that the diffusionist position is "exploratory and tentative and that no very solid body of evidence, and none incontrovertible, has as yet been discovered," Ekholm included in his list things that "excite [his] suspicion" and encourage an open mind about possible influences, such items and technologies as pottery-making, clay stamps or seals, iron pyrite mirrors, and bark cloth-making. However, he also included a list of cultural items and traits that must be attributed exclusively to indigenous invention.

My kinship with the departed Ekholm took me to New York, where I hoped to examine some of these artifacts and see whether his influence could still be felt anywhere in the American Museum of Natural History. Along with Betty Meggers, Clifford Evans, and Emilio Estrada, he had gone out on a limb in arguing for a major wave of Chinese influence, that of the Shang Dynasty (sixteenth to eleventh century BC), which he considered the most likely cultural source for the Olmec tripod pottery, jade-working, and fresco techniques. By the time I reached the glass cabinet I was looking for, somewhere in the maze of Mexican and Central and South American exhibits, I was so impressed with the variety and vibrancy of the art, I wondered how the possibility of a few Asian influences could be perceived as posing any sort of insult or threat to the reputation of indigenous peoples and their culture. Behind the glass were a few dozen artifacts from a site at Veracruz, Mexico, pottery figures whose faces looked decidedly Asian. Nearby were several wheeled toys and two tiny pottery figures on swings, with the briefest note suggesting possible Asian influence. These swingers, which had been found only in Olmec sites, were quite common burial objects in China, India, and Southeast Asia. I could hear the ghost of Gordon Ekholm chuckle.

Before flying home, I spent Sunday morning in downtown Manhattan at Ground Zero, reading memorials, looking at the photographs of victims, and eavesdropping on conversations. A young woman was talking compulsively about her brother, who'd been working several floors above where the first plane hit. I could not help thinking of the terrible innocence of wheeled toys.

All quiet on the bridge. The Tuvalese helmsman, Palili, a large man with a ponytail, stood motionless at the helm, his thick hands resting on the tiniest of steering wheels, which looked as if it had been designed for a child's toy car rather than a vessel a fifth of a mile in length. His eye was alert to lights on the horizon, though the likelihood of any showing up was slim. The *Pohang Senator* ploughed on alone through the black night and the even blacker waters of the North Pacific. The course was 077, the SOG (speed over the ground) 22.7 knots, the coordinates N41°24" E161°32", heading toward Japan and then on to the International Date Line. The controls were set on automatic pilot, small corrections being made constantly to account for the effects of wind and current. Nothing showed up on the radar except for an arcing brushstroke of light around the ship's position, indicating modest wave action. Behind a curtain, drawn so his desk lamp would not reflect on the windows of the bridge, Igor bent over the chart table, plotting our present course and position in pencil.

"Poison? Pages?" He looked up at me, elbows on the chart table, one hand on the parallel rule, triangle, and calipers, and twisted his rubbery face into a gargoyle smile.

I made a pun about poison pens, which took too long to explain. A thin strip containing the latest meteorological reports began to scroll off a small machine. It reported a low-pressure front building in Alaska and confirmed an earlier warning about a hurricane at N17° that was heading toward the coast of California. Advice from the ship's agent earlier in the day had been to take a more southerly route away from the Aleutians, which I'd been hoping to see as that seemed to me the most likely route taken by Huishen and his religious accomplices. The great circle route would take us to N51°, a few hundred miles west of the Queen Charlotte Islands, at which point we would begin a southeasterly course down the west coast of Vancouver Island toward the Juan de Fuca Strait.

"No poison, no pages." Igor was determined to lubricate my muse.

"Why not, I can't sleep anyway."

His watch duty on the bridge would be over at midnight, so Igor relieved the helmsman and asked him to make his rounds of the ship. I asked about his seamanship training, and he launched into a story about a pig, pausing to refill his cup from the coffeemaker. The terrified pig had been loose on the deck of a coastal training ship on the north coast of Russia, near Arkangel, hiding under the ropes, tarpaulins, and lifeboats. Igor would sometimes hear it grunt in the shadows behind him as he leaned against the gunwale. It had mastered stairs and, if sufficiently frightened, would even try climbing a ladder. Otherwise, it would make lightning forays into the open when it thought no one was looking.

"The peeg always theenk to stole something."

As part of its mission, Igor's training ship had been responsible for supplying remote lighthouses. This involved sporadic visits to deliver goods and people, including the middle-aged couple returning with the pig and a goat from a one-month holiday. At each port, the husband would get drunk and fail to return to the ship, so the wife and crew would have to locate him and carry him back. He could not face another two-year stretch of imposed solitude.

"You brave man go to Afghanistan."

I could not see where Igor was heading with this comment and wanted to hear the rest of the story about the pig. "Not brave, just crazy."

"My friend, good consciousness, very kind boy. After three years fighting in Afghanistan, Red Star Medal, come home crazy. No good consciousness now; only money, vodka, women." His was Russia's version of Vietnam, with identical casualties, physical and emotional. Maritime training had saved Igor from the army and from Afghanistan.

"What happened to the pig?"

"One day peeg run across deck, jump overboard." Crazed by hunger and fear, the pig was more successful than the lighthouse keeper in avoiding his destiny.

I returned to my cabin on E-deck, more awake than ever, and began to read Elaine Dewar's *Bones: Discovery of the First Americans*, a fat tome I'd brought along with just such an occasion in mind. It was more than marginally connected with my own research, as its subject is the peopling of the Americas. Until recently, most of us believed that all native peoples originated in Asia and had crossed over the Bering land bridge toward the end of the last ice age. They are often drawn fur-clad, spear in hand, pursuing hairy mammoths along the corridor that lay between the two great ice sheets east of the Rockies, and gradually dispersing south. Dewar challenges this view. My own reading and talks with maritime archaeologists had already led me to the conclusion that coastal migration was a more likely means of intercontinental travel. Because sea levels during the period of glaciation had been 50 to 150 meters lower than they are today, more land would have been visible and island-hopping considerably easier.

Daryl Fedje and fellow archaeologists, using a shipboard dredging scoop and sonar to map the ocean floor, had recently retrieved a stone artifact from what appeared to be an earlier coastline settlement some distance off the Queen Charlotte Islands in 50 meters of water. From what I'd learned about early rafts and ship technology, a watery voyage to the Americas seemed quite feasible, especially as there would have been abundant food available in local waters. What I was not prepared for was Dewar's suggestion, based on recent archaeological discoveries and more sophisticated analysis of ancient bones, that the Americas may have been initially peopled 25,000 to 50,000 years ago from the south and not by Asians or Mongolians.

According to mitochondrial DNA, or Y-chromosome analysis, ancient bones were showing up that were not characteristically Asian and that did not share the usual lineages. Ancient bones in Brazil were more likely to display an X-factor, which was present in African, European, and Austronesian DNA. Besides, Asian and African parasites, which could not have survived in cold northern climates, were evident in coprolites—fossilized feces—found in South America. The old foundations were shaking, but the establishment scholars, concerned for appearances and reputations, were digging in. In Dewar's view, "they simply refused to shake loose the last constraints of an intellectual prison. Their Bering Strait theory did not provide a useful framework, or narrative, to explain the human remains found in the ground. Yet they held on to it the way old prisoners find ways to stay in detention. . . . It was hard enough to stand up in public and declare that the oldest human remains in the Americas were not Mongoloid, were in fact closer in shape to recent Australians and ancient Africans than to modern Native Americans. So they clung to the rest of the theory as if their lives depended on it."

I turned off the reading lamp and crawled into my firm, narrow, and appropriately monkish bed. No ship movement tonight, only the steady vibrations of the diesel engine that turned the two huge screws driving us through the Sea of Japan.

Territoriality: Academia was not too different from politics, after all. Vested interests, old boys' networks, the closing of ranks. I had spoken with enough scholars to know that the subject of pre-Columbian Asian contact with the Americas was anathema, verboten. One of my correspondents, who insisted on remaining anonymous, did a master's thesis comparing Asian and Maya iconography, but her advisers warned that pursuing those interests for the doctorate would be suicidal: no jobs, negative peer assessment on grant applications, pariah status.

"I made a 180-degree turn," she confessed. "Maybe when I'm old and tenured and don't give a damn, I'll have another look."

David Kelley was my ace in the hole and proof that not all scholars behave like despots, drug lords, or tribal chiefs. He told me his old professor Carleton Coon at Harvard used to say, "When different groups meet they often fight, but they always breed." They also, it seems, leave behind different systems of belief, seeds of spiritual dissent. David's friend and fellow archaeologist Michael Coe, responding to a paper given at a Dumbarton Oaks conference in 1976, thought Asian visitors to the Americas had done the same: "I am really convinced that this idea or group of ideas came across the Pacific. I would be amazed if Chinese geomancy hadn't gotten into the New World, along with very complex ideas . . . So, I think that we ought to look at this mirror, on the grounds that so much additional evidence argues in favor of trans-Pacific diffusion, perhaps about the time of Christ, perhaps around the time of the founding of Teotihuacán."

In the corridor, I could hear the Russian second mates

returning from their lounge, talking loudly. Jobs well done, they could rest soundly now in the belly of the beast. They paused for a moment outside my door. There was a burst of laughter then all was quiet on the *Pohang Senator*, save the agonized metal containers carrying God knows what rewards for all our labors.

Eighteen

THE CHINESE HAVE a lot of words for *cape* or *point*, including *chia, chiao, chueh,* and *tou,* but the *Admiralty Pilot* booklets indicated that the Koreans outstrip them by a league or two. As we left our berth in Pusan and assumed a northeast course of 054, I counted at least ten Korean words for *cape* in the *Admiralty Pilot—ap, bi, dong, dan, du, gab, mal, gag, gi,* and *god*—a sure sign of Korea's seafaring heritage. With *god* thrown in, for good measure or bad, I was reminded of the taxi driver who had brought me back to the pier from my day's outing in the seaport. He was a spiffy dresser, decked out in freshly laundered powder-blue shirt and tailored pin-striped vest.

"I know English," he said, "just small."

I was pleased that he was taking the longer coastal route from the fish market to the Hanjin container terminal in the next bay rather than using the tunnels. He wanted to know my country of origin. When I told him, he launched into a hymn to Canada, the United States, and Jesus Christ, declaring he loved them all and confirming reports I'd read that this Buddhist country was now 30 percent Christian, the numbers no doubt a legacy of the Korean War and the overwhelming presence of U. S. forces.

Pusan had grown haphazardly, in response to the dictates of war and trade. I'd spent the previous evening drinking beer at a small bar on the infamous Texas Street, once a dangerous red-light district but now a rather benign tourist area where merchants are more active than sex-trade workers in plying their wares. Udo and I had decided to tag along with the Russian and Tuvalese crew members, who were itching to take advantage of an all-too-brief shore leave. Igor Falev, the cook, known as Galiz, decked out in a black leather vest, checkered bandana, earring, and dark beard, looked quite fierce. I was glad to have him on my side. Suslonov, the second mate, was heavy-set and sported two gold teeth that I imagined to be connected with a fight. I did not know what to expect from these Pirates of *Pohang*—brawls, blatant whoring, you name it—but I was hoping they would not get me into trouble.

First stop, the money changers, where an American dollar could be exchanged for approximately one thousand Korean *won*. Galiz shouted to a woman and disappeared with her into a doorway some distance down the street. I was surprised, because he had changed only a paltry ten dollars. Even then, I could hear his voice dickering over the price in English. I should have turned around, but my curiosity got the better of me. I slunk down the street and peeked around the doorway, fully expecting to see some sort of erotic quick fix. Galiz was speaking loudly and waving some sort of implement in the air. Light reflected off its sharp edges. Oh my God, I thought, a knife. However, he was dickering with the woman over the price of her carrot peelers. Eventually he emerged into the street with a huge smile and a new carrot peeler and a garlic crusher that he'd purchased for a dollar apiece. He dropped his prizes into my bookbag for safekeeping, then disappeared again to phone his girlfriend in Russia.

The area we walked through should have been called Little Russia rather than Texas Street, as most of the women and many of the merchants were either Russian or spoke the language fluently. Fish and vegetable stalls were closing down, but buckets of water still boiled with live eels. One of the merchants saw me peering into a large vat containing something that looked deceptively like chocolate custard. She gave me a toothless grin and indicated I could have the whole shebang for 30,000 *won*. Suslonov and Galiz commandeered a table in the middle of the street and ordered beer.

"Only Chekhov stand next Shakespeare." The cook did not share my enthusiasm for Dostoevsky and Yevtushenko. As light faded from the sky over Pusan, giving Texas Street an unearned intimacy, the conversation shifted to Russian politics. Galiz wondered who was responsible for installing Putin in the Kremlin. Suslonov raised his hand like the pope, index finger pointing skyward.

"I confess, it was me," he confided, taking a small mickey of vodka and four ceramic shot glasses out of his rucksack. "This top secret. I KGB agent, don't tell nobody." His remark was all the funnier since the hostess of this sidewalk bar refused to believe he was Russian and kept insisting he was Dutch or Polish. We offered a silent toast to his secret mission, another to his disguised nationality. Eventually I'd had enough beer and vodka to tell them Igor Bol'shakov's anecdote about the prostitute in the Canary Islands who could not understand her client's sexual ineptitude.

"Are you impotent?" she asked, stroking his knee.

"No."

"Are you gay?" Her hand moved up his thigh.

"No."

She stood up and grabbed her clothes from the bedside table. At the door, she turned and spat. "So, you're Russian."

The first officer, Mr. Braüer, was on the bridge. Our course toward Japan's Tsugaru Kaikyo was 054, SOG 21.7 knots. Mr. Braüer had his master's ticket as well, which was company policy in case anything happened to the captain. He had skippered a number of smaller vessels in the Great Lakes and through British Columbia's Inside Passage, transporting lumber from Nanaimo and Kitimat and grain from Prince Rupert to Korea. He lived forty miles from Lübeck in Schleswig-Holstein, equidistant from Hamburg and Kiel. I asked him if he liked the life at sea, the long separations from family.

Perched in front of several monitors, on what resembled a sliding dentist's chair, he looked like *Star Trek*'s Jean Luc Picard, except for the starched shirt and moustache. "In German we say, 'Only fools go to sea, and the real fools go in winter.'"

He told me he had been on a small freighter twenty years earlier, off the Japanese island of Etorofu-to, when he heard a loud noise and felt a jolt to the ship, as if it had struck a rock or been torpedoed. All the officers and crew had felt it too, but the usual safety checks and tests could find no problem. Later, on the radio, he learned that the ship had been directly above the epicenter of an earthquake that caused a tsunami, a tidal wave of such proportions that it killed 120 villagers on Etorofu-to.

"At moments like that," the first officer said, "we consider ourselves lucky and pity the poor fools on shore." Mr. Braüer would retire soon. He wanted to travel in North America and figured he'd need six months to do it properly. He made a slight correction at the helm in response to a strong current trying to pull the ship off course. I heard him later patiently explaining to Bob and Jeanne how the Japanese had invented large perforated steel buffers and installed them on the beaches, allowing some of the force of a tsunami through, thereby reducing damage significantly. Solid-wall technology would have crumbled under the assault. The same principle had applied to Tim Severin's bamboo raft.

Japan was part of the story I was pursuing, though there was no way of knowing what stops Huishen might have made in Japan en route to the Americas. With Hokkaido on the port side and Honshu on the starboard, I did not need the *Kazu Maru*, the fishing boat belonging to Kazukio Sakamoto, to remind me that, except for Russia, Japan was the Asian nation closest to the Americas and the most likely to have made contact, accidentally or otherwise. In fact, pottery had been found in Valdivia, Ecuador, that bore a strong resemblance to Japanese Jomon pottery dating back at least five thousand years. Betty Meggers, of the Smithsonian Institution in Washington, D.C., went to Ecuador in 1954, where she examined the decorative elements of the Valdivia pottery for which there were no local antecedents, including rocker stamping, cord and fingernail impressions, zigzag incisions, and crosshatching. Along with her husband, Clifford Evans; and Emilio Estrada, the archaeologist who initiated these discoveries; she suggested that a small group of Japanese, rudderless or dismasted, had been swept east by the Kuroshio Current, surviving the elements to establish a settlement upriver from the coast of Ecuador.

Despite objections to her methodology and denials of the feasibility of such a crossing, Meggers's hypothesis still stands as a major contribution to transoceanic theory. In response to skeptics, she takes pleasure in describing the successful voyage of the *Yasei-go III*, a double canoe equipped with only sails, rudder, and centerboard, which left Tokyo for San Francisco on May 8, 1980, traveling 4,842 miles and arriving at its destination fifty-one days later, on June 28. Propelled by wind alone, the *Yasei-go III* proved that Pacific crossings can be made by the simplest of crafts and in a relatively short time. The vessel even survived two hurricanes on the second leg of the journey from San Francisco to Acapulco and Ecuador.

When I asked Meggers how she had managed to continue her research in a hostile environment that had silenced so many scholars, she laughed: "I was lucky. Fortunately, the Smithsonian did not pay a lot of attention to what I was doing." Another scholar interested in the Japanese connection, Nancy Yaw Davis, had not been so lucky. She was discouraged from pursuing her interest in trans-Pacific theory and not welcomed into academia after completing a doctorate, not even in remote Alaska, where a person of her talents and credentials ought to have been in demand. However, Nancy was a fighter. What began as an interest in comparing Japanese mythology with that of the Zuni peoples in New Mexico burgeoned into a full-scale scholarly book called *The Zuni Enigma: A Native American People's Possible Japanese*

Connection (2000). If the word *possible* in the subtitle is an unfortunate reminder of the pressure independent scholars feel to proceed cautiously in a hostile academic environment, Davis does not pull any punches in her groundbreaking book. She discovered not only that the Zuni people share a rare kidney disease (mesangiopathic glomerulonephritis, a deadly form of renal failure) with the people of Kyushu, Japan, but also that, around AD 1350, their graves contained something remarkable: two distinct skeletal types. Along with a variety of other traits that make the Zuni different from other Native American peoples in terms of language, culture, and biology, these discoveries convinced Davis that "a group of Japanese reached the west coast of North America and migrated eastward in search of the middle of the world" and that they had merged and intermarried with the Zuni people.

The earthquakes and tsunamis Mr. Braüer had been discussing on the bridge are a constant in Japanese history and are deeply ingrained in the Japanese psyche. It did not take much imagination to see how a people might be pushed to such extremes by the forces of nature that they were willing, or forced, to emigrate in considerable numbers, searching for land that would not shake and oceans that would not rise up to swallow them.

There was much talk on the ship about the China Air flight from Hong Kong to Taiwan, full of kids returning to school, that had plunged into the sea days earlier not far off the route we had just taken from Kaohsiung to Pusan. Two hundred and six passengers and nineteen crew members had perished,

leaving nothing but a faint brushstroke of fuel on the enigmatic face of the South China Sea. The ocean was no
respecter of persons or of means of transportation, its calm as
deceptive as its storms; and the waters off Vancouver Island
were littered with wrecks. It was taking me less than three
weeks to make the crossing from China to Vancouver, a trip
that would have taken Huishen two or three months, perhaps
longer. If you're in it for the long haul, there's no rush; you
might as well take your time, visit the locals, spread the word.
I was prepared to believe that Huishen took the coastal route,
by junk or bamboo sailing raft, but I was still nervous about
my own safety, even in a commercial monstrosity with high-
tech navigational equipment.

Off our port bow was an Evergreen container vessel called
Hatsu Eagle, registered in London. It had obviously made the
passage. We had just overtaken, on our starboard quarter, the
Crane Ocean and were coming up fast on a large bulk carrier
called *Mozo Arrow*. With all this floating evidence for successful ocean crossing, I still needed more convincing by the
experts.

According to one of them, Clinton Edwards, "The mainland
to mainland crossing of the Pacific imposes no navigational
difficulties: the target is huge, and the only requirement is to
be able to sail consistently in a general easterly or westerly
direction, avoiding shipwreck or unknown islands." He does
not say how this "avoiding" might be achieved. "Another
very significant factor is speed. Aside from the possibility
that a storm might incapacitate a vessel, the greatest enemy
in long distance voyaging is time." After a while, you run out
of food and fresh water and, presumably, hope. Well, that's

reassuring, I thought—if the freezer is full and the electrical system and water distiller keep working, there's not a thing to worry about except storm, shipwreck, and *anjiao,* sunken rocks. Looking at a map of the entire North Pacific, the barriers to arrival, never mind brotherhood, still loomed substantial.

Udo, who had been down in the mouth all the way from Hong Kong to Kaohsiung, rallied during the next week. Kaohsiung and Pusan provided escape from the ship and restored his spirits. He continued taking the sun daily on the fo'c'sle, his padded deck chair nestled in among the bollards and hawspipes. He binged on fresh air and, when he saw me after lunch, leaped up from his chair, leaned out from the bow, and spread his arms in imitation of a bird or an angelic figurehead.

"Oh, Gary, it's so bee-oo-ti-fool! I very happy."

Udo was well placed on the *Pohang Senator,* where the language of command was English but where much of the official and idle conversation was in German. He understood a little Russian but not the Polynesian idiom of the crew from Tuvalu. As a passenger, he was stuck at mealtimes with Jeanne, Bob, and me, struggling along in English, but I could see he took in everything that was said by the German officers at the next table. Early on, I'd asked him the meaning of the word *moin-moin,* which I took to mean something like the French phrase *bon appetit.* Udo was not sure. He thought it was a workers' greeting, a sort of congenial prehistoric grunt acknowledging that the time had come to eat, as in *meal-meal.* When we looked it up in his small German-English pocket dictionary, the only words listed in the English translation were *baby* and *feeding,* which made me suspect that the greeting at lunchtime was a private joke at the passengers' expense, meaning something like "Feed the babies" or "Go suck a nipple."

While I was in lexicographical mode, I thought I might have some fun with Udo and the officers by coming up with an alternative greeting at mealtimes. After passing along the corridor on A-deck, where Galiz the cook had written on the board the word *ghoulish* instead of *goulash,* I entered the mess and was greeted with a half-dozen *mahlzeits.* I responded with my substitute greeting, *Das Nimmt den der Appetit,* which I thought meant something in the order of "A good appetite requires no sauce." This was supposed to be a not-very-subtle dig at the ubiquitous beef gravy that appeared on everything—on chicken, duck, turkey, even on fish. There was a moment of silence, then laughter and the clinking of knives on glasses. I thought my excellent pronunciation was being applauded. Only later did I learn that I'd made an unwitting insult, *May your appetite be spoiled.* In the small type, I'd selected the wrong phrase. What I'd meant to say was *Hunger is der beste Koch,* "Hunger is the best cook."

The colors of the sea were constantly changing, from dark gray to a deep bluish purple. The chart on the bridge showed a piece of Kamchatka in the top left corner; the rest was empty, with only lines of latitude and longitude and indicators of ocean currents. The Pacific Ocean, which for once was living up (or down) to its name, produced only a steady, moderate swell that intermittent breezes occasionally whipped to a light surface chop. The previous day a ship had appeared many miles to starboard, a container vessel shrouded in mist like a reflection, a ghostly doppelgänger; then it vanished.

Was it a contemporary equivalent of *The Flying Dutchman,*
roaming the seas with its crew of dead men and empty containers? I was ready to believe anything just to find some
variety on the horizon. I'd seen the periscope of a submarine
pass us on the way into Pusan, no doubt part of the Korean
naval convoy steaming along closer to shore, but Udo and
Bob accused me of imagining it. In weather like this, I
thought, you could have made the crossing in a kayak.

The tiny swimming pool on D-deck, with a very realistic
shark painted on the bottom, was finally filled with salt water
from the Sea of Japan, but it was so cold I used it only once.
When the ship rolled, the shark appeared to move in the
water. Aside from reading, scribbling, and walking to the
fo'c'sle, there was nothing to do but memorize the labels on
containers. This was not encouraging, because several of the
"reefers" carried a warning that had to be read vertically—
HIGH CAUTION—with the G, C, and N written backward. What
I needed, obviously, was Igor's *peeg,* mounted at the bow in
good Polynesian style, to sniff out some land a hundred miles
off, although pirate-chef Galiz would have made short shrift
of the critter, listing it on the breakfast menu board as "Pork
medals." Instead, I gathered stories from Bob and Jeanne
on the bridge, where they were busy scanning the horizon
with binoculars and making notes from the pages of the
Admiralty Pilot.

Bob had been based at Guam during the Second World War
and had fought in the U. S. Marines at Iwo Jima when he was
scarcely twenty. By the end of the war he had enough points
to return home and had no further desire to travel, until
many years later when he returned to the South Pacific to

look once more at those very places where he had crossed over the shadow-line. That's where he had met Jeanne, who had been traveling with a girlfriend. Unmarried and in their late forties, they had fallen in love.

"Perhaps it was in reaction to some of our more boring companions," Jeanne suggested, telling me about the woman in the group who had earnestly inquired of the tour guide somewhere in Micronesia, "Do the native people sometimes talk to each other?"

The Baptist missionary Hendon Mason Harris had spent his time somewhat differently in Korea. In 1972, having no further religious duties, he made the rounds of the antique shops to inquire about books and pictures. An obliging merchant asked him if he'd like to examine a book of old maps. What he saw stirred his imagination and altered his life as radically as if he'd discovered the Dead Sea Scrolls or the Holy Grail. In *The Asiatic Fathers of America,* Harris claims to have found the map, or a copy of the map, that Huishen used on his journey east to the Americas between AD 458 and 499.

The last map in the book the merchant showed Harris was called, appropriately, Everything under Heaven. The watery portions of the circular *mappa munde* had been painted green, with two red dots at the center indicating China and Korea. In addition to the Middle Kingdom and its neighbors, there is a ring of land that follows the circumference of the map, intended to represent all that is not China. The translations of place names—Marvelous Buttocks Land, Workers' Country, Frivolous Men Country, Land of Smoke-Blackened

People, Land of Straight Chest, Strange Forearm Land, Plowing Money Land, Courteous Heart Country, All Witches Land, Great Appointments Country—sound vaguely familiar and are enough to make you rush out and purchase one-way tickets, depending on your preferences. Other places, such as Land of Women, Giants' Country, and Fu Sang Country, might have been lifted from the *Liang Shu* version of Huishen's journey. There is even a drawing of the *fusang* tree, with long needles and an inscription to the effect that the sun and moon rise here.

Harris offers no proof of the age of the map, which some say is a copy of the *Shan Hai Ching* map in the School of Living Oriental Languages in Paris or a similar at the British Museum in London and no more than two or three hundred years old. Harris is given to a good deal of rhetorical sleight of hand and, when he is not thanking God for revealing the truth to him, uses words such as *authentic, infallible,* and *vindicated* to bolster his hypotheses. A particularly telling example of his method of argument is the following: "While the map is, in some respects, wrong, *yet in most essential respects it is so continually right* that we can immediately tell its authenticity." What interested me, as I reread the copy David Kelley had loaned me, was Harris's conviction that Asian expeditions to America had been multilateral: "Evidently there existed a confederacy, of East Indian Buddhists with the Chinese, Japanese and Koreans. These four nations, with the Amerinds, formed what we have denominated 'The Brahm-Handian Movement.'"

Although his arguments for Huishen's voyage are thin and somewhat derivative of the work of Vining and Mertz, Harris makes an important contribution here, as there is a considerable body of evidence to suggest Indian influence in the Americas. In addition to the Maya calendar, which David Kelley and the University of Frankfurt's Paul Kirchhoff consider to have been based on Indian calendrics, scholars argue that the Mexican game of patolli, the elephant stele at Copán, the *Ramayana* wall panel in Temple 0-13, and the stone deity with eight hands (both at Piedras Negras), as well as creation myths, the doctrine of the world's ages, and many other motifs in the Americas, all indicate Asian influence. India was not a country of landlubbers. Like China, India had not only the shipbuilding and navigational skills to make an ocean crossing, but also a firm reputation for far-reaching maritime trade. As Heine-Geldern says, "Ships that could cross the Indian Ocean were able to cross the Pacific too. Moreover, these ships were really large. An ancient text called 'The Periplus of the Erythraean Sea' mentions the large ships of Southern India which engaged in trade with countries of the East. A Chinese source . . . describes vessels from Southern Asia which were 150 feet long, and had four masts and were able to carry six to seven hundred men and one thousand metric tons of merchandise when the Buddhist Pilgrim Fahien returned from Sri Lanka to China, in 414 AD."

While Harris was not the companion I'd have chosen for a few beers on Texas Street, *The Asiatic Fathers of America*, despite its embarrassing style and sometimes racist conclusions, is further evidence of the fascination that Huishen's story, with its cryptic notations and enigmatic qualities, has had for amateur historians. Like Henriette Mertz, Harris believed that Huishen's first landfall was in the vicinity of

Cape Mendocino, California. Although he also shared Mertz's tendency to make excessive claims for Huishen's achievements, Harris might be forgiven if, struggling to evaluate his life's work as a Christian missionary, he read some of his own experiences into the story of an ancient and obscure Buddhist monk.

NINETEEN

"Moin-moin."

Mr. Braüer acknowledged my greeting as he stepped up to collect his toast and choose an orange. Pleased that I remembered the Bavarian phrase he'd taught me on watch, he repeated it, much to the amusement of his fellow officers.

Spicy sausage for breakfast and, according to the day's posted menu in the corridor, "steik" for lunch—a sure recipe for an attack of gout. Worse news was that we had run out of muesli, the only shipboard cereal I could endure. Bob and Jeanne, already seated when I arrived, were looking a bit grim, although Bob at least had his own supply of bran to top up the corn flakes. I'd had another sleepless night, thanks to the rolling motion and the grinding metals section of the Pohang Philharmonic Orchestra. Also, I must confess, I'd given in to a late and unwise cup of Igor's "poison" on the bridge.

As the ship lurched along in the pitch-black night, totally dependent on its navigational aids, mainly the radar, we had talked about families, money, ice, and what Igor called "individuability." Igor saw individuality as akin to what I would call "character," which he distinguished from mere personality. I had been reading the *Admiralty Pilot* and pointed out that there are eighty-eight words for *ice* in the Russian language, including translations for bay ice, pancake ice, fast ice, close pack ice, bergy bits, brash ice, growlers, weathered flows, and patch, tongue, ram, rafted, dried, and rotten ice. What did this say about the Russian character? Igor was not interested in ice. He wanted to tell me about a Russian woman, a famous actor, who had integrity. She would not take a part unless she fully understood and could empathize with the character she was asked to portray. The interview in the pop magazine *Top Secret* showed photos of her at various stages in her life, including one of a determined-looking little girl standing with her hands on her hips. Igor was impressed by her decision not to take a part in the filming of *The Master and Marguerita* until she knew for sure whether her character should be played as sane or mad. It sounded as if the Stanislavsky Method was alive and well in post-Soviet Russia. Sanity or madness was a subject too close to the bone of my project. I asked Igor about children. He had two, ages eleven and one.

"I try every ten years."

He was marking our current position in pencil on the map spread out on the chart table, some 240 miles southwest of the Aleutian Islands: N46.15, E171.29. I envied Bob's and Jeanne's luck outbound from Seattle, when the *Pohang Senator* had taken the more northerly Great Circle route, passing through the Aleutians into the Bering Sea, then through the Kuril Islands into the Sea of Okhotsk, entering the Sea of Japan via La Perouse Strait at the north end of Hokkaido, a route akin to that which the island-hopping Huishen and his colleagues would have taken. Money, calculated on the basis of weather, safety, and available port facilities, dictated our ship's speed and course as much as it dictated Igor's lifestyle and long apprenticeship to the sea. His modest income was many times that of the average Russian. As I sipped my poison, he tried to explain to me that he lived in the "sleeping area" of St. Petersburg, not exactly downtown but not in the suburbs either. It took me several tries to come up with the English phrase, "residential district."

Mr. Noa, the chief steward, removed several soiled plates from the breakfast table. Jeanne had told me that Mr. Noa was an ordained minister, and the previous day, when he'd graciously switched our afternoon beverage from coffee to tea, he'd commented on the goodness of the Lord. He also confided that most of the crew from Tuvalu—a cluster of islands in the South Pacific between Fiji and the Marshall Islands—were believers. No one lived more precariously than the Tuvalese, whose islands would be the first to disappear in the event of a significant rise in ocean levels; they needed all the help they could get, including divine intervention. Although I felt a little guilty that I could not share his faith, I was glad to have Mr. Noa, with his benign presence and biblically significant name, in charge of survival rations afloat. With him aboard, we would make it to Seattle, or at least Ararat. His sense of order pleased me too, as had that of the women at the fish market in Pusan who took such care in folding the thin sheets of dulse into rectangular shapes no bigger than a hardcover book.

"Damn," Jeanne said, "I've spilled my yogurt again, this time on my clean blouse." She grabbed several paper napkins and started dabbing furiously at an invisible spot. "My balance is no good. It must be because we're repeating the day. I have enough equilibrium for a twenty-four-hour day, but not a forty-eight-hour one." We were about to pass the international date line in a few hours, and Captain Walther had announced that there would be two Wednesdays this week. Jeanne had had her heart set on a repetition of Thursday, which would have meant ice cream for dessert two days running.

"You have to expect these problems, Jeanne, when you're dealing with a living organism." I offered her my auxiliary napkin. "Yogurt has its own agenda."

I was thinking again about David Kelley, in his book-lined house in Calgary, whom I had arranged to interview on film. Though I was a complete stranger, David insisted that I stay with him and his wife, Jane, while we talked and prepared for the interview. He wanted me to make full use of his library. David had retired some years earlier from the University of Calgary but kept up with his discipline and continued to write articles and reviews for journals. He was also a legend in archaeological circles because he had been one of the first Americans to champion the work of Yuri Valentinovich Knorosov in the cracking of the Maya code. As he said in *Deciphering the Maya Script*, a groundbreaking work, "I believe that he had a clearer view of the nature of the script than any other man of his period." Neither Knorosov's rigorous departure from orthodoxy nor the cold war climate of the 1950s and 1960s deterred Kelley from celebrating the Russian's achievement.

David was not the least bit surprised by, or dismissive of, my interest in the story of Huishen. Instead, he plied me with books and articles and suggestions, using the intervals to question me about literature and the arcane. What did I think of Shakespeare's *Merchant of Venice*? Did I think that the name Shylock might come from the same root as *Shiloh*, meaning "messiah"? And don't forget it was Portia, not the Bard himself, who posed the question, "How fair a face does falsehood wear?" I'm afraid I proved a disappointment to David on that score. Nonplussed, he took another tack.

"There is a site in Kashmir called the Tomb of Jesus. Just imagine, if there were a genuine relic of Christ's body, you could determine the DNA of God!"

He also spoke of the loss of his son Michael, dead at age twenty-six of AIDS, and worried aloud that he might not have provided sufficient moral and emotional support. After Michael's death, he had addressed an AIDS symposium in Lethbridge, Alberta. I was touched by this shared confidence. I had come with all these trivial questions I wanted to ask David but was learning so much more by just letting him talk about his life. While he instructed me on calendrical glyphs in Monte Alban, on the connection between the Maya 6 Rabbit and the Burmese 6 Hare, and the dating of Lady Beastie, the ancestral goddess of 761 years who gave birth to the three main gods of Palenque, I also learned that at the age of eight he had wanted to be a herpetologist. This tidbit of information seemed strangely appropriate given the ups and downs, the discoveries and losses, of an academic discipline such as archaeology, which like life itself, was a game of Snakes and Ladders.

The Maya script is a case in point. Efforts to break the code had taken almost two hundred years, with progress and setbacks that had more to do with personalities and academic politics than with scholarship. The rogues' gallery of would-be decipherers includes many of the great names of Mesoamerican archaeology. One of them, Cyrus Thomas, had been a strong proponent of the phonetic approach to Maya glyphs in the nineteenth century, but his intuitions were not confirmed until the 1930s, when Hermann Beyer identified glyph repetitions that seemed to indicate that their function might be syllabic and syntactical rather than symbolic. Eventually, Yuri Knorosov made the case for a phonetic-syllabic reading of the glyphs and the torch was picked up by Tatania Proskouriakoff, David Kelley, and others. David's first breakthrough came with the reading of a particular glyph for *east*. According to Michael Coe, David's former classmate, "This was a tremendous achievement: a personal name was found to have been written in a stone inscription by scribes operating under the rules discovered by Knorosov; it was an achievement that presaged the present generation of decipherers. And it brought us closer to one of John Lloyd Stephens' dreams, that histories recorded in the Colonial documents might be linked in some way to events in the ancient Maya cities."

David's description of his work on the invention of the Mesoamerican calendar went right over my head, but his deep respect for the receiving culture did not. He considered the Mesoamerican calendar superior to its Eurasian counterpart as a time-keeping mechanism: "I now think that the relevant contacts might have been made as early as the second century AD and that it still seems to me that voyagers from northern India must have been primarily responsible for bringing the many Eurasian ideas which provided the basis for the invention of the Mesoamerican calendar." He was not troubled by the absence of the kind of hard evidence on the ground of pre-Columbian Asian contact, such as ships, port facilities, and an abundance of ancient artifacts, demanded by some of his colleagues. I asked him why.

I had taken David and Jane to dinner in downtown Calgary but was concerned about the time and his health, as he was having problems with his heart and had been scheduled for angioplasty. When he saw me checking the time, he put his hand on my wrist, covering the watch face, and said, "I think the evidence is of so high a quality that it will eventually be possible to prove at almost any necessary level of proof that the Olmec, Maya, and Eurasiatic systems had a common origin."

All this was encouraging, because Huishen and his associates had come from Kabul, which was one moment under Persian rule, the next under Indian. Could it be there were legends of previous voyages to the Americas already circulating among the members of the cultural and religious elite of his community, even at Bamiyan? This might have influenced not only Huishen's determination to travel to the Americas, but also his decision to remain there for forty years. Familiar elements, including the possibility of a welcoming committee, or at least of a receptive audience, might have made the transition to the Americas easier and the duration more attractive.

According to the published specifications I was given before embarking, the ship's engine was capable of cranking out 55,000 horsepower. I could not imagine a combustion engine five hundred times as powerful as the one in my car. As conversations ground to a halt and shipboard novelties (all three of them) wore thin, I asked the chief engineer if Bob Cox and I could have a tour of the engine room. Klaus-Dieter Hasse, who had already donned his coveralls, met us in the ship's office on the top deck. He explained that we would need to wear ear-protectors, but that he would give us a detailed briefing in the control room where the noise was not quite so deafening.

The *Pohang Senator* was equipped with a nine-cylinder diesel engine larger than my house. The crankcase was so large that each cylinder had its own door, big enough for a man to enter upright. There were spare parts handy. Pistons the size of a giant garbage can, with a three-meter stroke; rings, bearings, a twelve-foot spare exhaust valve. Two smaller auxiliary engines were required to generate electricity, as the heavy diesel fuel had to be heated before it would ignite and, in addition to the ship's own heating and cooling systems and water distiller, the refrigerated containers in transport drew a lot of voltage. We could see these things from the insulated control room, where we stood like a pair of extraterrestrials, ear protectors jutting out from our temples like protruding eyeballs. It all seemed unreal, like some science-fiction extravaganza viewed on a television screen. Descending into the belly of the beast was something else, a maze of catwalks to service the pipes, valves, fuel lines, generators; steep, narrow metal stairs dropping still furhter down to the level of the crankcase, electrical shop, and three water systems: salt water, low-temperature fresh water, high-temperature fresh water. Occasionally Mr. Hasse would stop in front of a piece of equipment or a gauge and lean in to shout something that I could never understand into one of our ear protectors. Because Bob wore a hearing aid, I knew he was faking as much as I was when he nodded his head to indicate he'd got the message.

Along the lowest catwalk, less than ten feet above the bare hull, we stopped to examine the drive shaft, which was fifty feet long and three feet wide with bearings the size of a Volkswagen

Beetle. I was surprised at the slow speed of the turning shaft, about 150 rpm, compared to the 2,500 rpm that is normal at cruising speeds in an automobile. Mr. Hasse said that the ship carried 4,800 tons of diesel fuel, using about 160 tons per day. I could not translate this into anything that made sense until later on the bridge when Mr. Braüer said the ship used sixty gallons of fuel per mile. At a speed of 23 mph, this amounted to 1,380 gallons per hour. This explained not only the huge pall of smoke and soot emitted from the stack behind the bridge, but also why container ships are now required to stay as far as possible from inhabited coastal areas. One ship at full speed was the equivalent of the emissions of 690 automobiles—or worse, as diesel is not a clean-burning fuel.

I had been putting off this inspection tour until mid-ocean and more northerly latitudes, where I thought the heat in this mechanical inferno would be less intense, but air-conditioning had made the lower depths almost comfortable. Mr. Hasse thought he might have to replace one of the valves in Seattle, an eight-hour task that would preclude shore leave for him and several of the crew, one of whom was now making a small repair on a catwalk to our left, oblivious to his audience of three. As the engine pulsed above us, I imagined him one of those heroic red blood cells or genetic regulators on duty somewhere amid the body's vitals, making sure that the arteries were not clogged and that the kidneys continued their filtering.

"Where's the clutch?" I asked Mr. Hasse when, having hung up our ear protectors, we emerged again into the light and relative silence of the top deck. "How does the ship go in reverse?" Forgetting he could hear me perfectly well, I made the motion of bringing my two closed fists together to simulate parts of the engine and transmission coming together to transfer power to the driveshaft. Mr. Hasse laughed.

"There is no clutch," he said. "It's a straight drive arrangement. The engine must basically stop and then be forced, using directed air pressure, to turn and begin firing in the other direction, thus reversing the propeller." He might have been describing what was necessary to change attitudes to the idea of pre-Columbian Asian contact.

"Starboard, five degrees," the pilot announced. In the dim light and early-morning mist, the *Pohang Senator* was moving rapidly in Canadian waters toward the San Juan Islands.

"Starboard, five degrees, sir," replied the helmsman.

Captain Walthers and the pilot were conferring. Palili, with his ponytail, was at the helm. It was all very cordial and civilized. Two nights earlier, I could not sleep, more from excitement than from discomfort. Suslonov, the second mate who claimed to be a KGB plant, was on duty in his shorts and baggy gray sweatshirt, seated in the master's chair, studying the radar screen and electronics. His large white running shoes with clear plastic air pockets in the heels, having gathered into their orbit all the available light in the small space, seemed to have acquired a life of their own.

"I like dogwatch. I alone, nobody answer to."

The helmsman liked to avoid being ripped off as well. In Russia, he said, a tin can is considered the best place to hide your money. This common wisdom and resurrected practice gained significance because the words for *tin can* and *bank* in Russian employ similar sounds. His parents had lost all their savings in a bank default; so had he. In Russia, he said, the government always wins; there is no protection for investors built into the system. One percent of the population is very wealthy, there is a tiny middle class, and 90 percent are desperately poor. I could see his gold teeth flash in the dim light as he spoke. Maybe in ten years, he said, if things don't improve, there will be another revolution. The leaders already had their suitcases packed—and had foreign bank accounts. How did that make him feel?

"Is bullshit." He spat out the words into the gloom of the dimly lit bridge, as much for his own benefit as mine. "I respect Salvador Allende. He defend palace to the end."

Hopelessness about the situation back home had engulfed him completely, unexpectedly, like a tsunami. Not even his luminescent white shoes could ward off that gloom. In the background, a Russian radio station was playing French music. I tried to change the subject, asking him about hockey.

"I like for Canada in hockey, too." He sighed, relieved, launching into an impressive string of great Canadian players, most of them with Slavic names.

By now we had sailed down Puget Sound and docked in Seattle. Having failed miserably to spot killer whales for Udo or even to point out my house at the southern tip of Vancouver Island, which had been obscured by a low-lying bank of fog, I invited him to stay over at my place at French Beach if he made it to Victoria. Before parting, we stopped for lunch at a small deli on First Avenue in Seattle, not far from the Pike Street Market, but Udo was too wired to eat. We wanted to stretch out the moment, though the language barrier—mainly my lack of German—was inhibiting. So we talked in simple terms about Bob and Jeanne and the ship.

When she disembarked, Jeanne was wearing the new white cotton work gloves I'd bought for her in Korea. She had warned me early in the trip about the amount of grime that accumulated on the railings and had requested in Kaohsiung and Pusan that we not use the long metal stairs, which had a tendency to bounce, until she had reached the bottom. That way, she could maintain her balance without holding on. I purchased the pair of gloves from a stall at the fish market in Pusan, knowing she had only one more chance to use them on board. She had warned us that she did not like good-byes, so wasted no time hailing a waiting taxi. As she turned to leave, Jeanne gave me a big hug and threatened violence if I came to the San Francisco Bay Area and did not contact them. She offered me her precious yogurtmaker, a spare purchased for the trip, which she planned otherwise to leave on board for the next set of passengers. I told her I didn't think I could trust myself handling such dangerous and unpredictable material.

As I was not leaving the ship until Vancouver, I spent a couple of hours perusing the shops on First Avenue, including one that was full of Afghan carpets, many of them with elegant modern designs. The shopkeeper, as it turned out, owned a factory in Kabul, which employed weavers who worked from his designs. In the Pike Street Market, buskers plied their trades; and fresh salmon were tossed from merchant to merchant over the delighted faces of the crowd. The woman next to me shrieked when a flying fish went astray and landed in her arms, but it turned out to be made of Styrofoam. Along the harbor, between the Aquarium and the Bay Pavilion, I passed an innocuous, tortured-looking statue of Columbus, his body a modernist combo of steel joints and levers, suggesting, to me at least, that his belated discovery of the Americas had been a rather lackluster and mechanical proceeding, especially if he was already in possession of Zheng He's or someone else's charts. Since Huishen had made the journey ten centuries earlier, and because so many others also had the jump on him, Columbus could be forgiven if he looked a little rusty and out of sorts.

As I walked along the waterfront, I calculated that I had already traveled almost thirty thousand miles, visited seven countries, sampled several dozen cultures, and gone deeper into history than I'd imagined possible in such a short time. However, events had put my experiences in quite a different light—the light of politics. Afghanistan had been invaded, the Taliban replaced by a patchwork governing council; there was even talk of rebuilding the *Buddhas of Bamiyan*, though the infrastructure of the ruined country needed attention first. Rumors were flying, too, that Iraq was next in line for invasion, referred to euphemistically by the U.S. administration as a "regime change." I knew a little more than when I began about the links between politics and religion and could see how race and skin color were likely to shape immigration policy and security measures into the future. I also knew I had five weeks to prepare for my daughter Bronwen's wedding, which would take place with or without the bank of fog we had sailed past at French Beach. The fog of history would have to wait.

While I sipped my fresh orange juice and laid waste to the pasta salad at the restaurant, Udo translated a nautical blessing that had intrigued me and that was still echoing in my mind a day later as the ship turned twenty degrees to starboard toward the Lions Gate Bridge in Vancouver. It was a German expression that had to do with ocean voyages, a universal wish for safe passage. I had asked him to write it down for me on a table napkin at the restaurant: *"Auf de* Pohang Senator *und immer eine handbreite Wasser unter dem Kiel"*: "May the *Pohang Senator* always have a hand's-breadth of water under its keel."

The phrase would reverberate long after I'd paid my respects to David, Igor, Suslonov, Galiz, the captain, and Mr. Braüer, and as I followed the clues south to Mexico and Central America in search of my elusive monk.

THE BUDDHA ON THE ROAD

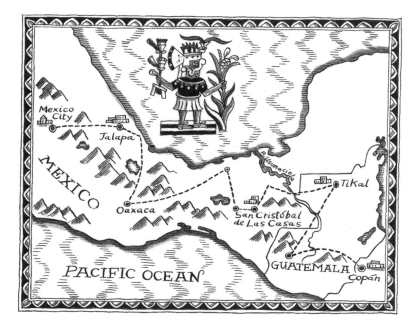

TWENTY

I ROSE EARLY to hire a launch to take me upriver from the out-post of Frontera Corozal in the Mexican state of Chiapas to Bethel in Guatemala. Outside the office of the *Cooperativa*, there were few signs of life. Five chickens lounged in a mute chorus line, three standard browns and two mangy Asians, whose black flesh showed through their sparse feathers. Against the pale blue wash of the building, they might have been posing for a still life. A brown hen balanced on one leg while her two foreign companions, pre-Columbian melanotic chickens for sure, checked their bodies for lice, a pre-breakfast snack. Twenty-four narrow *lanchas*—red, blue, or green—were tied up along the riverbank, their sterns angled down-river by the current. Some had curved *palapa* awnings; others were covered with black plastic tarpaulins as protection against tropical sun and rain. In the nearest *lancha,* about twice the width of a standard dugout, a man was bent over in the stern bailing, the intermittent slap of emptied water from his bucket barely audible over the hum of the swollen river.

I presented my passport to the most officious-looking of the three bored young Mexican soldiers dozing in their stick shelter, each laden with a pistol, grenades, flare, bandolier, and AK-47 rifle. He flipped from page to page, looking intently at each visa. This was the moment I'd been dreading since my departure from Asia shortly after 9/11, but no British,

Canadian, or American customs officials had noticed the Taliban visa.

"Afghanistan, Pakistan, China." I expected a significant pause as he stood to attention and adjusted his gun belt, but the young soldier simply smiled in recognition of the names, stamped the passport, and handed it back to me.

"Un viaje muy lejos," he said.

A long journey indeed. I nodded, shouldered my backpack, which had been given a cursory inspection by one of the other soldiers, and picked my way gingerly down the muddy bank of the Usumacinta River. I thought of all the rivers I had crossed and recrossed during this pilgrimage: the Indus, the Kabul, the Huang He, the Li Jiang, and the amazing Yangtze—arteries carrying life and death, seldom in equal measure.

As the small launch shifted to accommodate my additional weight and the powerful currents of the north-flowing Usumacinta River, my mind was half on the vegetation and half on the fate of archaeologist Charles Frey, who drowned in 1949 when his canoe capsized during an expedition to nearby Bonampak. Wearing a life jacket and being ensconced in a more stable boat with a flat bottom and outboard motor, I was concerned less with drowning than with the possibility of being mistaken for supper should the boat strike a submerged log, run aground on a sandbar, or flip in the tricky currents. Ten days earlier, I had photographed crocodiles in Sumidero Canyon en route to San Cristóbal de Las Casas, a city in the highlands of Chiapas, and I'd seen enough movies about piranhas to make me suspicious of this murky jungle waterway that served as a partial border between Mexico and Guatemala. Most of the original forest, or *selva*, had disappeared, though here and there a vast snag strained skyward in protest, its naked branches supporting a vulture's nest. The muddy, swollen, olive-green water surged against the banks, cutting into the earth, dislodging ancient roots.

We eased into the river, drifted a few yards downstream, then surged ahead, ploughing south against the current with the aid of a new forty-horsepower outboard engine. I was the sole passenger. I could feel the full force of the river resist our passage, millions of gallons of water and sediment—now a pea-soup color against the darker green of vegetation—sweeping past us toward lowland estuaries and the Gulf of Mexico. The banks of the Usumacinta, which had been predominantly clay on the journey to Yaxchilán, now displayed intermittent patches of deeply pocked volcanic rock, reminding me that I was heading upriver toward even more unstable ground, where, if politics does not kill you first, geography might do the trick. A white ibis taking a break on his floating log watched us pass under an overhanging branch that extended thirty feet out into the waterway. Javier, my Chol Lacandon skipper, was obliged to cut the engine several times to clear weed from the propeller shaft, so we would drift broadside in the current for a while before surging ahead like dancers in a dialectical ballet.

This was a borderland in more ways than one. Stepping off the ship in Vancouver, I had been suddenly overcome by the impossibility of my project. It was not Huishen, Asia's elusive Pimpernel, troubling me. I had reached a point at which I doubted I would ever write the book he and his legend hinted at. That faint glimmer of possibility had taken me once around the world and twice across the North Pacific. Was I any closer to solving the mystery? Against a backdrop of post-9/11 fear, uneasy peace in Afghanistan, threatened war in Iraq, and a maddening cycle of suicidal attacks and revenge in Israel and the Palestinian territories, my imagination and bag of literary tricks were simply not up to the task of writing a whimsical narrative about an obscure Buddhist monk. And now, to add to my confusion and unease, I was traveling through another blighted landscape, a site of carnage, of genocide that had begun with the arrival of the Spaniards and had never ended.

About the same time, I had another visitation from Huishen that set me thinking about many things, not least of which were the writing of history and what he might have experienced in the Americas that helped to shape his vision.

There are ways to describe this carnage we call birth. My mother's teeth bite into the cord, the rope of words. My body revolves in blue air. Raven tears at a dead shape, gorges on absence. There are no tongues in trees, no sermons on the wind. The operatic style bowed out with polite war. Lice breed under armor, lay their eggs in folds of sour cloth. I try to tell my story to the emperor, to render visible villages shrouded in mist or the great city shimmering and unreal in waves of heat. You'd think we did not speak the same language. He's no fool. I spoke briefly of the Land of Women, the People Who Give Everything Away, and a substance that makes it possible to pass unimpeded through matter. I could sense him giving me a thorough once-over, watching my lips open and close, staring with absolute impunity at the flesh of my dead eye. He was forthright as a child in demanding explanations. I told him I'd seen enough, that after a certain point two eyes are an impediment to sustained thought and understanding. It's no secret the new emperor is having a crisis of confidence — he wishes to abandon his divine calling for the monastic life. I'm afraid I'm a serious disappointment to him in that realm as I prefer ale to alms, parables to prayer. I smell of women, not incense. Talk of blindfolds makes him nervous.

There was no good reason to suppose, from the short account in the *Liang Shu*, that Huishen might have lost, or deliberately plucked out, an eye during his sojourn in the Americas. Yet this peculiar detail casts an uncanny light not only on the idea of bearing witness, but also on the matter of writing history, implying that the road to "truth" may well pass through the land of fiction. And that, perhaps, we begin to see only when we close our eyes, become partially or totally blind. Blindness has a good deal of radiating power, raising the question of whom we acknowledge as a reliable witness, blind Homer and Milton or the sighted historian. I was not quite prepared to admit that the choice made no difference, though I was convinced that every account of the past contains distortions, partial truths, first by having passed through the forge of language—as white light passing through a prism fractures into the colors of the spectrum—and second by having the unavoidable stamp of an individual creator.

The parable or allegory of the storyteller, with its focus on sensory detail and psychology, explores the limits of the possible and is as essential to our understanding of the past as any carefully researched document. In his essay "Poetry and History," Frank Kermode argues that the task of poetry, and of creative works in general, is to *make history strange*, to smudge its clarity, make us look a second time, forcing us to "read it against the grain of the manifest." As these nightly "letters" suggested, Huishen belonged as much to the poets as to the historians.

All this was comforting. I hoped I'd find in Mexico and in Central America some trace of Huishen and his fellow Buddhists. Having spent forty years in the Americas, Huishen probably migrated to, or at least visited, Teotihuacán and the major centers of the Maya, who ruled these territories from AD 300 to 900. I decided to examine museums and ruins from Mexico City to Yucatán and, if time permitted, Tikal and Copán, to satisfy myself that pre-Columbian Asian contact was not just a chimera. As I pondered this daunting task, I received two decisive and serendipitous e-mail messages.

The first was from Betty Ferber and Homero Aridjis, expressing an interest in my project, inviting me to visit them in Mexico City, and informing me that an important announcement had just appeared in the pages of *Reforma*. Archaeologists Rubén Cabrera and Saburo Sugiyama had discovered three human remains beneath the Pyramid of the Moon at Teotihuacán, the famed City of the Gods not far from the Mexican capital. The three skeletons were seated with legs crossed in full lotus posture, along with a small jadeite figure carved in the same position, all four facing west. I located the article on the Internet and printed a copy, which included photographs of Cabrera, the bones wrapped in tinfoil, the jadeite figure nestled in packing material, the reinforced tunnel, someone at work in the pit, and Sugiyama emerging like a beaming and exultant gopher from under the earth. Of course, I assumed these human remains were Asian monks and that the jadeite sculpture was an approximation of the Buddha. Had it not been for the proposed date of AD 300 in the article, I would have immediately volunteered three of Huishen's Afghan companions as likely candidates for sacrificial burial, in honor of the construction and consecration of level five of the sacred pyramid.

The second intriguing message was from another Mexican poet and publisher, Gabriel Zaid, who was curious about my project. Gabriel, signing his e-mail Z, invited me to meet him and added, as an afterthought, "Many years ago I saw at the Mitla Museum a small Olmec piece in a yoga position that could not be a semblance but the real thing: *urdhvapadmasana* (lotus flower inverted). Nobody had an explanation for it." Felicitous portents! I felt as if I were on the receiving end of messages from the gods, special deliveries sent to me—not along the Silk Road this time—but via the Information Highway.

It was mid-October 2002 when I arrived in Mexico City. I called Betty and Homero and was promptly invited to dinner. They had met in San Miguel de Allende through a friend of Betty's while they were both students. Homero later served as Mexican ambassador to the Netherlands and Switzerland, which he said mostly involved putting a good face on bad news. In 1985, he cofounded *Grupo de los Cien*, an international group of one hundred artists and intellectuals engaged in the protection of the environment, which often brought him into conflict with the Mexican government. This was no superficial commitment for Homero. "Ecology is poetry," he said. "Nature and poetry are closely linked. I defend water, soil, trees, animal life by making them the central issues of my poems." Betty, a New Yorker, had completed a PhD in medieval literature at Columbia but became interested in psychology, eventually completing a master's degree in the subject and working part-time as a family counselor. She was also Homero's principal translator.

As soon as I arrived, Betty gave me a copy of the original *Reforma* article that included a line drawing of the three figures and the jade sculpture as they were found in the pit, with the headline announcing blatantly, in bold type, "TIENEN POSTURA EN FLOR DE LOTO."

Not only were the human remains sitting cross-legged in lotus posture, but also their hands were open at the sides, palms facing forward. The description of the jadeite figure, meditative with eyes closed, was blunt and noncommittal: "Anthropomorphic figure in green stone." While the posture of the carving resembled Buddhist sculptures, the head with its limited facial relief, broad nose, and thick lips bore a faint resemblance to the famous Olmec heads of La Venta, Veracruz. Not surprisingly, because the Maya were given to depicting their priests and leaders seated in an approximate lotus posture, the archaeologists concluded that the three figures were evidence of hitherto unsuspected contacts between Teotihuacán and the Maya, though no one could yet explain how this might have happened.

I was not so easily dissuaded. Buddhism seemed to me a possible explanation for the complete absence in Teotihuacán of the cult of personality so prevalent in Palenque, Tikal, Copán, and many lesser sites, where rulers had obsessively caused their every move to be recorded in paintings, stelae, and glyphs. No tombs of rulers had been found in Teotihuacán and no self-aggrandizing art. Whoever built the City of the Gods had chosen to remain silent and invisible. So who were these sacrificial victims? What was their status? And why were their hands not tied like those of the victims found in the other pits? Could this mean they had died willingly? I was determined to put these and other questions to Cabrera. The whole business was so exciting that I paid far too little attention to the lovely meal of stuffed rolls, lentil soup, sliced cactus, and guava that Betty had served. Rufus, my hosts' huge German shepherd, brought me back to reality by licking my hand and lifting the napkin off my lap with his nose.

"When we were in Beijing and Shanghai," Homero confided, "I kept saying to Betty, 'That looks Mexican.' Finally, she had to tell me to stop. It was the same in Japan, but in this case the faces—the eyes, the cheekbones, the heavier lower lip . . ." My host excused himself and disappeared upstairs to retrieve a ceramic cylinder he'd bought twenty years earlier. He'd noticed it on a shelf amid carvings of the rain god Tlaloc because it bore no resemblance to those other pieces. It showed a decidedly Asian face with a Fu Manchu beard. Homero was convinced it was evidence of Chinese, or at least Asian, influence. As he took me out to the walled patio garden to examine the piece in natural light, *picaflores*—hummingbirds—were sipping the nectar of bougainvillea and various tropical flowers thrusting up amid the bamboo. I could hear the voice of María Sabina on an old Folkways recording in the house, which Homero hoped would demonstrate for me certain tonal qualities of the Mazatec language that, to him, sounded almost Chinese.

Because the Olmec and Maya rooms were closed for renovation at the National Museum of Anthropology and History in Mexico

City and because Rubén Cabrera could not see me until the middle of November, I made quick trips to Jalapa and Parque La Venta in Villahermosa, winding through various landscapes and climatic zones—desert, grasslands, cornfields—all peppered with the most bizarre clusters of cacti: the classic agave with its elegant octopus arms, dense shrubs resembling a rugby scrum or some creeping disease, tall, spindly trees with bulbous, hairy heads that looked as if they'd been struck by lightning. Fertilizer factories, roadside shrines, and the occasional small town, its white adobe walls plastered with bright red Coca-Cola advertisements and billboards that promised the Good Life to consumers of Mexican beer, were all that broke the monotony of the vast tracts of private land. Not until I reached the damp, east-facing slopes of Veracruz State did the Atlantic rains and lush vegetation take over, auguring a different set of options, an alternative to those of the high plains and the oxygen-deprived capital.

The Olmec, known as the mother culture of Mesoamerica, appear to have originated in the lowlands of Veracruz and neighboring Tabasco. No one knows how their civilization, which lasted from 1200 to 150 BC, came into being or why it disappeared; but experts agree that it constituted an amazing flowering of art, architecture, writing, religion, and social organization. The university's Museum of Anthropology in Jalapa contained a dozen large Olmec heads—some smooth basalt, some pockmarked—each weighing several tons and carved from stone that had to be transported hundreds of miles. One of the heads had been strategically placed out of doors in a patio full of bamboo and bird-of-paradise. Scholarly debate continued about the possible African origins of the protruding lips and broad, flattened noses, though they looked to me not unlike faces

I'd seen in China and Japan. However, it was not the Olmec heads that had brought me east to Jalapa. With considerable excitement, I picked my way past the flayed god, the coiled serpent, and one of the notorious "smiling women," who beamed disconcertingly from her bower of bones. There was also a clay sculpture of a woman who had died in childbirth and was now numbered among the gods. Though her own head was missing, she appeared to be carrying the head of her child in a basket.

Then I saw what I was looking for: two wheeled toys and several pottery figures on swings, dated 200 BC to AD 300, either Olmec pieces or creations from the early Maya period. These ceramic figures were close relatives of those that had captivated the late Gordon Ekholm and that I had seen in New York. Ekholm believed they were Asian in origin. Art historian Paul Shao, who shares this view, has discussed the wheel at length because isolationists insist it would have been in use in the Americas had pre-Columbian contact really taken place. Its absence, they argue, is proof that contact never happened. Shao disagrees, making the point that the wheel would have been useless to the indigenous peoples of Mesoamerica because they had neither horses nor oxen to use as draft animals and because the swamplands, jungle, and mountainous terrain would have made road-building and maintenance impossible. Yet here, plain to see, were wheeled toys—a sleek cat with tail flying out behind and a second, indeterminate animal. The Olmec, with no use for the wheel themselves, could well have employed it for the amusement of children or as a trinket for the deceased.

The same logic applied to swings. One pair of swingers, arms linked and toes thrust forward, looked decidedly Asian, heads shaved except for a tuft of braided hair down the middle and more gathered at the sides. No more than four or five inches tall, the two boys were wearing only loincloths and belts around the waist. The other pair, sisters perhaps, were fully clothed, with large floppy hats and neck ornaments. The only solitary figure on a swing, decked out in a patterned dress and hat, had the brightly rouged cheeks of a doll. Her dress was decorated with straight red lines and what appeared to be inverted triangles and their watery reflection; over each breast was a small insignia that resembled an Asian swastika, the ancient symbol of peace. Common funerary items in Asia, the swingers and wheeled toys appear rarely in Olmec graves and not at all among the late Maya and other cultures of Mesoamerica.

I was reluctant to leave the cool highlands of Jalapa, but I had no choice. Villahermosa, my next destination, situated inland from the swampy coastal plain of Tabasco, was dusty and hot. The bus delivered me early enough to visit the city museum, which contained a number of items that also struck me as decidedly Asian in aspect or inspiration, including two small but well-endowed pre-classical clay figures. With voluptuous thighs and an air of sensuality and abandon, they owed more to India than to either China or Mexico. One of these voluptuaries sprawled with legs crossed at the ankles, her head in the lap of another woman, one hand touching her hair, the other nestled in her crotch. The seated woman, whose breasts rested on the head of her partner, leaned back, eyes closed, with a blissful expression. In a small alcove, reached by a separate set of stairs, I also found a number of Maya pieces, including one that had the aspect and shape of a Buddha. I was so taken by the similarity that I stood to one side as several touring American women paused in front of the sculpture. When I asked if it reminded them of anything, they declared, without a moment's hesitation, that it resembled the Buddha.

Since the ruins at La Venta, an Olmec city on an island in the Gulf of Mexico, were not easily accessible and most of the artifacts had been removed to other locations, I was determined to visit Villahermosa's *Parque La Venta*, where a gathering of Olmec sculpture had been installed cleverly along simulated forest paths next to the city zoo. The artifacts gained something from the "natural" setting but were less impressive than the pieces I'd seen in Jalapa. Unfortunately, the zoo itself was closed. During my rounds of the park, I managed to glimpse a prostrate jaguar in his cage, his jaw twitching in sleep. He was no doubt sticking to union regulations against undue exertion on weekends and holidays. Among the nonunion animals, only the spider monkeys—their legs like pipe cleaners—and the white ibis by the lake maintained their daily routines. I was walking back to the park entrance and thinking I'd wasted my time coming to Villahermosa when I saw a small building to my left, just beyond a sculpture of the park's founder and architect. I couldn't believe my good fortune.

To my surprise and delight, I found in the open-air museum a replica of the controversial group of Olmec jade figures and celts (chiseled tools) from La Venta that I'd hoped to see in the Olmec room under renovation at the National Museum in Mexico City. The original exhibit had caused a considerable stir when it was on temporary display in 1996 at the National Gallery in Washington, D.C. Even in its copied state, the effect was staggering, unlike anything I'd seen among the Olmec, Maya, and subsequent Mesoamerican cultures.

The group consisted of fifteen figures carved from light-colored jade, mostly pale green, and one from what appeared to be porous red volcanic rock. The figures were arranged dramatically, with the red figure facing the rest of the group. Behind the leader, like a bulwark, were six standing chisel-edged jade implements, the celts, on which were engraved designs or markings that looked like primitive writing. This unique group of figures, with no obvious religious or funerary significance, had been discovered three feet underground at La Venta and remained an enigma. Mike Xu, a scholar at Texas Christian University, was convinced that the jade celts contained Shang inscriptions, and he had invited Han Ping Chen, a specialist in the Shang Dynasty writing, to Washington to examine this group. The Chinese scholar had not looked at the markings on the jade celts for more than a few minutes when he announced, "I can read this. Clearly, these are Chinese characters."

Han Ping Chen insisted that one of the messages appeared to be connected with a special event, probably the founding of some sort of community. Using his tattered dictionaries, Han identified the character for *ruler* or *chieftain* and another character meaning to *found* or *establish*, along with a pictorial symbol representing *kingdom* or *country*: two triangular mountain peaks underscored by a line representing a river. According to Charles Fenyvesi, who wrote of the visit in *U. S. News & World Report,* "If Chen is right, the celts not only offer the earliest writing in the New World, but mark the birth of a Chinese settlement more than 3,000 years ago."

How did Shang script reach Mexico? The Shang, who practiced ancestor worship and divination with oracle bones, held power in areas bordering the Huang He from 1554 to 1045 BC. Their art, particularly the bronze work, is considered very sophisticated. When the Shang were defeated, the conquering Zhou not only slaughtered much of the Shang population, but also destroyed all the written records they could find. Some have suggested the fleeing Shang elite escaped by boat on the Huang He and when they reached the ocean simply kept sailing east. Fenyvesi makes reference to a recent excavation near the ancient Shang capital of Anyang, where the charred remains of a library containing inscriptions on turtle shell were unearthed. The body of the librarian, who had been stabbed in the back, was still lying in the doorway clutching ancient writings to his chest, the fate of many a book lover throughout Chinese history.

The negative response from academia to Han Ping Chen's thesis was not surprising, except for its intensity. One Americanist scholar accused Han, and the Chinese in general, of having ulterior—that is, political—motives for identifying the script as Shang. Two more scholars dismissed the translation as "rubbish." And Michael Coe, once a supporter of the idea of Asian influence in Mesoamerica, dismissed the whole idea as "insulting to the indigenous peoples of the Americas." Things were definitely heating up. According to the establishment line, here was further evidence that diffusionists and their supporters, lacking hard evidence, were nothing more than charlatans whose foreign attributions served only to *robarle su patrimonio cultural,* to rob the indigenous person of his cultural heritage.

In an article published in 2002, Mike Xu distances himself from the hastily rendered translations of the La Venta jade celts and from Han Ping Chen himself, who seems to have lost credibility, overstayed his visa, and gone underground in the United States. Nevertheless, Xu still maintains his belief in the Shang origin of the script and suggests that the underlined triangular figures are more likely to represent a *mound, hillock,* or *grave* than a *kingdom*. Instead of the script indicating the founding of a city, Xu proposes the following translation: "Let us practice divination at the stone temple over the burial mound and make sacrificial offerings to hear from the spirit of the ancestors."

Is it possible that the Shang were responsible for, or at least significant partners in, the sudden emergence of the sophisticated Olmec culture in Mesoamerica? Many reputable scholars, including Mike Xu, Betty Meggers, and Gordon Ekholm, are convinced that they were.

As had been the case in Asia, politics was never far from my mind in Mexico. Protests were a daily occurrence in the capital. I could hear the music and speeches from the roof of my hotel near the *zócalo*. It was the same in Oaxaca and San Cristóbal de Las Casas, the staging-ground for many military exercises by the Zapatistas in Chiapas. Despite conciliatory statements by the government, the Mexican army was on high alert. The city itself had been quiet, but the surrounding area and the roads leading into San Cristóbal had all the appearance of an armed camp or occupied country, with military command posts and checkpoints every few miles. I spent two days outside Ocosingo—a flashpoint for confrontations and the unofficial nerve center for the Zapatistas—staying at a small resort called Rancho Esmeralda, run by an American couple named Ellen

Jones and Glen Wersch. I was there to visit the Maya ruins at Toniná, but the presence of the army was distracting; so too were stories of neighbors being intimidated by supporters of the Zapatistas and encouraged not to allow passage through their property to the ruins.

Ellen and Glen had built Rancho Esmeralda, with its cabins, paths, and gardens, over a seven-year period and were looking forward to harvesting their first crop of macadamia nuts. They loved Mexico and had sold all their property in the United States to finance this new venture, which employed many of the local inhabitants. Theirs was a hands-on affair, the owners engaged in every aspect of the operation, including the cooking and serving of meals.

"Have a look at this," Glen said, as I settled into one of the lawn chairs with a beer. He had just returned from Ocosingo in his pickup truck with a load of groceries. He was lean and tall, wearing a checkered work shirt that would not stay tucked into his jeans. "It will give you a bit of perspective on the struggles going on here."

It was a 1994 article by George A. Collier from *Cultural Survival Quarterly*, explaining some of the reasons for the Zapatista uprising:

> The rebellion galvanized nationwide critiques of Salinas de Gortari's policies of economic restructuring and led to demands for fair elections. Peasants in Chiapas and elsewhere have taken over town halls in protest against the old-style "politics as usual" which guaranteed posts to those loyal to the PRI [*Partido Revolucionario Institucional*]. Because the Zapatistas negotiate from a nearly inaccessible

heartland that the Mexican military has little possibility of controlling without a massive campaign of counterinsurgency, the rebels hold a strong suit in their bid to redirect the forces that shape not just their region but the nation as a whole in its articulation into the international economy as an exporter of petroleum and a signatory to the North American Free Trade Agreement.

Collier's article proved prophetic, as the Zapatista Rebellion contributed to the eventual collapse of the PRI, if not its policies. The election of Vicente Fox in 2000 resulted in a few changes to the infrastructure that were mostly cosmetic, including sewage and electrical repairs in San Cristóbal and a new technical college in Ocosingo, but the military presence actually increased. In addition to the sixty thousand troops of the Mexican army deployed throughout Chiapas, there were still right-wing paramilitary groups plying their grisly trade in the region.

While visiting the ruins at Bonampak and Yaxchilán, in the less confrontational, though equally troubled, region of eastern Chiapas, I'd spent two nights at the Escudo Jaguar Hotel in the village of Frontera Corozal. A roar from the soccer field indicated that someone had scored. The rain had let up, but drops were still descending from the steep *palapa* roof of the restaurant. I ordered another *cerveza* and put my notebook aside to eavesdrop on a tour group from Baltimore and Washington, D.C., that had just arrived in a chartered bus. The young American guide was telling a joke about a new archaeologist who had arrived in the region. The archaeologist did not speak the Lacandon language, so he depended on a mixture of Spanish, English, and inspired guesswork to get his points across and to gather information. In response to a question he mistakenly thought to be about his place of birth, he said "Arlington," which brought a huge smile to the face of his interlocutor. Soon the Lacandon man returned with another villager who posed the same question. When the answer was given, both men looked at each other and burst out laughing. When the same routine was played out before a large assembly of villagers, the archaeologist decided to consult one of his colleagues who spoke the language. Did the Lacandon have some previous knowledge of Arlington, Virginia? No, but *ali* translated in Lacandon as "heavy testicles," a condition caused by a particular river worm that crawls up the penis and into the scrotum, where it hatches its eggs. Eventually the scrotum becomes so large it has to be carried in a wheelbarrow.

Later, when his charges had retired for the night, I asked the young American about his training. He turned out to be a Canadian named Mark Zender, fluent in both Chol and Yucatec, who was working on his doctorate in archaeology at the University of Calgary. He had given a paper in the United States that was so highly regarded that he had been hired to conduct an elite tour of the major Maya sites. He was surprised to learn I had met several of his colleagues and had interviewed David Kelley.

I thought of all the Asians who had washed up on the coasts of the Americas over several thousand years and wondered how many had looked at each other, compared notes, and said, "Small world, eh?"

TWENTY-ONE

I WAS AS NERVOUS crossing into Guatemala as I had been flying into Afghanistan. A popular uprising by the Maya in
Guatemala had been brutally suppressed in the 1980s by the
U.S.-backed military, its abuses reported in *The Catholic Worker*
and in books such as Carlos Fuentes's *Latin America: At War
with the Past* and Eduardo Galeano's *Guatemala: Occupied
Country.* Galeano's book includes an account of atrocities written by Father Thomas Melville, a Maryknoll priest forced to
leave because of his revolutionary sympathies. Father Melville
tells of the deaths and disappearances at the hands of two paramilitary groups, *Mano Blanco* (White Hand) and *Nueva
Organización Anticommunista*, (NOA), of "2,800 intellectuals, labor leaders and peasants who have in any way tried to
organize and combat the ills of Guatemalan society." He con-
demns not only the Guatemalan elite, but also the Catholic
Church and the government of the United States for their com-
plicity. He and his brother, another priest, decided they could no
longer be "silent accomplices of the mass murder that this system generates." Fortunately, Melville was given the option of
leaving, but not before he'd made his famous pronouncement: "I
am a communist only if Christ was a communist. I did what I
did and will continue to do so because of the teachings of Christ
and not because of Marx or Lenin. And I say here too, that we
are many more than the hierarchy and the U. S. government

think. When the fight breaks out more in the open, let the world know that we do it not for Russia, not for China, nor any other country, but for Guatemala. Our response to the present situation is not because we have read either Marx or Lenin, but because we have read the New Testament."

I'd written and published a poem about the murder of Guatemalan activist and shop steward Marlon Mendizábal. According to *The Catholic Worker*, the Coca-Cola Company's way of dealing with strikes at the plant was to hire army lieutenants to direct warehousing, personnel, and security. Mendizábal was one of forty-four members of the National Confederation of Labor murdered by right-wing death squads. Not surprisingly, when I scrambled up the bank of the Usumacinta River at Bethel, my imagination was working overtime. I feared my name would be on every list, that I might be arrested or have the white hand of doom stamped on my backpack.

What I found was a sleepy, sprawling hamlet with no military outpost to match the one I'd just left in Mexico. My search for the *aduana* (customs) took me along a dirt road that I shared with brown and black pigs, turkeys, chickens, kids, and a plague of scrawny, diseased dogs. Customs procedures were even more casual in Guatemala than in Mexico, the major concern being that I contribute to the local economy by exchanging dollars or pesos for *quetzales*. No lists were checked, no fingerprints taken. The official could barely wait to stamp my passport before descending again into unconsciousness in his hammock.

Two hours later, I was on a minibus headed for Flores, the major rallying point for trips to the great Maya ruins at Tikal. The trip through scrubland—cleared jungle, now mostly swamp and no longer useful for anything but grazing—was uneventful, except for a flat tire, a pit stop for repairs, and the beating taken by passengers and vehicle on the rough gravel roads. Asian cattle peered through the railings of a ramshackle feedlot. Beyond them, the bleached white skeleton of a giant ceiba tree lay uprooted in a field, its trunk as broad and white as a cement culvert. Two women bent over a stream, scrubbing clothes on rocks. A man rode past on a donkey, a machete tucked into his belt, the animal's legs clicking like machine parts, causing no up-and-down movement. So far, everything was on the level.

If you see the Buddha on the road, kill him. This shocking piece of advice, which seems to have emanated from the master himself, was meant to encourage a skeptical view of spiritual self-promotion. It certainly did not apply to the serenely attractive young woman I found meditating atop Temple II in the Grand Plaza at Tikal. She had assumed the lotus posture, eyes closed. Her white blouse, bare arms, and high forehead, absorbing the full force of the sun as it rose above the jungle canopy, were luminous, radiant. I had not noticed this apparition, this apotheosis of goodness and light, as I inched heavenward on all fours, not daring to look down or pause for fear I would panic and lose my nerve. If I didn't faint first and tumble down the stairs to my death, as had a number of unfortunate tourists on Temple I before it was closed to the public, I'd be paralyzed halfway up the steep 125-foot incline and have to be rescued.

I flung myself onto the broad stone platform, my heart pounding as much from fear as from exertion, and chucked my backpack and camera against the wall of the sacrificial chamber. I could not imagine how I would ever drum up the courage to descend with the height and perilously steep incline in full view. Perhaps that's why so many sacrifices had taken place up here: those who made it to the top preferred the knife to the stairs. As the blood vessels in my retinas stopped whirling, I looked around. Several young people in their early twenties were spread out on the platform trying not to look concerned about the condition of the wheezing mountain goat that had materialized on their ledge of sky.

It was a glorious day. I'd watched the first rays of light from atop Temple IV, where various birds—mostly parrots and toucans—swooped from tree to tree and a coati, a relative of the raccoon with a long, flexible snout, hung around cadging food from those tourists oblivious to the signs. The jungle glistened as sunlight reflected in a billion drops of dew in the thick canopy. Now, only twenty-five minutes later, the intense heat had licked up every bit of moisture.

"Isn't it wonderful?" Marissa Dolan unwound herself from the lotus position to extract some bottled water from her tote bag. "I see we're using the same camera. Would you like to see how it looks through a good zoom lens?" She unzipped the bag, slid the long lens from its case, and passed it to me. I attached it to my camera and zoomed in on two crows that had just landed on the roof of Temple I, a hundred yards away. One had its head buried under a wing; the other was toying with a piece of twig at its feet. I could count the fleas.

Marissa, who grew up in Florida, introduced me to her husband, Colin, a Canadian. They had driven down from Ottawa with another couple and their dog. I was intrigued, having thought of making a similar trip myself, but when I looked at the map and calculated the distance, I had realized that half my available time would be spent behind the steering wheel. Their friends were off somewhere with the dog, which had been refused entry to the site. I asked Colin if he was familiar with the inverted lotus posture, as I had never seen it in a photograph or in the flesh. He immediately performed a headstand and was in the process of trying to twist his legs into the lotus position when I begged him to stop, as he was less than two feet from the edge of the platform. Laughing, he obliged but said he hoped I'd got the general idea.

"You mean self-torture?"

When I told Marissa I was on the trail of a Buddhist monk, her face brightened. She wanted to know if I had been meditating at the various sites on the way south. I'm not a Buddhist, I confessed, just a searcher. I asked what their theory was on the sudden demise of Maya civilization. Marissa recommended *The Mayan Factor: Path Beyond Technology* by José Argüelles, a copy of which I had picked up in the museum bookstore a few days earlier in Palenque but had not read.

As I was to learn that evening in my hotel room overlooking Petén Itzá Lake in Flores, Argüelles, who writes in English, is convinced the Maya were sent to Earth for a reason: "to make sure that the galactic harmonic pattern, not perceivable as yet to our evolutionary position in the galaxy, had been presented and recorded." When their task was finished, these galactic masters simply left. I hadn't the slightest idea what he meant, as Chiapas and Guatemala were full of Maya, but I kept reading. Argüelles rejects the idea that climatic change or "a slave revolt against despotic leaders" contributed to the demise of the Maya. Having emerged from a personal hell of alcoholism and domestic chaos, Argüelles came to view himself, like the Maya, as a spiritual navigator in search of a system of thought that would help him, and others, through perilous political times.

Argüelles links the months of the Maya calendar with the twenty amino acids and the sixty-four six-part code words or codons of DNA. His leaps of logic are as breathtaking as his rhetoric: "If the *Kuxan Suum,* like a resonant galactic walkie-talkie, could be the transmitting agent of the information necessary to transport high-frequency synchronization scouts from a system outside of ours to our planet, it also bears resemblance to the Hopi *Sipapu.*" If I thought I was dizzy atop Temple II with my new Buddhist friends, Argüelles's charts—so many spiders, vaginas, exploding eyeballs, and dancing figures disappearing up the yin-yang of the universe—would be enough to induce permanent motion sickness.

That Argüelles's flaky book should be so widely known and easily available and not Ronald Wright's *Time Among the Maya* is perhaps a comment on our skewed values, our lack of direction. Wright's book gives a detailed account of life among the Maya of Belize, Guatemala, and Mexico. Beginning with a dig in Lamanai in northwestern Belize that showed evidence of three thousand years of continuous occupation, Wright moves through Maya communities, relating present conditions to historical events, all the while giving a sense of the rich texture of Maya daily life and spirituality. While lamenting the ongoing war against the Maya conducted by right-wing, racist regimes, he celebrates their resilience and adaptability: "Today five million people speak Maya languages, and many of them still preserve calendrical and religious knowledge as old as their civilization."

In the epilogue to *Time Among the Maya*, Wright speaks passionately of the people and their struggle: "One could say that the Maya are shattered: by the white men's countries drawn between and around them, by their own many languages, by the creeping replacement of Maya with Spanish (or English in Belize), by the loss of the calendar in some places and its retention in others, by the many faiths they have kept and acquired. The Maya may be shattered, but they have always been so. Disunity may be a weakness but it is also their strength. The Spaniards conquered the Maya again and again but never broke them. Even in Guatemala, where the war of conquest has been renewed, Maya culture survives."

Having, like Argüelles's mystical DNA, my own dubious ends to attain, I wished Colin and Marissa well, took a deep breath, and picked my way diagonally, as if I were a novice skier traversing a steep slope, down the perilous steps to the Grand Plaza where chairs were being set up for an official ceremony, though not of the sacrificial sort. There would be no bloodletting or severed heads today. Three Maya in ceremonial costumes prepared the ground for a dance and small ceremony. As dignitaries took their seats in the front row, three spotted turkeys of the Petén, which resemble—and certainly like to think of themselves in the same league as—pheasants, strutted past.

I'd been warned by friends about the criminal element in Guatemala City. Even my daughter Bronwen had a personal story to contribute about being robbed on a second-class bus within the city limits. However, my two days in the dreary capital turned out to be enriching.

I checked into the Hotel Chalet Suizo, a comfortable if spartan refuge, then took a taxi to the Popol Vuh Museum, where I found two unexpectedly bizarre pieces. These low-relief, pot-bellied figures called *gordos,* or "fat ones," struck me as meditative and Buddha-like, with half-closed eyes, well-defined lips, and deep ridges between the nose and bulging cheeks. A note in Spanish indicated that they were associated with a "cult" and had been found near Escuintla and the Central Highlands, not far from the Pacific coast. I couldn't shake the feeling that these mysterious figures were significant to my research. I was determined to learn more about the cult. Could it have been inspired by visitors or refugees from Asia? I thought I could detect a faint resemblance between the *gordos* and the Olmec heads of La Venta. None of the museum staff could enlighten me, but an elementary-school teacher conducting a tour of Grade 3 students thought the *gordos* were fertility figures. She told me I'd find similar artifacts at the new Kaminaljuyu Museum, which had been built as a token reminder of the ancient ruins now lost beneath an urban wasteland of super-hotels and freeways. She was right; several *gordos* were locked in glass cases under the watchful eye of an armed guard, who patrolled the upper balcony. There were also several quite different, angular heads that looked as if they'd been sculpted by the same artist who made the famous heads of Easter Island.

Given these discoveries and my determination to visit their place of origin near Escuintla, I made short shrift of Guatemala City, where the casualties of war were reflected in high levels of unemployment and where it was an act of folly to go in search of a bank machine or be out and about after dark. I could not decide which was worse, the menacing vagrants or the pushy evangelical cabdrivers. At least the vagrants would clam up in response to a small donation. I checked out of the Hotel Chalet Suizo early and traveled south by private coach to the Honduran border, where the crossing was straightforward for buses, though not for vehicles that might provide a hiding place for drugs or refugees. A dozen plainclothes men, swinging sawed-off shotguns and pistol-grip rifles, slouched near the rope barriers or lounged in the shadows. As I was paying my entry fee, I heard my name being called. Colin and Marissa, Buddhist fellow travelers, were behind me in line, also heading to the ruins at Copán.

The previous night, after consuming a bad imitation of a pizza, I had awakened with indigestion and another message from Huishen, this time with advice I might well have considered:

A Buddhist travelogue is a contradiction in terms. Discover the universe by staying home, et cetera, et cetera. There's bullshit enough in that to contain a grain of truth. After all, what have I learned from forty years of wandering Earth that I could not have picked up amidst, this host of worthies? That's good—shouts of "Hear! Hear!" Cups and fists pounding the tables. Still, even the most jaded among you would have been shocked to meet The People Who Give Everything Away, a tribe of barbarian big-time spenders who loved to make jokes at our expense and called us, among other things, maggot eaters. They'd never seen rice before, or shaven heads. Taay Gitgha, whose name trans-lates literally as "Son of Coho," but whom I called Nang Dlgiis, *the "one who swims," was the chief's son and taught me much about the language, its glottals and clicking sounds. Fifty words a day; syntax would come later. A species of shelf fungus, which grows on the north side of dead trees, served the purpose for writing. Characters shrink as the fungus dries and hardens. Any day you'd see a dozen children copying calligraphy in the dirt and mimicking my pronunciation. Nang Dlgiis's niece, a precocious three-year-old, would scrunch up her face and offer a more-than-passable imitation of me repeating the body's parts. When she got to the word for genitals, she'd run to the water's edge and squat to pee. I know the feeling. Excuse me while I extricate myself from a portion of Peng's execrable opiate.*

Copán, though by no means as dramatically situated as Palenque, remains the most famous and controversial of the Maya sites, mainly because of Stela B. Yax K'uk' Mo' (Blue Quetzal Macaw) has been identified as the founder, if not the first ruler, of Copán, which is situated inland in the Honduran jungle just south of the Guatemalan border. The date of his assuming power has been calculated to be September 9, AD 426. If Huishen made it this far south during his 458 to 499 sojourn in the Americas, he may have met the as-yet-unidentified third ruler of Copán, as well as Cu Ix, the fourth successor of Yax K'uk' Mo'. However, the fame of Copán is related to two later rulers, Smoke Imix K'awil and his brilliant but ill-fated son and successor, 18 Rabbit (Uaxaclajuun Ub'aah K'awil), both of whom transformed the city and were responsible for promoting the arts, including tree-stones, or stelae, which have been aptly described as "dramas in stone."

The most famous of these tree-stones is Stela B, so long a focus of dispute among diffusionists and isolationists, the former identifying elephant trunks, the latter declaring these sloping appendages to be nothing more than the curved beaks of indigenous macaws. The debate over Stela B, which has raged for more than a century, features prominently in a new book by a Chilean architect turned amateur historian Jaime Errázuriz Zañartu. *The Pacific Basin: 4,000 Years of Cultural Contact* boldly revisits the issue, asking on its front cover, "Why do educated people see a macaw where the ordinary person sees an elephant?"

The question, it seems, will not go away. After an hour spent examining this amazing tree stone, so intimate, playful, and three-dimensional—reminding me of Chinese ivory carvings, some of them free-moving shapes within shapes—I had to confess to be one of those ordinary folk who see elephant trunks in Stela B. How 18 Rabbit and his artists might have come in contact with an elephant or the image of an elephant I could only surmise, but even in its weathered form, the shape, texturing, and curl at the end of the trunk indicate a creature not found in Mesoamerica. Earlier archaeological drawings and photographs of Stela B are even more convincing, as they clearly show, perched on each head, the turbaned figure of a mahout, or elephant driver. I could still make out these tiny mahouts, but time would soon erase them. In *Lost Kingdoms of the Maya*, George and Gene Stuart include a striking photograph of Stela B that shows a great kiskadee—a tiny yellow bird with black-and-white head markings—with a blade of grass in its mouth, about to alight in the nest it is building in the curl of one trunk.

As I picked my way among the ruins, where excavations have recently revealed tunnels and a perfectly preserved smaller temple with its original colors still intact, I encountered, at the base of a giant ceiba, the carving of an almost toothless and slightly demented old man grinning—one of the ancients said to be holding up the four corners of the world and obviously pleased to be having a break from his onerous task. A carved human face looked out from the stone wall, strikingly realistic, its chin consisting of three separate mineral deposits—age lines, cataclysms—an indulgence on the artist's part that seemed to say: You never know what a man is made of. Nearby was an older, more weathered face, with a protruding hand carved from the rock beneath, another of those hands reaching out from the past that had spoken to me so often in China. Much of the work was sensual, realistic, anything but monumental. These details, along with the stelae and a dozen crudely carved heads that looked like maniacal cartoon drawings, gave Copán a degree of intimacy, humor, and domesticity I had experienced in no other ancient ruins in Mesoamerica.

Maya achievements in writing and sculpture under 18 Rabbit's patronage of the arts may have been surpassed, but the evidence to prove it has been destroyed or lost. The writing was of particular interest to me. According to Linda Schele and David Freidel in *A Forest of Kings: The Untold Story of the Ancient Maya*, "a lineage of scribes occupying Compound 9N-8 built an extraordinary family temple dedicated to God N, the patron god of writing, and hence, of history itself." These scribes were responsible for preserving the dynastic record and, ironically, for restoring 18 Rabbit to his rightful place in history. After his ignominious demise—he was captured and sacrificed on May 3, 738, by Cauac

Sky, the very man he had installed at nearby Quiriguá—18 Rabbit's reputation plummeted for almost twenty years. Thanks to the scribes and to the political savvy and architectural prowess of Smoke Shell, son of his successor Smoke Monkey, 18 Rabbit's shameful defeat was effectively erased from the records in Copán. This careful rewriting of dynastic history is still legible in the Temple of Hieroglyphic Stairs, where the risers contain 2,200 glyphs, the longest pre-Columbian stone text to have been found in the Americas. Here the brilliant but ill-fated ruler, whose existence had been briefly expunged from history, assumes his rightful place between Smoke Imix K'awil and Smoke Monkey.

According to his loyal scribes, 18 Rabbit remained a great leader. Let others remember his defeat; the Maya of Copán would celebrate his achievements in art and governance. So reads the official record. It is enough to make one ponder the writing of history, ancient and contemporary. The few pages that remain of Huishen's brief history of his travels to the east tell us little of what he saw and even less of what he thought of the people and social systems he encountered. How was the account of his travels shaped by his audience? What would the emperor and court historians expect to hear from an itinerant Buddhist priest, and what would they consider worth recording? Was he simply performing? Was his story intended to inform his adopted countrymen of what lay outside their realm of experience and influence, letting them know that the Middle Kingdom was not, in truth, the center of Earth? Was he projecting an image of himself that might garner approval? Or, perhaps, all of the above?

If history is subjective, the obvious corollary is that all history is also personal history. Before leaving Mexico, I'd been rereading David Herzberger's book *Narrating the Past: Fiction and Historiography in Postwar Spain*, in which he discusses the various strategies novelists had used to rewrite Spanish history to make it look as if Franco's regime represented the fulfilling of destiny, the final flowering of all that is good in Spanish culture. They had, by extension, painted left-wing political dissent as an aberration. When Franco died and a more democratic system began to evolve, novelists of a social-realist cast committed a similar error. By dismissing the Franco era as an unfortunate deviation from the true path, they denied those negative authoritarian elements that were deeply ingrained in the Spanish psyche and culture. One essentialist myth replaced another.

It seemed to me that New Spain was undergoing similar ruptures in terms of the writing of its own history, much as archaeologists were struggling with new discoveries in the field. From a period when Asian contact was accepted and too much credit was ascribed to possible foreign influences, fierce defenders of the uniqueness of Mesoamerican culture emerged. These scholars championed the inventiveness of indigenous peoples and refused to admit to any outside influence. Much of their defensiveness had to do not only with personal ambition and fear in the face of a conflicting master narrative, but also with justified pride in the accomplishments of Native Americans. Yet new evidence was emerging that repeated foreign contacts had begun earlier and with more than one point of origin. The idea of coastal migration was challenging the hegemony of the

Bering land bridge theory of human arrivals, and artistic and linguistic comparisons between Asia and Mesoamerica could no longer be so easily dismissed.

No one wants to be told—never mind have it proved—that he is wrong. Eric Thompson resisted the truth about Maya glyphs until his deathbed; and it seemed to me, regretfully, that the academic establishment might prove equally resistant to new information about pre-Columbian Asian contact.

TWENTY-TWO

I WAS eager to get back to Mexico City. I wanted to talk with Rubén Cabrera about the human remains and the jade figure he and Saburo Sugiyama had discovered beneath the Temple of the Moon in Teotihuacán. I also planned a second stop in Oaxaca, where I'd been promised help in locating the missing figure in *flor de loto invertido* (inverted lotus posture) that the poet Gabriel Zaid had noticed thirty years earlier in the Mitla Museum and that he believed to be Asian in origin or inspiration. Having checked out Stela B's elephants and the revisionist scribes of Copán, I was also determined to see, on my journey north, more of the mysterious *gordos*, originating on Guatemala's Pacific slope. However, I had not expected to encounter one so promptly—and on the bus. Although the bus had left the station half-empty, so many *campesinos* were picked up along the highway by "Jennifer"—a recycled Bluebird school bus from Burlington, Ontario, now painted pink and renamed—that I had to put my backpack on my lap and pile two small bags on top of that. As a result, I was taking up more than my share of the seat. An enormous woman in a floral dress, determined to recover lost territory, gave me a nasty look, propped her feet on the seat across the aisle, and pushed.

Suddenly I knew how it felt to be two-dimensional. Meanwhile, her small son was standing in the aisle with a puzzled look on his face, because the furious exertions of a bus with no shock absorbers had caused his pants to fall around his ankles and he couldn't abandon his tight grip to pull them up. The heat was deadly. Outside Escuintla, an urban blight on the Pan-American Highway whose Maya name means "headful of water," "Jennifer" lost power and glided to a stop beside the road. Both driver and swamper hopped out with a bag of tools, tape, and wire and disappeared astern for half an hour, where they conducted the necessary rituals to get us to the next stop. The usurping *gorda* was still not satisfied and seemed determined to reduce me not just to the status of cardboard, but to pulp.

There were no hotels in Santa Lucía Cotzumalguapa, so I rented a bed at *Hospedaje Reforma*, where my feelings of claustrophobia in a windowless room were surpassed only by my nausea from the pervading odor of mold. Mario, a good Catholic Maya with a wrecked Datsun that looked as if it had died and been reluctantly resurrected, was waiting for me on the street. He and his doomed chariot looked so desperate that, ignoring my survival instincts and the temptation to flee, I climbed in. The doors, purely decorative, hung on rusted frames. I could see pavement through the repatched floor. Stripped to the essentials and beyond, the taxi was a triumph of faith over technology. Nothing on the dashboard worked: no speedometer, no horn, no turn signals, no fuel gauge, no sunvisors, no windshield wipers. We set off up the road in a series of epileptic jerks because the clutch plate was worn smooth and almost no compression remained in the aching cylinders.

At the gate of Finca El Baúl, an armed guard halted the taxi, made a quick assessment of the situation, and waved us back fifty yards. He grimaced as if we might be contaminated and refused to approach. Mario went to the gate and presented his papers, explaining that I had come all the way from Canada to see the sugar refinery's sculpture garden. While we waited, several other vehicles were admitted. Routine checks were made on Mario's licence and vehicle registration. He was told that something was amiss, a discrepancy in terms of dates. We would not be allowed in. Mario, humiliated and knowing this had less to do with regulations than with the arbitrary exercise of power, would not let the guard see his anger. I went to the gate to present my "credentials"—a passport and a couple of letters of reference—aware that anything I might say on my own behalf would be undermined by the dilapidated state of my transportation. At least the guard did not ask where I was staying. After several calls to the administration building and another twenty-minute wait, the gate swung open and we were permitted to pass, for one hour.

We jerked and sputtered our way uphill past the sugar refinery. The deafening noise and sour-sweet smells were familiar to me, as I had worked for two summers at the BC Sugar Refinery on the waterfront in Vancouver. Mario hauled up in front of a building without walls, a staff canteen, and bought himself a subsidized lunch while I examined the sculpture garden. There was nothing unusual in the collection, certainly no *gordos*, and no illuminating text to explain the collection, just the kind of unimaginative, lackluster display you might expect from a company that did not require good public relations to justify exploiting the locals. I took photographs of a few sculptures and an ancient locomotive, then joined Mario for a cheap lunch.

As we coasted downhill to save gas, Mario released a tirade against the abuses in his country. He even made up a poem about them, the theme of which was decidedly biblical: What is small is great, what is great shall be brought low. He explained to me how difficult it was in Guatemala to be an honorable man. Only thieves and the rich survive. Then he told me of a novel he had read, or dreamed, with the ironic title *Aun Lloren los Ricos, Even the Rich Cry*. At the same moment, the taxi hit a pothole and emitted an ominous death rattle.

We both howled with delight.

Our next stop took us through several cane fields, where the Datsun could not make up its mind whether to explode or disintegrate. With every bump, the key popped out of the ignition and our survival would be up for grabs while Mario held the steering wheel with one hand and rummaged between his feet with the other. Only repeated interventions from the Holy Mother kept us from puncturing the oil pan on protruding rocks. We emerged from the tunnel of tall cane into a clearing at the foot of a small hill, where two Maya cowboys had tethered their horses and were having a smoke in the shade. Beneath the overhanging branches a third man performed rituals before an enormous stone head partially buried in the earth, only its eyes, nose, and sarcastic upper lip still visible. The stone was black from centuries of smoke, candle wax, and offerings but sported several flowers draped over the forehead like psychedelic bangs. The worshiping cowboy had placed candles in a starburst arrangement around the embers of a small fire and was swinging a 48-ounce juice can full of burning incense—copal, no doubt—attached to a piece of bailing-twine. As he swung the incense back and forth over the embers, he alternately droned and prayed for forgiveness.

"Dios perdón, delitos de trabajo, delitos contra mi familia"— "God forgive me for sins committed on the job, for sins against

my family." Rituals over, he picked up the tall candles and, one by one, dropped them onto the embers. As I watched in fascination, the stalwart and devout Mario at my side grunted his disapproval of the antics of his Maya brother.

"*Es ignorancia,*" he declared, turning back to the car.

I was not going to be tempted into a debate about the relative merits of Maya and Catholic superstitions, especially in Spanish, so I let it pass. Having been insulted by the guards, Mario could be forgiven for needing to feel superior to someone.

At Hotel Francia in Oaxaca, which boasted D. H. Lawrence as one of its illustrious former guests, my thoughts were not on Mesoamerican culture and its Asian influences, but on my own body art, specifically the constellation of flea bites and red marks left from scratching that extended from shoulders to ankles— souvenirs from *Hospedaje Reforma* or the long second-class bus ride from the border town of Tapachula and on through the mountains of western Chiapas. While I counted volcanoes, stops for passengers, and military checkpoints and shivered as the bus climbed higher and higher, *una fiesta de plugas*—a little carnival of fleas—was in full swing in the warm, damp tropics of my road-soiled garments. It was second class for me; for them, first class all the way. Not even a hot shower and liberal applications of Polysporin would reduce the itching.

However, I was happy. After a nervous encounter with a platoon of army reserves outside the museum at Finca Las Illusiones, Mario had surprised me with a whole garden of *gordos* at the nearby town of La Democracia. Olmec-style heads and pot-bellied *gordos*—twenty in all—were placed at regular intervals around the plaza in front of the museum, which was closed on Mondays. Now I was waiting for the Oaxaca Museum to open so I could talk to the director, Jesús Martínez Arvizu, who had promised to try to locate in storage the figure in inverted lotus posture from the Frissell collection in Mitla. Jesús was very sweet but told me that the matter was now out of his hands—it would take three days to locate the figure, and permission could be granted only by Eduardo López Calzado, Director of the Oaxaca branch of the Instituto Nacional Antropología y Historia. I'd booked into the Hotel Francia for November 20 without realizing it was a national holiday. All the government offices were closed, and the city was in a festive mood, with parades of athletes, clubs, and school bands. I wrote a letter to Señor López, offering to pay for labor, photographic costs, and postage, and left it with the concierge at the institute.

I divided my afternoon between an Internet café and supporting a protest rally in front of the government offices. Half a dozen organizations, including the Zapatistas, were protesting the effects of globalization on the Mexican economy, assassinations by paramilitaries, and unlawful detention of their members. I had spoken with Zapatista supporters in San Cristóbal de Las Casas but was unable to travel deeper into the organization's heartland. To escape the heat in Oaxaca, I spent several hours studying Zapatista propaganda on the Internet, which included a Web site with a huge number of public utterances by *Subcomandante* Marcos and open letters he had written to Vicente Fox and former president Carlos Salinas de Gortari.

There was no denying the humor and wit in these documents, as well as the absence of stridency, self-promotion, and ideological ranting. Their rhetoric was quite different from that of the scribes of Copán, apologists for the vanquished Maya leader 18 Rabbit. Psychology and humor were the distinguishing characteristics of the Zapatista Web site. The reports denied any Zapatista association with foreign constituencies, political, military, or religious, and claimed that "the use of masks to hide our faces is in keeping with elemental security measures and as a vaccine against *caudillismo*," the cult of the strong man so deadly to political reform.

One letter seemed to me particularly telling, as it demonstrated an important human dimension in the movement. Deftly, *Subcomandante* Marcos plunks his reader in the middle of a kitchen where he is being harassed by various armed *compañeras* for scolding Heriberto, a small boy who justifies his torture of ants by saying, "I'm not bothering them, I'm patting them." While the women berate Marcos, Heriberto absconds with a bag of candies intended as a birthday present for one of the other children. "I have been sighing with nostalgia," Marcos says, "remembering the good old times when the bad guys were bad guys and the good guys were good guys. When Newton's apple followed its irresistible trajectory from the tree toward some childish hand. When the world smelled like a schoolroom on the first day of class: of fear, of mystery, of newness." Meanwhile, Heriberto has returned with the now empty candy bag only to snatch a bag of balloons. Amid the maps, gun belts, ashes of pipe tobacco, and rank-smelling ski masks, Marcos wryly observes, "This is not a general headquarters, but a kindergarten."

The difference between the Zapatistas and the Taliban, in terms of strategy and ideology, was striking. The Zapatistas were nonsectarian, democratic, and antiglobalist in sentiment;

they wanted land, justice, and education for indigenous peasants who had long been impoverished and marginalized. And they had a leader who was neither despotic nor fanatical, who resisted armed confrontation whenever possible. Marcos had a sense of humor and, I gathered, no long-range political ambitions. However, a few weeks after my return home, the Zapatistas, frustrated with military interference and government inaction, would reoccupy San Cristóbal de Las Casas for long enough to hold a press conference and then, sadly, take permanent possession of Rancho Esmeralda resort, intimidating the staff and forcing American expatriates Ellen Jones and Glen Wersch to leave before having a chance to harvest their first crop of macadamia nuts. As much as I admired Zapatista strategy in general and Marcos in particular, the irony of dispossessing two apologists for your cause was not lost on me.

Something unusual about Oaxaca—the air, the altitude, the ghosts—plays havoc with the subconscious. During the Day of the Dead celebration two weeks earlier, I had had a strange encounter. A Zapotec woman in the *zócalo* accosted me, shouting *"Sangre! Sangre!"*—the Spanish word for "blood." I had just been to the cemetery, where bands were playing jazz and ragtime tunes and the graves were festooned with flowers and ringed with masked celebrants. Later that evening, I had a few beers and, before going to bed, self-administered minor surgery, using my nail clippers to remove a skin tag in the groin area. Although I had used rubbing alcohol to clean the area and sterilize the clippers, I woke up several times from a nightmare in which the characters in D. H. Lawrence's novel *The Plumed Serpent* and the woman from the plaza, whom I now saw as a female shaman, joined forces in shouting at me about blood. I woke with a temperature, convinced I had blood poisoning. I tossed back the antibiotics I'd been saving and tried to get back to sleep.

When the alarm rang, there were two more messages from Huishen, no less cryptic than usual, that I had scribbled into my notebook.

Pundits dismiss the world of action as a world of stones, my dear Guo. But the saying itself's an act that brings a rain of stones on the unwary. Witness the stony silence that greets us at court. Am I not a man of action? Do I not marshal legions of words and send them marching against ignorance, their infectious rhythms stirring hearts, driving a wedge of fear into the enemy? Poets are put to death for inventing a new measure—or worse, sent to the borderlands to collect taxes. What are we doing here, old friend, wasting time when there are beds to bivouac in, tender fish to be filleted? Misery, the Buddha says, originates in desire unsatisfied; extinguish desire, and misery perishes with it. Yet propagation of the Buddha's wisdom involves a desire to save the wretched. Such desire is said to be impersonal, free from egotism. Or so the story goes.

The second message, which appeared to emanate once again from Peng's drinking establishment in the Chinese capital of Jingzhou a year or two after Huishen's return from the Americas, surprised me.

It's Friday and the one-eyed bonze, as they call me, has not yet put in an appearance. Business is slow. Peng can count the regulars on one hand. But Guo Guo, the dwarf musician, will be there. He plays a horse-hair fiddle designed to accommodate his diminutive size and squat fingers. The man is brilliant—with heartbreaking lyrics, perfect pitch— but is forced to play the fool and perform for the privileged, the pretty ones. Ugly by conventional standards, he is a favorite among the courtesans we visit. He sits in their laps and allows himself to be fondled or dressed up as a child, all the while copping a feel or two and making crude sugges- tions. His melodies bring tears to their eyes and make the money and juices flow equally. When Guo Guo plays, the neck and head of the fiddle emerge from between his legs and a kind of spell settles on the rowdiest guzzlers in the bar. "My limbs may be stunted," he says, stroking the neck of the fiddle, "but my equipment, otherwise, is standard issue."

When I explained these dreams and my strange encounter in the *zócalo* to some friends back home who were frequent visitors to Oaxaca, they put it all down to too much beer and too little Spanish.

"She was offering you a drink," one insisted. "The word was not *sangre*, but *sangría*."

A first-class bus delivered me and my fading body art to Mexico City in six hours. I checked once more into the Hotel Catedral and prepared myself for the interview with Rubén Cabrera. I wanted to know how he and Saburo Sugiyama had located the entrance to the underground passage in the Pyramid of the Moon at

Teotihuacán, whether they'd used high-tech sonar or some other equipment. I hoped Cabrera would be able to tell me why the three human figures he had found in a pit on level five did not have their hands tied behind their backs like other sacrificial victims. When the right moment came I would ask him why no tombs of rulers had been found at Teotihuacán. Could the City of the Gods have been ruled by priests for whom the cult of personality was anathema? I did not want to show my diffusionist colors too soon or Cabrera might clam up, but I was determined to ask if these figures, seated in lotus posture with hands open at the sides, could be foreign missionaries, Buddhists perhaps. As for the small jadeite figure in lotus posture, had anything of this sort ever been found before?

José Antonio, whom I'd met at Copán, had arranged for one of his associates at the civil aviation office, Raúl Martínez, to accompany me to Teotihuacán as interpreter. Raúl phoned the night before to ask if he could bring his son and daughter, who were studying English and were very interested in my project. I had no objection, though it occurred to me that Cabrera might be overwhelmed or intimidated by an audience of four. I faxed Raúl the questions in English, went out to purchase a small audio recorder, and set my alarm for 6:00 a.m. so I could go over the questions. The interview was scheduled for 11:00. At 9:30, Raúl phoned to say he was stuck in traffic. By the time he arrived with Marissa and Raúl Junior, there was no way we could reach Teotihuacán on time. I was sure Cabrera would give up on us. Most of Mexico City's twenty million people seemed to have descended on the *zócalo*. Congestion was so bad we had to go in reverse for two blocks to find a route that was not blocked by street merchants, but Raúl managed to reach Cabrera on his cell phone to explain our predicament.

By the time we arrived at Teotihuacán, my air of confidence had completely disappeared. We crowded into the small office of the Ceramoteca, where, to my surprise, Raúl's son assumed the role of interpreter. He and his father had translated all the questions into Spanish and printed them out. I'd planned to begin my interview with a *chiste*, a little joke, asking if scientists were allowed to get excited by such discoveries. By the time it was translated, the joke, thin even in English, evaporated. In the midst of the second question, Cabrera interrupted to ask the purpose of the interview. This threw me off slightly, as I thought I'd explained my purpose in letters and phone calls. He said that *National Geographic* had already committed money for first rights to the story, so I would have to agree not to publish anything before their article appeared. I assured him I wanted the information for a book that was not yet visible on the horizon.

Cabrera was a short, puckish man, probably my age or older, surrounded by shelves of books and small boxes, which I assumed to be full of skulls, bones, and sundry artifacts. He answered each question very carefully. From the half-smile that played around his lips, I was convinced he'd pegged me at once as part of the lunatic fringe. In response to my question about the absence of rulers at Teotihuacán, he said there were two theories. The first, his preference, was that the tombs of individual rulers still remained to be found. One of his colleagues, on the other hand, believed that Teotihuacán had been governed by committee, by a group of leaders. Cabrera did not think there was any reason to believe in the presence of foreigners other than Maya.

The sacrificial victims whose hands were bound would have been captives, whereas the three human remains I was interested in were probably high officials who had gone to their deaths voluntarily, considering it an honor. The small jadeite figure was quite unique and would require further study, but, no, it did not appear to be Asian. In fact, it had more in common with Olmec figures than with anything else. As much as I wanted this to be a jade Buddha, I could see his point. It's Saturday, he apologized, and, because none of his colleagues were at work, it would not be possible for us to view the discoveries, which were stored under tight security.

I was not ready to leave, but I could see the interview was at an end. I looked at Raúl Junior, who had his hand on the door.

"The drawings," I persisted. "Surely the drawings published with the *Reforma* article make the three human remains and their unique seating arrangement, with hands open at the sides, resemble Asian Buddhists. What is the significance of that?"

"Oh, those." Cabrera's bemused expression was transformed into a full smile. "Those are not our drawings. They were produced by the graphics department at the newspaper."

Twenty-three

As we make our way along the hard-packed sand, leaping over streams that empty into the sea, Nang Dlgiis spots a black bear feeding on a fresh salmon. We are downwind, so the animal does not pick up our scent or observe us behind a beached cedar log. From this angle we can see how delicately the she-bear removes bones before eating the salmon, pausing to scratch between the rows of nipples. A pile of broken clamshells lies on the cedar trunk inches away, probably left by ravens or gulls. On impulse, Nang Dlgiis brushes the surface with his fingers, scattering fragments of shell down the far side of the log. This gesture elicits a shrill cry that brings us both to our feet and the black bear loping toward us. As she rears up, with only the bulk of the tree separating us, I can see milk dripping from one of the distended nipples. Observing the enraged creature, I am quietly grateful for the girth of cedar that wind and tide have deposited on this exact spot. The bear ponders her options. Sunlight reflects off myriad dry scales adhering to her paws. I expect the stench of kept animals, but only the smell of raw fish reaches my nostrils. Nang Dlgiis is first to move, stepping sideways to absorb the creature's attention, then tossing a handful of sand into its eyes, while I bring the length of dead branch down behind the bear's ear, stunning her. We

*do not stay to count the cubs startled from their slumbers in
the humming sand.*

After I shook the dust of Mexico and Guatemala from my feet,
I was on the road again, the whale road. My own instincts, and
Huishen's repeated messages, took me back to the Queen
Charlotte Islands, a dot on the map of the northwest coast of
British Columbia, known to the indigenous people as Haida
Gwaii. This, properly speaking, was where the intensive phase of
my quest for Huishen had begun three years earlier. That ear-
lier visit was very much on my mind.

On that occasion, I had swung my rental car into the driveway
of the Skidegate Museum complex, ploughing in good faith
through several small lakes that had formed on the unpaved
road. I parked across from six long polyethylene tents built to
protect the new totem poles and their carvers from the rain. It
was December 2000, only four in the afternoon but already
pitch black. I sat still for a moment, in the darkness, listening
to the heavy, insistent rain pelting down on the metal roof of
the car. A friend in Vancouver suffered from SAD, seasonal
affective disorder—not enough sunlight, a problem associated
with northern or southern extremes that can be quite debili-
tating. Here on Haida Gwaii there was a local variation known
as RAD, "rain all day," or, more appropriately, RADED, "rain all
day every day." I extracted a folding umbrella from my kit bag
and edged into the deluge, soaking a sandaled foot in the process.
One tent seemed to be alive, breathing. Decorated with a string
of winking Christmas lights, its rib cage expanded and con-
tracted in time with the insistent bass of an old familiar rock
tune I could not name.

I was curious to look inside but had only a couple of hours left to inspect the museum before my poetry reading was due to begin in Queen Charlotte City. Besides, I did not want to interrupt some Haida Michelangelo during a moment of inspiration inside this womb of blue plastic. I splashed through the puddles and up the entry ramp. The museum was closed, but a poster on the door presented me with a soggy imitation of my own face and with information advertising the evening's event.

As I retraced my steps to the car, the entrance slit of the decorated tent parted just enough to give birth to a head and a shaft of yellow light.

"You must be the poet."

Bathed in this luminous pool and attached to the talking head was a shape with a long black ponytail, clothed in jeans, sweater, and rubber boots, beckoning to me. He stepped aside to let me enter. Atop the totem pole, a plastic ghetto blaster vibrated alongside an intricately carved dorsal fin and a scattering of audiotapes.

"Jefferson Airplane?"

"No, The Doors."

I introduced myself, though the poster had apparently made this unnecessary. My Haida Michelangelo turned out to be Michael Nicoll Yahgulanaas, cartoonist, environmental activist, and now assistant carver. We talked for an hour. He had given up a decade of his life fighting the logging companies that were clear-cutting Lyell and Moresby islands. Now he was determined to pursue his own creative impulses. As the music pounded, Michael instructed me on the basic symbolism of the pole and on his role as assistant carver.

The Jim Hart pole, he explained, represented the community of K'uuna 'llnagaay (Skedans) and two of that village's Raven clans. This particular "talking stick" was busy, with three top-hatted watchmen at the tip. Beneath these humorous lookouts, in descending order, were Full Moon, Raven, Mountain Goat, Killer Whale with two dorsal fins, and, bearing the entire burden, a rather benign-looking Grizzly. This string of symbolic creatures, conjoined for aesthetic or culinary purposes, appeared to be either on intimate terms or devouring and being devoured by their colleagues in the food chain.

We agreed to meet the next day for lunch in Queen Charlotte City, a string of dilapidated shacks, businesses, and a school stretching out along a shoreline dotted with the rotting stumps of vanished jetties. There was a beauty in the very transience of the place. Over homemade vegetable soup and multigrain bread, I told Michael about Huishen and my interest in pre-Columbian Asian contact with the Americas. I was convinced, I said, dipping my bread in the soup, that, if Huishen's voyage actually took place, Haida Gwaii would have been a major stop along the way. Michael compressed his vegetarian sandwich with its wayward lettuce and too-healthy bread to a bite-sized thickness and said nothing, but I could see amusement in his eyes and in the play of movement around his mouth, as if he was trying not to smile.

"We have a story here on Haida Gwaii of an Asian monk, in ancient times, spending more than a year on the islands. He's supposed to have helped the ancestors of the White family build stone cairns across the mountains. You know, blinds or markers so they wouldn't get lost in fog during the bear hunt."

I accused him of pulling my leg. He broke off a piece of the sandwich and paused before popping it into his mouth: "Your family name even shows up in the story."

I shook my head. I could see this trickster was up to no good, but I had to admire his deadpan delivery.

"Henry Geddes, a relative of the White family, not only remembered the story, but saw the cairns himself." Michael dismantled the remainder of the sandwich and ate the ingredients piecemeal, looking up at me.

"Of course, he's dead now."

I still believed he was putting me on. After a century of anthropologists and archaeologists making reputations by copying and transcribing Haida, Tlingit, Tsimshian, and Kwakiutl legends or making off with their artifacts while the indigenous peoples' physical survival hung in the balance, I could understand any amount of suspicion and irreverence in the face of new inquiries. So, you want a story about Asians on Haida Gwaii? I'll give you a story. While we're at it, how about the Vikings? I think we had Viking visitors as well. When I made this observation, Michael laughed.

"You're not the only one interested in the subject." He stood up to leave. "Ask David Phillips. He runs a B & B in Masset. They even made a small film."

Before I could ask who "they" were, Michael excused himself and headed back to work on his carving, inviting me to Haida Gwaii for the installation of the new poles. As a parting gesture, he gave me a cedar chip from the Jim Hart pole with his name and e-mail address written on it with a felt-tipped pen.

A Haida business card.

I could not get the cairns out of my mind. I returned to Haida Gwaii a few months later with my friend Martin Duckworth, a filmmaker from Montreal who had become interested in my project. David Phillips was slicing eggplant in the kitchen of Copper Beach House B & B in Masset, laying the slabs with their deep burgundy skin on top of a layer of pasta and cottage cheese. He was a large, imposing man who reminded me of those eighteenth-century portraits of Samuel Johnson. Someone to be reckoned with. David was Johnsonian not only in girth, but also in taste and opinions. He liked to pontificate. He was suspicious and proprietary at first, even when I explained that I had been studying and making notes on Huishen and his alleged journey to the Americas for twenty-seven years. As proof, I showed him the short excerpt about Huishen I'd included in my anthology *Skookum Wawa* in 1975.

David took exception to my use of the word *alleged*. He was a true believer. He pronounced Huishen "the greatest missionary of all times." Then he shared some articles he had gathered on the subject, all of which I'd seen previously. The conversation was peppered with local projects he was involved in, including fund-raising for a new hospital, and with the names of distinguished guests at the B & B, including Canada's Asian-born governor general. This lively exchange was accomplished, I should add, while David generously prepared and served Martin, other guests, and me a magnificent dinner. As a host, David was of an age that predated even Samuel Johnson. In fact, he would not have been out of place among Chaucer's Canterbury pilgrims.

In 1992, David, a film crew, and He Zhixiong, a young visiting scholar from China, had organized a small expedition to the boglands at the head of Masset Inlet. A documentary of the abortive expedition was made for the Open Learning Institute in

Vancouver, a short, charming film that shows David and the others sailing up the inlet and He Zhixiong staring meaningfully into the distance, one hand resting on the mast. I had met Zhixiong and spent some time with him driving up Vancouver Island to visit friends. He had trained in social work but was a dreamer and an idealist. He had become so intrigued by the Huishen story that he translated articles and chapters of books into Chinese and published them alongside Chinese essays on the same subject. Had I known he was to be the only Chinese person I would speak to who knew the Huishen story intimately, I'd have questioned him more thoroughly. As it was, he gave me a copy of the collected essays—*Patient Huishen: Who First Arrived in America?*—that included an English translation of the introduction.

"It's not a fairy tale like *Arabian Nights*," He Zhixiong insisted as we stopped to visit friends in Lantzville. He was wearing a white T-shirt with the block letters MAYAN CULTURE framing a colorful procession of Maya religious leaders and nobility.

He Zhixiong's translated introduction was very useful, citing more than a dozen Chinese authors attracted to the debate. While Chinese opinion seems divided on the question of Huishen's voyage, at least one scholar, navigational historian Fang Zhongpu, believed that pre-Columbian Asian contact with the Americas had been taking place for at least three thousand years. While He Zhixiong dismisses the doubting Thomases and takes his place among the believers, he admits that all the evidence is not in, that "more clues will present themselves if scholars can dig further . . . and this historical mystery will definitely be unmasked in the years to come."

The members of David's and He Zhixiong's expedition, finding nothing, decided they had consulted the wrong person concerning the possible whereabouts of the cairns. Martin had plans for a more ambitious film. He hoped to raise enough money to bring Zhixiong from Boston, where he and his wife were doing graduate studies, to take part in a larger expedition, this time over the ridges of Haida Gwaii. The National Film Board, the CBC, and the History Channel were being approached to underwrite the project. We were cautiously optimistic. Even if the cairns were found, we had to admit, there was unlikely to be sufficient proof to link them indisputably to Asian visitors, especially a fifth-century itinerant priest, as there was unlikely to be graffiti saying HUISHEN WAS HERE.

Martin loped ahead with his bulky camera, looking for ledges and rocky outcrops from which to shoot the passage of our minuscule expeditionary force. Otherwise, he lay flat on the path filming boots and calves as we passed. July 2003. Not much was happening in the calf department, however, as we were all fully wrapped against the damp fog and cool wind sweeping off the Pacific. Small wonder the Queen's Own Guard preferred hats made from the thick coats of Haida Gwaii black bear, evolved over millennia to protect against the cold and penetrating dampness of the northwest coast. I'd seen Martin's work. He loves close-ups and will hang for what seems like hours on a twitching lip muscle or disappear up a nostril, spelunking the nasal cavity to search out the roots of a renegade hair. Now he was trying to record the ups and downs of emotion as we hit one snag after another:

Michael Yahgulanaas unable to join us at the last moment, Ian cursing the fog and inadequate survey maps, me nursing a badly bruised ankle, torn rain gear, and a container of coffee tipped accidentally in the cab of the truck that delivered us to road's end.

We had been told of the existence of a cairn in a high meadow back of the logging camp and were anxious to inspect it. When I mentioned this to the camp manager, he laughed.

"I built that cairn myself ten years ago, with the help of my kids and a couple of friends. A recreational project, I guess you'd call it. Definitely not Asian."

Disappointed, we decided on one more trip into the muskeg in the saddle between Dinan Bay and the Pacific. We made an early start to take advantage of the light and weather, now suddenly clear and, for coastal mountains, warm. I was carrying nuts, sandwiches, granola bars, chocolate, and juice for the others, except Ian, who insisted on Pepsi. He had brought rope and a small tarp in case we were forced to camp overnight, so the perishable foodstuff could be strung from a low branch of a cedar. A desperate or enterprising black bear might still reach the food by climbing, but we were counting on the lure of summer berries to satiate and distract it. I had brought along several canisters of bear-spray, just in case.

"Bears are not like mosquitoes," Ian advised. Midday sun had brought out his freckles. "Point it downwind and don't spray it on your arms."

This was a difficult assignment for Ian, a reminder of his honeymoon camping adventure on the ridges with Rosie, who came down with a disabling disease shortly after their marriage. Ian is a superb nature photographer, but I couldn't resist teasing him about his practice of preparing the scene, removing broken branches and debris.

"Art is nature rearranged," he insisted, as we crossed a dodgy patch of muskeg. Ian hadn't even unpacked his camera. He was giving this event over to Martin and the technology of moving, talking pictures, rather than the terrible eloquence, the impacted drama, of the still shot.

I had binoculars, extra film, and a couple of small scrapers in my backpack. The folding army-surplus spade was attached on the outside of my pack by two clips. Martin was toting empty plastic food containers in his pack in case we decided to bring back concrete evidence of the cairn, though there were ethical questions and professional archaeological practice to consider before carting off a stone or two.

"Expecting to find a relic?" Martin adjusted the battery belt and thrust the camera in my face. "Hipbone of the Buddha, per-haps? If Huishen traveled this far, wouldn't he have carried something light, like a tooth?"

A camera trained on the hair in your nostrils is not easy to ignore. I assumed my best gargoyle expression. "I suggest we call our little expedition—our rock group—the Stupa Faction."

Ian rolled his eyes and quickly absented himself, descending the bank toward the creek bed. He was pleased. Spirits had def-initely lifted; we were off to a good start.

It had been warm on the eastern slope, the lee side, away from the prevailing westerlies. On the way up to the saddle, with no cloud cover, we'd had the full advantage of early-morning sun-light, which was glinting off the still waters of Masset Inlet. With binoculars, I could make out in the distance, emerging from a bank of low-lying fog, a small outboard boat with two bumps amidships. Fishermen, jigging for cod or trolling slowly for the ever-more-elusive salmon. It was worth the effort, even if we found nothing—the visual spectacle, companionship, freedom. No wonder Huishen dallied for forty years in the Americas, if only monasteries and religious responsibilities awaited him at the other end. Over a year with the Haida, so the story goes. Long enough to have an impact and to construct enormous canoes for the return journey, hugging the coast, the dragon's tail of islands, a clever game of currents, wind, star fixes, and a little luck, if luck is allowed in the Buddhist vocabulary.

"Quick, over here!" Ian was shouting several hundred yards ahead of us, where the path, a narrow forest trail forged over centuries by deer and bear, emerged onto one of several dozen rocky knolls that dot the muskeg. He pointed to a small mound covered in green moss. Martin was down on one knee shooting me as I ran, my pack bouncing wildly and putting me off balance because I had forgotten to fasten it at the waist. I miscalculated and sank to one knee in mud.

"Talk about timing." Ian grinned, extending me a hand.

When I extracted my right foot, both hiking boot and sock were missing. I thrust my arm into the water hole and rummaged around until I'd found the boot. It emerged from the mud with a sepulchral gurgle. The sock had vanished.

I removed the other boot to let them both dry out in the sunlight. The surviving sock was hung from the branch as a marker, a victory flag. I was barefoot now—barefoot and itinerant. All I lacked was a begging bowl.

Ian lowered his backpack and stepped back to let me examine the mound. It was certainly in the right location, on a narrow ridge of rock in the muskeg. The trail would be easy enough to

follow in fog until it opened onto this broad expanse of saturated ground, where a turn in the wrong direction could result
in a dunking or worse. It was smaller than I'd expected. Only
three feet high, and rectangular rather than square. The size
may have been determined by the scarcity of small stones at
this altitude. The mound was slightly rounded on top and had
a covering of green moss, like a bun with green St. Patrick's
Day icing—a Buddhist St. Patrick.

Martin, camera thrust out from his shoulder like a rocket
launcher, was circumscribing, sidestepping, an almost perfect
circle about a hundred feet in diameter in the muskeg, as if
enacting some ancient Druidic ritual. Cinema in the round.
With the camera covering his face, he could have been one of
those ancient dancers behind a wolf or bear mask, with a long
projecting snout. All he needed were drums, though my own
heart, which I could hear pumping blood into my eardrums,
was doing a good, if private, imitation. So far, no one had
touched the mound. If it was a cairn, constructed in ancient
times, it could be damaged by removing the blanket of moss
and exposing it to the elements. I found myself wishing we had
brought along a professional. However, our hesitation had
more to do with aesthetics than with science, no one wanting
to break the spell of the mound, rubbed smooth, clothed by
time, still glistening with dew.

Off to my left, Michael Yahgulanaas, who had been unable
to accompany us, was sitting cross-legged, in full lotus posture,
doing a sketch of the cairn. I blinked again. The apparition
waved, then vanished. This gesture did nothing to dispel my
suspicion that this Haida trickster had been here before.

» » « «

Two nights earlier at Myrna's B & B in Port Clements, I had intercepted a bevy of messages from Huishen, who, sensing the end of the journey, wanted to get in his full two cents' worth. The first communiqué, damaged somehow in transmission, concerned a potlatch and a ceremonial naming, followed by an enemy raid that caused the death of Nang Dlgiis and his three-year-old niece Raven's Tail-Feathers. I knew the story, including Huishen's obligation of revenge, but could not find the right words, so I let it pass. The second message was clear enough:

I listen to the motley crew of early risers, some half-asleep or still tucking in garments and tying up their hair. I locate the reclining figure of Guo Guo by his labored, erratic breathing and draw the covering over his shoulders. In my mind, in this company of decrepits, I am still sailing eastward, toward the entering place of the Great Mother. I can't escape the irony that I've left the unbounded hospitality of the People Who Give Everything Away with an enormous weight of debt on my shoulders. I take refuge in the words of Lao-Tzu: "Before and after are in mutual sequence."

I did not mention these wisps of gossamer or the ghostly presence of Michael, to my friends. The last thing I needed was a lecture on island politics, sound thinking, or cultural appropriation. When you've spent years imagining an Afghan monk sailing under the Chinese flag and preaching to the Maya or the Haida, why trouble yourself over a moment of cultural indiscretion at 50 degrees north latitude? Instead, I kept the messages tucked away in my notebook alongside a piece that had come to me on the plane north from Vancouver, as we banked to make a landing at Sandspit. The tip of Moresby Island was set in a bed of cloud like a piece of precious green jade, thanks to the Creator and to people like Michael who had put their lives on the line and their careers on hold to stop the logging.

Feng-liu, *the flowing of wind, which also means "elegance."* *Water moving under the boat, air above. Myself afloat on the turbulent watercourse, the Dao. Nothing in classic texts compares with this for grandeur. Ancient trees draped in moss. Rock slides altering the course of the fecund river. And moving alongside us, hooked black noses, red swollen bellies breasting the river's tumult, Nang Dlgiis's escort, destruction's sweet seed.*

The fifth message delivered to me at Myrna's B & B, while insistent rain drummed on the glass panes of the greenhouse roof, suggested a greater empathy and broader spectrum of travel than I had imagined:

I could not stomach the doctrines of Pan-ti, for whom the body was a sea of misery the soul must navigate. I love the myriad things of this world. Even the land of ice, fierce and featureless, whose barrenness ought to have appealed to the Buddhist in me, teemed with detail. Stacked stones that mock the human form radiated presence. The solitary figure half-clad in lichen stood as marker or monument for frigid mariners; the cluster, as a place of ambush for wandering herds. Gifts, not refusals, fleet creatures feasting on death, the man dressed in skins placing his offering of flesh on an ancient cairn. Fingers lopped off on gunwales reappear as dolphins, whales.

I'd done my homework. Before returning to Haida Gwaii I had ransacked libraries, talked with indigenous people, corresponded with experts such as Paul Tolstoy and Jeremy Sabloff, and interviewed diffusionists such as David Kelley, Betty Meggers, Nancy Yaw Davis, and Stephen Jett. At the last minute, Gavin Menzies was added to this list. I interviewed him in Washington, D.C., en route to visit my new granddaughter, the indomitable Isabelle, three months old and trailing clouds of glory. By the time Menzies' book, *1421: The Year the Chinese Discovered the World*, was published in the fall of 2002, he had produced anything but an open-and-shut case; in fact, most of the evidence he presented for Asian influence in the Americas merely confirmed, as Stephen Jett and others have argued, that there was much earlier, and repeated, Asian contact. The U. S. edition, subtitled *The Year the Chinese Discovered America*, was fast becoming a commercial sensation, though it had not been well received by the critics.

We met in The Archives, a small restaurant a stone's throw from the White House, where the ambient noise was minimal. I was glad to be inside, as a cold front had settled on the capital, freezing the gas lines in my B & B, so I'd spent an uncomfortable night without heat—though not half so uncomfortable as the protestors in front of the White House who opposed a U. S. invasion of Iraq. I liked Menzies, who was open and candid, though I had reservations about his book. He had not proven his case, but I was grateful to him for stirring up public interest in transoceanic contact.

"I'm a kept man," he was saying. "My wife handles most of the business while I do my writing and research. I'm also the cook. My speciality is fish soup."

I asked if he was prepared to put the word *proven* to the question of Zheng He's voyages. In his National Public Radio interview, he'd claimed that 85 percent of those responding to his thesis were in agreement. I asked him exactly what he meant by that, pointing out that most of those who disagreed would not have responded at all and, of those who did reply, the majority would have been assenting to the likelihood of early and repeated Asian contact rather than with the Zheng He circumnavigation thesis. To his credit, Menzies agreed, but insisted that his Web site—bursting with new information—and the research he was funding would confirm his hypothesis in the near future.

When it was time to leave, Menzies, the once-famished naval cadet, abandoned his unfinished plate of veal medallions, but he had by no means given up on his Zheng He investigations. He was as busy as I was, copying down the names of people and books and ideas that had come up in our conversation. He had another lecture to give before visiting his own new granddaughter in Hamilton, Ontario.

I felt a certain kinship with this mariner turned historian, as we were both interested in altering the paradigm of discovery for the Americas. I was convinced that evidence for repeated early Asian contact, with Huishen as one likely candidate on the list, was mounting, reaching a critical mass. The recent discovery of shipbuilding tools considered to be eight thousand years old, excavated at Eel Point, San Clemente, one of the Channel Islands along the coast of California, was strengthening the argument for coastal migration from Asia. Bones, the calendar, pottery, parasites, Asian melanotic chickens, art and architecture, corn, bark-beating, rare diseases, and a host of other phenomena suggested two-way transoceanic traffic. And, given the two-hundred-year margin of error in carbon-14 dating, the human remains found in Teotihuacán, initially pegged at AD 300, might still be considered relevant to my quest, bringing them well within the time frame of Huishen's forty-odd years in the Americas.

My journey from Kabul to Kashgar, from China to Chiapas, had taken me through war zones, co-operatives, refugee camps, fried-chicken franchises, grottoes, and Haida villages. A kingdom of ten thousand things, to be sure. However, nothing had been so nourishing as the friends I had made along the way, including the mysterious Huishen, who visited me one last time as I turned in my bunkhouse cot at the logging camp in Dinan Bay, waiting for the release of sleep.

Master, wherein is wisdom best achieved, in movement or in stasis? The master, without lifting his eyes, contemplates the outcrop of rock his disciple stands on. One sandaled foot blocks his view of patterns in the rock's surface, displaying its own throbbing network of veins and a small diagonal scar.

Is the tree wise or the running deer a fool?

The disciple steps back from the rock, scratches his head, and experiences sensations of dizziness, shortness of breath.

The same blood that courses through his feet oblivious to all
else feeds and cleanses his brainpan.
What he tastes, in that moment, is his own ignorance.
And lo, it is good.

A little to the left, Ian squats beside his backpack and drinks from
his can of Pepsi. Martin stands next to me, waiting. I feel no pressure from him to speak or do anything. He is as aware as I am of
what's at stake, having become so caught up in my quest that
he scoured the libraries in Montreal looking for materials on
pre-Columbian Asian contact. Every two days there would be
another message from Martin. Would I have a look at this pro-
posal he was making for funding? Had I read *Man across the
Sea*? What did I think about Meggers' Valdivia-Jomon and
Shang-Olmec theories? Had I noticed that Joseph Needham,
initially skeptical, had given the nod to cultural diffusion in
his final publication, *Trans-Pacific Echoes and Resonances*,
thereby joining the ranks of the lunatic fringe he had himself
named? Martin encouraged me to read Peter Matthiessen's
The Snow Leopard, convinced it was somehow crucial to our
project. Matthiessen never saw the snow leopard during his
arduous trek into the Himalayas. It was all very Aristotelian,
the journey being the thing. Better scholars and historians
than I have been unable to show, definitively, that Huishen
made this voyage. I stand here, barefoot, humbled by what I
have learned along the way, by those I have met, but not
daunted. Pant legs rolled up, naked feet rampant, I am free
at last of shoes, their embarrassments, their painful memories.
I look at my companions in this quixotic adventure—
sunburned, mud-spattered, expectant. If the mound is indeed a
cairn, can we prove it was built by Huishen or an Asian monk

rather than by St. Patrick himself?

I've come so far that I'm not only happy to be caught in this radiant moment of stasis, this bright bubble of possibility, but also reluctant to force the issue, to risk destroying the illusion. Instead, I unzip my backpack and take out the single Milsean demerara buttercrunch bar, a gift from my sister-in-law, that I've been hoarding for just such an occasion. The label explains that *Milsean* is Gaelic for "sweet things" and that its Irish emblem, the claddagh ring, a heart held in two hands and crested with a crown, is a symbol of love and friendship.

I break the bar into four pieces, putting one aside for the once-again invisible Michael, who helped make this moment possible. Then, in a gesture of mock communion that Huishen and St. Patrick might have understood and appreciated, I share them with my friends.

ACKNOWLEDGMENTS

I would like to thank the Canada Council and the Center for Canadian-American Studies at Western Washington University in Bellingham for encouragement and support during some of the research and writing of this book. To family and friends who kept in touch and tracked my peregrinations in Asia and Mesoamerica, I am deeply grateful. Some of the Afghan material appeared, in slightly altered form, in *Event* and *Border Crossings;* my submission to the latter was subsequently shortlisted for a National Magazine Award. I thank the editors for their support.

A detailed account of my debt to journalists, friends, and scholars in various fields, including pre-Columbian Asian contact, would require a separate chapter. Names that must be included here are David Kelley, Betty Meggers, Paul Tolstoy, Carl Johannessen, Stephen Jett, Nancy Yaw Davis, Michael Xu, Michael Coe, Paul Shao, Otto J. von Sadowsky, Joseph Needham, Lu Gwei-Djen, Ho Ping-Yü, Wang Ling, Edward Vining, Henriette Mertz, C. R. Edwards, Charles Boland, Patrick Huyghe, Ronald Wright, Tim Severin, Karl Taube, Joe Sneed, Jeremy Sabloff, Hendon Mason Harris, Gordon Ekholm, Ivan Van Sertima, George F. Carter, Louise Levathes, Reverend Master Kōten Benson, Carmen Malvar, Gavin Menzies, Gunnar Thompson, James Delgado, Grant Keddie, Daryl Fedje, Robert Temple, Guujaaw, Michael Nicoll Yahgulanaas, Diane Brown, Xi Chuan, Ding Yan, David Phillips, He Zhixiong, Geri Walker, Ian and Rosie Gould, Martin Duckworth, Knut Fladmark, Tom Keppel, David Herzberger, Elaine Dewar, Sunny Shuyu, Hayden White, Peter Burke, medics and staff of *Médicins Sans Frontières*, the International Committee of the Red Cross, Ralph Maud, Bryant Knox, Habibulakbar and Gulalai Habib, Richard Callaghan, Nancy Dupree, Dr. Salim Khan, Hassan Sobman, Terry Glavin, Stephen Hume, Scott McIntyre, Jennifer Viegas, Peter Caley, Chris Drennen, Barbara Stephen, Dave Woodman, Marina A. Peresheina, George Woodcock, Khawar Medhi, Sultan Mohamadi, Yousef Asefi, Sabir Latifi, Jeremy Green, Robert Bringhurst, Maureen Mayhew, Scott Lawrance, Edwin Doran Jr., Morris Swadesh, George McWhirter, Betty Ferber, Homero Aridjis, Gabriel Zaid, Raúl Martínez *y familia*, José Antonio Diaz de la Serna, Rubén Cabrera, Jaime Errázuriz Zañartu, and Hadiadic Reza.

Special thanks must be recorded here for Mark Abley, who generously read a ragged version of the manuscript and had the honesty and integrity to demand something better; I've tried to oblige. Thanks, also, to Ron Smith, always so good at fine-tuning. To my literary agent, Kathryn Mulders, I am indebted in so many ways. To my editor and friend Phyllis Bruce, I offer my gratitude for the moral support of belief and for her great reserves of wit, acumen, and diplomacy. To Lisa Cupolo, Noelle Zitzer, and other staff at HarperCollins who believed in the project and helped with the midwifery, I am extremely grateful. And finally, to Jan, who helped with the final editing and so much else, I affectionately dedicate this book.

INDEX

Index

Index

GARY GEDDES is an award-winning poet, writer, editor, and critic. He has written and edited more than thirty books, including the bestselling *Sailing Home* and several literary anthologies. His work has been dramatized on CBC and BBC Radio and on stage, and he has won more than a dozen national and international awards, including the Americas Best Book Award and the Gabriela Mistral Prize. Most recently, he was Distinguished Professor of Canadian Culture at Western Washington University in Bellingham. Gay Geddes lives in Sooke, British Columbia.